4/91

WITHDRAWN

The Cost of Competence

The Cost
of Competence

Why Inequality Causes Depression,
Eating Disorders, and Illness in Women

Brett Silverstein, Ph.D.

Deborah Perlick, Ph.D.

New York   Oxford
OXFORD UNIVERSITY PRESS
1995

Oxford University Press

Oxford   New York
Athens   Auckland   Bangkok   Bombay
Calcutta   Cape Town   Dar es Salaam   Delhi
Florence   Hong Kong   Istanbul   Karachi
Kuala Lumpur   Madras   Madrid   Melbourne
Mexico City   Nairobi   Paris   Singapore
Taipei   Tokyo   Toronto

and associated companies in
Berlin   Ibadan

Copyright © 1995 by Oxford University Press, Inc.

Published by Oxford University Press, Inc.,
200 Madison Avenue, New York, New York 10016

Oxford is a registered trademark of Oxford University Press

Library of Congress Cataloging-in-Publication Data
Silverstein, Brett.
The cost of competence : why inequality causes depression, eating disorders,
and illness in women / Brett Silverstein and Deborah Perlick.
p. cm.   Includes bibliographical references and index.
ISBN 0-19-506986-2
1. Women—Mental health—Sociological aspects.
2. Sex role.
3. Achievement motivation in women.
4. Self-esteem in women.
5. Eating disorders.
6. Somatization disorder.
7. Depression, Mental.   8. Anxiety.
I. Perlick, Deborah.   II. Title.
RC451.4.W6S58   1995   155.6'33—dc20
94-44235

1 3 5 7 9 8 6 4 2

Printed in the United States of America
on acid-free paper

To Dr. Stanley Schachter,

who taught us to follow our noses

and go where the data lead

Acknowledgments

The work described in this book was based on the efforts of a large number of women, primarily graduate students. They expended great effort working on the scientific studies cited throughout this book. They also spent many hours talking to us about their lives and those of their mothers. Their names appear in the References as coauthors of the cited studies, but a few deserve special mention because they have remained involved with the research over many years. Lauren Perdue, Shari Carpman, and Joanne Clauson are colleagues, and friends, who have contributed much to this work.

Richard Gordon and Rudolph Bell read an earlier version of the book and offered suggestions that have greatly improved it.

Our editors at Oxford University Press have helped to whip this book into shape. Rosemary Wellner, the copy editor, smoothed out our language and tightened up our arguments. Joan Bossert, our editor, has been involved in every step of the writing and production of this book, and has greatly helped in shaping the final version.

February 1995   B. S.
Mamaroneck, New York   D. P.

Contents

The Cost of Competence

Introduction

We have been studying depression, disordered eating, and a host of other maladies for over fifteen years and collecting newspaper clippings and scores of books along the way. We thought it fitting to open with a favorite and intriguing quote, whose origin we hope will surprise the reader. In a book published in 1992, the physical and psychological symptoms suffered by one 35-year-old woman were described as follows:

> ER lost her appetite; when she did eat, she frequently could not keep her food down . . . she was depressed . . . we would call her loss of appetite, which continued for years, "anorexia" . . . [she exhibited] frequent vomiting . . . felt profoundly tired, suffered headaches, and had days when she wondered about her will to live.

She also felt very inadequate, and, later in life, according to her daughter, was indifferent toward sex.

If the book that contained this description was one of the many written about the epidemics of depression or disordered eating that have afflicted so many women in recent decades, this snippet might not seem unusual. But it is a biography of an eminent woman—and the description deals with symptoms experienced by Eleanor Roosevelt in the second decade of this century. It is surprising because for several generations she came to symbolize the possibilities open to a talented, intelligent, hard-working woman.

She was all these things but her early life was not an easy one, although born to a wealthy family. She had a cold, distant relationship with her uneducated, very traditional mother who "wanted little more than to enjoy . . . dances and dinners, tennis, and the hunt." In contrast, she idolized her father (President Theodore Roosevelt's brother), despite his drinking and severe psychological problems, in part because "he promoted . . . her education." She was also inspired by her Aunt Bamie (Theodore's sister), an intelligent, dynamic woman who felt "galled" about being "denied access to work," and by Marie Souvestre, the self-described feminist headmistress of the boarding school she attended.

Like so many other talented, ambitious women throughout history, she "felt torn between the traditions of her mother . . . and her own inclinations—as awakened by her father and Marie Souvestre," which were reinforced by the very active feminist movement of the 1920s. Reflecting traditional influences, she reported that as a young woman she "took it for granted that men were superior creatures." She did not attend college because she was unable to "defy her relatives who scorned a college education for women," an inability she later referred to as "one of the biggest disappointments of her life."

Perhaps as a result of this traditional upbringing, she suffered low self-esteem in young adulthood, a period when "she never missed an opportunity to mark her own ignorance." Even later in life, she "generally minimized her own contributions and her own achievements."[1]

The premise of our book is that Eleanor Roosevelt's feelings of inadequacy, beliefs about female inferiority, difficulty identifying with a traditional mother during a period of rapid change in gender roles, and idealization of a father, who seemed to be the only one who appreciated her intellect, were not unusual in the past and are all too common today. Also common were her symptoms—depression, disordered eating, and such somatic problems as severe headaches. We argue that these symptoms, along with some others, are components of a single disorder or a series of related disorders that for centuries has plagued women who have been brought up in gender-biased societies.

Throughout history, bright, talented, ambitious women have sought to achieve in areas traditionally reserved for men—academically, professionally, and politically. During some periods, such women were relatively rare, whereas during the past 150 years their number has grown, particularly during the 1920s and after

World War II. Some women were able to overcome the barriers standing in their way; others were not. But even extremely successful women and those who lived during times of "women's liberation" have learned from family members, teachers, employers, and the mass media that women receive much less encouragement for, and access to, the power and prestige associated with nondomestic achievements than men do.

In this book, we discuss the large number of women who have paid a price exacted by these gender biases. Specifically, we have been struck by the persistence of a combination of symptoms—including depression, anxiety, disordered eating, headache, and several other psychological and somatic symptoms—that afflicts many women who define themselves nontraditionally, who aspire to achieve in areas historically reserved for men. This syndrome, which we sometimes refer to as "anxious somatic depression," first develops when girls confront the psychosocial and physiological changes of adolescence. We argue that, faced with societal and familial prejudices against "acting like men," some of these women develop doubts about themselves and ambivalent feelings about their femininity.

Reviewing medical writings of the past, we show that for centuries, as long ago as the fourth century B.C., a syndrome involving depression, anxiety, disordered eating, body aches, and other psychological and physical symptoms has been known to afflict women at adolescence. This syndrome went by many names, including chlorosis, hysteria, a subtype of neurasthenia, and possibly consumption. Recent writings of anthropologists and cross-cultural psychologists and psychiatrists describe a very similar set of symptoms in adolescent females in many contemporary developing nations. As in medical writings of the past, the disorder has been given many names in the anthropological literature, disguising just how common it is. But under whatever name, past or present, the syndrome has been described as afflicting young women who confront the biases facing females who strive for accomplishment in areas traditionally reserved in their cultures for males.

While we use much historical evidence to support our conclusions, this book is meant to shed light on contemporary problems. But in looking at recent scientific findings in psychology and medicine, we found that modern science did not relate various symptoms as a single syndrome, as was the case for so many centuries. Was this an improvement on earlier work, or an oversight? Although there has been a recent trend toward focusing on the coexistence of related symptoms, in most cases the individual symptoms—depression, disordered eating, headache, insomnia, breathing difficulty, and so forth—described earlier in history as part of one syndrome have been studied in isolation. When these isolated investigations are compared, however, it becomes clear that even in contemporary industrialized nations all these symptoms exhibit a pattern very similar to that reported in previous centuries and in other cultures: Beginning at adolescence, they become common among women who aspire to achieve academically and professionally, particularly those who feel that being female has limited their achievements and the amount of respect they receive for those achievements. Furthermore, studies of people born throughout the twentieth century indicate that these symptoms become very prevalent among women who grow up during periods of changing gender roles, like the present. Because this syndrome is not recognized by contemporary science, we sometimes refer to it as the "forgotten syndrome."

To add depth and detail to our understanding of the forgotten syndrome and of the gender dynamics underlying it, we have studied case histories, including many well-known published cases. We look at Sigmund Freud's studies of hysteria, cases of such noted therapists as Hilde Bruch, Erik Erikson, Ludwig Binswanger, and Peter Blos, as well as contemporary case histories of our own patients and those of our colleagues. Case studies provide rich, detailed material about women's lives. By searching for similarities among the large number of cases we have studied, we avoided, to some extent, the pitfalls of particularity inherent in generalizing from a single instance. What we found most intriguing were the striking similarities in women who lived centuries apart and received many different diagnoses—similarities not only in the symptoms they exhibited, but in their attitudes toward marriage, childrearing, and sexuality, and in the feelings they and their families had about what it means to be female in general, and about female achievement in particular.

These findings led us to study the lives of eminent, high-achieving women; to date, we have examined biographies, autobiographies, diaries, and collected correspondence pertaining to the lives of almost 40 women most of us would agree were highly accomplished. Their areas of achievement ranged from science (e.g., Marie Curie) and health (Florence Nightingale, Clara Barton) to politics (Queen Elizabeth I, Golda Meir) and poetry (Emily Dickinson, Elizabeth Barret Browning). We use these case histories to bring alive the results of our empirical, statistical research. This biographical material offers rich, interesting detail regarding the problems experienced by these women, most of whom wrote of themselves or were described by biographers as suffering from such symptoms as headache, disordered eating, and depression, which they termed "profound," "deep," "extreme," "severe," or "suicidal."

We also distributed questionnaires and psychological tests to female students attending several high schools and colleges and to women beyond college age working at hospitals, clinics, and universities. This material, derived from over 2000 women who checked off scales on our questionnaires, lacks the flavor of the case studies. But it does allow us to use scientific methods for relating the women's reports of how they and their families felt about gender and female achievement to careful measurements of depression, disordered eating, and other symptoms. Furthermore, only a select group of women end up being the subjects of biographies or published case studies. The questionnaire method enables us to determine whether the similarities we found in the lives of such women also apply to the "average" women who filled out our questionnaires.

We wish to make this book as interesting and accessible as possible to a wide range of readers, so we briefly describe the results of our scientific studies and those of other researchers in the body of the book, and consign to the Appendixes many of the technical details regarding methods, measures, and statistics. Appendixes and detailed references are included to demonstrate that our conclusions are based not only on historical, cross-cultural, and case-study evidence, but on a great deal of empirical, statistical research published in scientific journals and presented at professional meetings. One strength of our book, we believe, is that material derived from such a wide variety of sources, using several different methods, all points to similar conclusions regarding the existence of a syndrome of anxious somatic depression and its connection to gender roles.

Nontraditional women have often been placed in the position of feeling split between their femininity and the aspects of themselves defined by academic, professional, and political achievement, which are often labeled, even today, as "masculine." For some of these women, this conflict has led them to devalue aspects of their own feminine identities and those of their mothers. They have come into adolescence and adulthood in societies valuing traditionally "masculine" pursuits more highly than domestic and other traditionally "feminine" pursuits, mirroring cultural values at large. In addition to reinforcing these gender biases, societies have placed physical and ideological barriers in the paths of women striving to achieve in the more valued masculine pursuits. Psychologically speaking, what are we to make of all this? We argue that the heightened psychological and physical problems of women that occur at adolescence in such societies result from the widely acknowledged heightened importance of gender role and gender identity that coincides with adolescence.

Our central thesis is that the ambivalence engendered by negotiating the passage through adolescence in the face of the emotional dilemmas centered around gender role and identity all too often finds expression in a combination of psychological and somatic symptoms. This is particularly likely to occur during periods of change in socially prescribed gender roles, when the increased importance placed on achievements in traditionally masculine pursuits produces increased conflict among nontraditional women, who must come to terms with aspects of the self regarded as "feminine" and those labeled by society as "masculine." Understanding the mechanisms of identity development and the conflict surrounding identity we call "gender ambivalence" helps to explain why it is females who suffer from the symptoms, why the suffering begins at adolescence, and why the constellation of symptoms becomes more prevalent during periods of great change in gender roles. Specific details about the likelihood of developing particular symptoms at particular ages during particular periods of history may depend on a variety of social, biological, and historical factors, ranging from family dynamics to genetic predispositions, to the changing state of the economy.

Many of the points we make here, as well as our methods, are bound to raise controversy. We are aware, for example, that in drawing attention to the psychological symptoms of high-achieving women we risk being misconstrued as labeling these women and blaming them for their problems. But the high prevalence among women of the symptoms we focus on—depression, disordered eating, headaches, and so on—is already widely acknowledged. If these symptoms are actually part of a larger syndrome, many contemporary women may be suffering from a disorder that is not currently recognized and may not be receiving adequate treatment. The potential benefits that may result from addressing this disorder, and from stimulating research into the means by which social and cultural biases against some forms of female achievement may underlie it—including the prevention or alleviation of some of the suffering and the elimination of a great deal of expenditure on medical treatment for what is really a social and psychological disorder—seem to us to justify the risk of being construed as labeling women. We are not suggesting in any way that women are somehow frail and are thus vulnerable to a whole array of symptoms. Nor are we "medicalizing" their symptoms, for these are symptoms for which women themselves have sought relief.

Writers on a particular subject sometimes examine historical material to gain insight into particular problems through an analysis of similarities in patterns taken by these problems across different periods in history. Historians would caution about the use of such methods, arguing that individuals and their behaviors can only be understood within the context of their particular historical setting. While this is an important concern, we believe that in this instance much evidence points to similarities between the problems experienced by women living during different centuries who have attempted to achieve in areas traditionally reserved for men. In our judgment, insights gained by studying patterns of similarities in women's lives across time outweigh the disadvantages of overlooking some historical differences between these women. Some readers may be uncomfortable with our focus on similarities over time because such a focus is often associated with theories that emphasize biological predispositions as the sole or major cause of disorders. But because most societies have accorded preferential treatment to males over females who strive to achieve intellectually and professionally, similarities in the problems experienced by women over the centuries are as likely to result from psychosocial as from biological forces. Furthermore, the differences we found between generations of women who grew up during different periods of this century clearly point to the important role played by psychosocial forces in causing anxious somatic depression.

As is inevitably the case in any work that draws on a body of knowledge of several fields, we have been forced to be highly selective in our treatment of any one field. Comprehensive reviews of the many important contributions to the understanding of, for example, the vicissitudes of the development of gender identity, the biological underpinnings of depression, disordered eating, and the other symptoms we discuss, or the changes in women's roles initiated by the Industrial Revolution are beyond the scope of this book.

   Although the symptoms of anxious somatic depression range
far beyond anorexia, bingeing, and vomiting, readers may be most
familiar with disordered eating and the quest of females for slim,
noncurvaceous bodies because these symptoms have received so
much media attention recently. We begin by demonstrating that,
contrary to popular and scientific accounts, these symptoms are
not new and that our modern obsession with being thin and the
concomitant eating disorders experienced by many women today,
and in the past, are related to the limited traditional definition of
what it means to be female. Disordered eating is just one of the
costs of competence paid by talented women who strive to
succeed.

Part I

THE FORGOTTEN SYNDROME

1

Curves and Competence

Actress Lillian Russell may have been the most popular sex symbol this nation has ever known. From the early 1880s to the late 1890s, the shows she starred in were often sold out, newspaper gossip columns overflowed with details of her life, and her photograph frequently graced major magazines. At the height of her popularity, one Western coal miner shot a friend who had the effrontery to claim Lillian Russell was not the most beautiful woman in the world. She was even selected to make the first public long-distance telephone call, singing in New York City to President Grover Cleveland who sat listening in the White House.[1]

Her popularity rested on her beauty. One columnist wrote unabashedly, "She looks like Venus after her bath," while another gushed, "If Lillian Russell does not cease to take on new phases of beauty every month or so, there will be no reason why the flowers of Spring should bloom." Even a half-century later, the *New York Times* described her as "the raging beauty of her period."[2]

A modern audience, overexposed to media hype, might not be surprised at the adulation accorded Miss Russell but for one detail: By today's standards, Lillian Russell was plump.

Recalling a pilgrimage to New Haven he made to see Lillian Russell appearing in a play, Clarence Day wrote in the *Saturday Evening Post*:

There was nothing wraithlike about Lillian Russell. She was a volup-
tuous beauty and there was plenty of her to see. We liked that. Our
tastes were not thin or ethereal. We liked flesh in the Nineties.[3]

As indicated by Day's quote, the ideal female figure of the late
nineteenth century was quite different from what it is now. One
visitor from England described American women in 1875 as "con-
stantly having themselves weighed," which only becomes surprising when we read on: "and every ounce of increase is hailed with
delight."[4]

The inconvenience, poor health, and self-disdain experienced
by many contemporary women who go from diet to diet, con-
stantly weighing themselves and hailing with delight every ounce
lost in an attempt to develop and maintain thin, ethereal figures
are put into tragicomic perspective by the ephemeral nature of the
standard of beauty they suffer so much to attain.

Unfortunately for Lillian Russell, she reached the peak of her
popularity as the country was to witness a most dramatic change
concerning our standards of beauty. As early as 1899, a reporter for
the *New York Journal* wrote: "Lillian has no beauty below the chin
. . . she moves her grand-opera amplitude with the soft heaviness
of a nice white elephant." And by the 1920s, the *New York Times*
was reporting announcements by fashion experts of a new ideal, an
"American Venus" standing 5 feet 7 inches in height, with measurements of 34–22–34 and weighing no more than 110 pounds.
The same article suggested that fashions began to change about the
time that Lillian Russell's popularity started to wane.[5]

More accurately, Russell's public image changed from that of a
raging beauty to an authority on exercise and weight loss. Her
adoption of the new exercise fad of bicycling was front-page news.
She began to give interviews about her myriad attempts to lose
weight and, in 1909, the *New York World* carried a story on her
latest regime—rolling over 250 times in the morning. In 1912, pre-
dating Jane Fonda by over sixty years, the Kinemacolor Company
featured Lillian Russell in a series of motion pictures in which she
demonstrated calisthenic exercises and deep-breathing postures.[6]

Whatever regime she followed, there was no way that Lillian
Russell could have slimmed down enough. Beauty standards were
changing too rapidly. By the 1920s, one writer described the reign-
ing standard: "Henceforth slimness, leanness and flatness are to be
the order of the day . . . the figures of our flappers and subdebs
shall be slender and slinky and lathlike and the line of grace no

longer the curve but the prolonged parallelogram."[7] This description could not be more different from Clarence Day's memoir of
the tastes of the 1890s, just as the figure of the flapper, the standard
for the 1920s, could hardly differ more from Lillian Russell's physique.

The changing standard had its impact on many women besides
Lillian Russell. The 1920s were characterized by one author as "the
period of female reduction."[8] By 1920 and 1921, when the standard
of beauty had already become very thin, half of the freshman
women entering Hollins College in Georgia were underweight
based on the actuarial tables used at the time. By 1925 and 1926,
the proportion of underweight women had increased to an incredi-
ble two-thirds. At several other colleges, the weight of women also
decreased during the 1920s.[9]

Some male authorities expressed horror at the change in the
bodies of college women. Dr. R. McKenzie of the University of
Pennsylvania told the *New York Times* in 1921, "If we compare
the typical student of our women's colleges with the deep-chested,
vital type that has come to us through the royal succession of Ven-
uses like the Venus of Milo, we are apt to become pessimistic over
the future of the race."[10]

Even greater concern over the future of the human race was
reported in a 1925 *New York Times* article that carried the offensive headline: "Women more ape-like . . . than is man."[11] The
story began:

> The trouble with woman—take it from Sir William Arbuthnot Lane,
> consulting surgeon to Guy's Hospital, is that "she is much more sim-
> ian than man, and by natural instinct imitative." That is why women
> endanger their health and the much mooted future of the race by try-
> ing to look like boys with the aid of barber's shears, rubber corsets
> and other contrivances.

Over the centuries, authorities writing about the health problems of women have often attributed these problems to female inferiority, and used startlingly offensive language in the process.
This led some authors, justifiably repelled by those descriptions, to
focus their attention on the obvious biases evidenced by these experts. While this is an important issue, it may have had the unfor-
tunate effect of distracting us from the problems the women experienced. That an authority draws unwarranted, even offensive,
conclusions about the causes of a problem does not discount the
existence of that problem.

Severe problems did develop among young women of the 1920s who sought to be thin. Based on a 1925 survey, the Delaware County Tuberculosis Association concluded that high school girls in Chester, Pennsylvania, were "starving themselves" in an effort to maintain "stylish silhouette figures" until they were dangerously underweight. Dr. Harry Schulmann, the Secretary of the Association, said that until the age of 15 the proportion of underweight boys and girls was roughly equal. But, at 15, the girls began the "slimming process," and 18 percent were found to be "under the danger line" with regard to weight.[12] The League of Nations reported that in the United States tuberculosis had decreased among all populations except young women; the lack of decline in this group was attributed to "the modern habit of slimming."[13]

The health effects were strongest among college and working women, which was worrying to the business community. Speaking to the American Dietetic Association, Emma Holloway, supervisor of Institutional and Dietetic Courses at Pratt Institute, reported that she had been called in by large companies to discuss the widespread fatigue experienced by their female employees. She concluded that because the women were "so afraid of being overweight" that they were "not willing to be even normal in weight," they were "starving themselves." Based on a series of laboratory studies he performed on female office workers, Dr. Thaddeus L. Bolton, head of the Department of Psychology at Temple University, concluded that "working efficiency is lowered by the dieting fad."[14] As a result of such conclusions, life insurance companies tried to convince their female employees not to diet. As F. L. Rowland of Fort Wayne, Indiana, told the fourth annual convention of the Life Office Management Association:

> Women of 25 and under who are underweight are poor insurance risks. . . . Dieting is one sure way of becoming underweight and so we argue strongly against it, especially so far as our employees are concerned. Several cases of tuberculosis have been directly traced to dieting.[15]

By 1926, the problem had become so widespread that the American Medical Association convened an emergency meeting at the New York Academy of Medicine to discuss the health problems resulting from the attempts of women to drastically reduce their weight. Conference participants reported hundreds of cases of "mental breakdown" attributable to weight reduction. They inveighed against the methods being used by women to control their weight, ranging from self-starvation, overexercise, and rolling machines, to the taking of thyroid and gland extracts, iodine, and other drugs and stimulants, including the use of cigarettes to excess.[16]

Thus, slim standards, starving sophomores, fad diets, phony products, and even exercise films featuring famous actresses characterized not only the decades of the seventies and eighties most of us have witnessed, but the 1920s. To begin to understand the real cause of these problems, however, we must look beyond standards of attractiveness to another similarity between our recent history and the Roaring Twenties—a rapid change in women's roles.

Women's Changing Roles

Feminists were active early in this century, making, according to one magazine article, a "constant clamor about maiden names, equal rights, woman's place in the world,"[17] and attempting to pass an equal rights amendment to the Constitution. Although no E.R.A. was passed, the fight for equality brought about dramatic changes in the roles of women. According to the popular philosopher and historian Will Durant, writing in 1927,

> If in imagination we place ourselves at the year 2000 and ask what was the outstanding feature of human events in the first quarter of the Twentieth Century, we shall see that it was . . . the change in the status of women. History has seldom known so startling a transformation in so short a time.

Among the changes that Durant noted were increased opportunities for women:

> Within a generation or two the weaker sex has made such progress in conquering a position in industry, in pervading almost every field of it except the brutally physical occupations. . . . A million alert and happy girls are filling with color and charm the class-rooms and dormitories and campuses . . . their athletic bodies leaping with the sense of a fuller life.[18]

In many respects the "women's liberation" movement we treat as innovative and the product of recent decades occurred with equal force in the twenties. Women resisted taking their husband's name, tried to pass an E.R.A., entered colleges in large numbers, and worked in occupations traditionally closed to them.

Thus, changes in the standard of feminine beauty from the voluptuousness embodied by Lillian Russell to slim and noncurvaceous flappers obsessed with dieting paralleled important changes in the role definitions of women. In the same year that *Century* magazine carried philosopher Will Durant's statement about the change in the status of women, the *Saturday Evening Post* ran an article by S. G. Blyth, who reported a parallel change in women's attitudes toward their weight:

> In the year 1912 . . . the world seemed to be populated mostly by
> . . . fat persons who were trying to get thin and thin persons who
> were trying to get fat. . . . In 1927 . . . the world is populated largely
> by fat persons trying to get thin and by thin people trying to get thinner. . . . This is the period of reduction, especially the period of female reduction.[19]

Women's Roles, Women's Bodies

The flapper, the epitome of fashion in the twenties, was a woman in a shapeless shift with short hair, a style described as "sexless" and "mannish."[20] Many observers saw a connection between supposedly "mannish" standards of beauty and the increasing frequency with which women took on roles traditionally considered masculine. In the same article that rhapsodized over women's progress, Will Durant wrote, "There is more joy . . . in motherhood than in careers that harden the body . . . into the unlovely likeness of an emasculated male." The assumed connection between body build and the performance of traditionally "masculine" tasks was so prevalent that one female author felt compelled to caution her readers: "Nor does it necessarily follow, scientists tell us, that a woman with a flair for the creative or the scientific, or with a genius for abstract thought will have a masculine physique."[21]

The striking parallel between women's role definitions and women's bodies continued throughout the century. But, by the middle of the 1930s, both role definitions and standards of attractiveness had begun to revert to what they had been at the century's beginning. First the Depression, then World War II, slowed, then temporarily reversed, the professional and educational progress made by women. Women, particularly professional women, lost their jobs in disproportionate numbers during the Depression and did not begin to regain them until after World War II.[22] Although women worked in factories during the war, they did not hold professional jobs or attend college in great numbers. The rate of college graduation among female high school graduates went from 17 percent in the mid-1920s to 13 percent in the mid-1930s and then to 12 percent in the mid-1940s.[23]

The return to traditional roles brought the return of traditional fashion, including traditionally fashionable female bodies. As early as 1931, the U.S. Bureau of Home Economics was predicting in the *New York Times* that

> Milady of fashion . . . will eat a lot of wheat to bring back the curves lost by reducing diets. "Economists have agreed that one of the outstanding reasons in the decrease of cereal consumption was the modish slender figure," said Dr. Florence B. King of the home economics staff. . . . "Of course, this Autumn's drastic change in contour will have just the opposite result."

The article's headline was amusing: "Women expected to eat into wheat surplus to restore curves for Eugenie silhouette."[24]

The relationship between female eating patterns and gender roles was unwittingly described in another headline in the *New York Times*, this one in 1937, that listed without relating them the two most interesting results of a study made by the Northwestern National Life Insurance Company: "Business girls turn from reducing diets; 75% eager for marriage, survey shows."[25] Other sources were quite aware of the relationship between fashion, the economy, and women's roles. As described in *Fortune* magazine,

> There is even a case to be made for women's skirts as economic barometers. . . . In the fall of 1929 every skirt in the country fell with a plop—and so did the stock market. By 1931 women were wearing leg of mutton sleeves and fake bustles, and now in 1935 hips and breasts have returned.[26]

In 1938, *Vogue* magazine, an important barometer of female fashion, reported that

> Paris has decreed a new woman. . . . Perhaps they have sensed that growing ennui which has attended so much freedom. . . . The new woman . . . will be vested and gloved and corseted. . . . There must be frou-frou and femininity . . . woman is rediscovering herself, her personality and her sex.[27]

But by 1942, eleven years after it had reported the findings of the U.S. Bureau of Home Economics that dieting women were responsible for a wheat surplus, the *New York Times* reported the opposite finding by the Metropolitan Life Insurance Company that, during a period of war rationing, "The average overweight woman is digging unnecessarily into the country's food supplies."[28] It appears that, whatever form they took, the economic problems of society were attributed by journalists to the supposed eating habits of women.

As most readers already know, the 1950s, 1960s, and 1970s were decades of dramatic change in women's roles, with a sharp increase in women attending college and holding professional jobs. During that period, females portrayed in all the mass media became slimmer, including *Playboy* models, Miss America finalists, and the most popular movie stars.[29] It appears that as go women's roles, so go their figures. Lillian Russell, Clara Bow, Marilyn Monroe, and Jane Fonda may have been popular not only because of their talent, but because their bodies reflected the changes experienced by women of their times.

To help us portray these changes in women's dimensions, we depict in Figure 1 the curvaceousness of the models who have appeared in *Vogue* magazine over the course of the century. This graph was constructed by dividing the width of the busts of the models portrayed in the magazine by the width of their waists. Thus, during the reign of Lillian Russell at the turn of the century, the average model had a bust twice as wide as her waist, whereas in 1925, heyday of the flapper, the average model had a bust that was barely larger than her waist. The bars in the figure depict the decade-by-decade changes in the proportion of American women graduating from college.

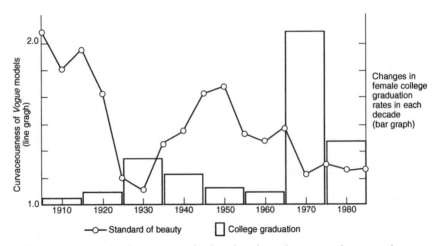

Figure 1 Changing beauty standards related to changing educational opportunities for women over the course of the twentieth century.

In decades when the bar graph gets higher, the line graph gets lower, indicating that the greater the increase in the proportion of American women graduating college, the slimmer the standard of female beauty portrayed by the models in *Vogue*.[30] The juxtaposition of the line and the bars graphically points to the same conclusion as our review of the mass media: Changes in women's roles bring changes in women's bodies.

We argue that this relationship between women's education and women's bodies is rooted in a stereotype of women as intellectually incompetent and an associated linkage between incompetence and female physique. Studies done in recent decades demonstrate that, although modern writers no longer feel compelled to caution that intelligent women do not necessarily have masculine physiques, this stereotype has nonetheless not disappeared but has simply gone underground, becoming more subtle so that many people still hold to it without realizing that they do.

Do We Equate Curvaceous with Incompetence Today?

In 1972, one well-known psychological study found that at least three-fourths of the people of each sex agreed that, compared to men, women are more illogical, have more difficulty making decisions, are less ambitious, and less skilled in business. Even in the 1990s, women who serve as presidents or general managers in large corporations report that the main obstacles toward career advancement they face relate to "the fact of being female."[31] These stereotypes regarding professional women are accentuated when women look very "feminine." Personnel consultants asked to judge the job qualifications of a group of women based on their photographs rated the women who were presented in more feminine styles—long hair, soft sweaters or ruffled blouses, dangling jewelry, and makeup—as less independent, more helpless, more illogical, and less managerial than the same women presented in less sex-typed styles (e.g., tailored clothes with a jacket, little makeup, and short hair).[32] Like the style of her hair and the cut of her clothing, a woman's physique may also accentuate her femininity, influencing perceptions of her occupational status. Of female college students asked which of the two women in Figure 2 was more likely to be a homemaker, only about one in fifteen chose the slimmer woman, whereas almost half—seven times as many—chose the more curvaceous woman.[33]

The continuing connection between physique and perceptions

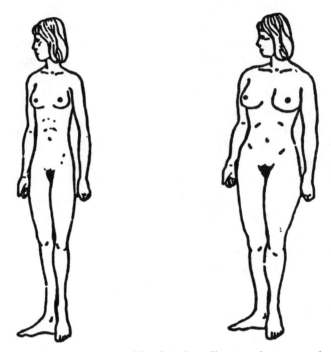

Figure 2 Women compared by female college students as to homemaker status, level of success, and level of intelligence.

of intellectual competence is most clearly demonstrated by a series of studies in which Chris Kleinke and Richard Staneski asked students at several colleges to make judgments about three women, based solely on photographs. While some students saw photographs of a woman in her normal, small-busted state, others looked at photographs of the *same* woman made to appear large busted with the use of cotton padding, allowing Kleinke and Staneski to determine if a woman's bust size was used as a key factor in judging her. The students evaluated several dimensions of the women, including competence. The study found that students rated large-busted women not only as more immoral and immodest than small-busted women, but also as more unintelligent and incompetent.[34] No wonder *Fortune* magazine in 1935 reported that the symbol of the modern office was the "competent . . . intelligently dressed woman," not "the blond stenographer with the . . . redundant breasts." More recently, one author advised women seeking to cultivate *The Professional Image:* "If you have a large bust don't accentuate it."[35] In the eyes of many people, curvaceousness signals femininity and both are stereotypically associated with traditional roles and professional incompetence.

The Effects of Stereotyping on Women

The assumed connection between competence and curvaceousness leads those women particularly concerned with intellectual and professional achievement to eschew curvaceous bodies and to feel uncomfortable with their feminine physiques. For example, one study found that women who are interested in careers traditionally considered more appropriate for males, such as pharmacy, prefer smaller breasts and buttocks than do other women.[36] Other studies found that women who are very concerned about what other people think of their achievements, or who worry that others don't think that they are intelligent, also tend to prefer slim figures and are dissatisfied with their own bodies.[37]

The connection between curvaceousness and competence that appears to be part of many women's self-concepts also affects their health. For example, today, as in the 1920s, women oriented toward intellectual and professional achievement have often been found to be particularly likely to manifest symptoms of disordered eating.[38] The amount of importance female college students reported that they placed on intelligence and professional success was related to the extent to which they reported purging—controlling weight through the use of laxatives, diuretics, or self-induced vomiting—and the extent to which they were underweight.[39] Moreover, when we asked another sample of college women to indicate the importance they placed on various characteristics, women who reported symptoms of disordered eating were more likely than other women to rate professional success and intelligence as very important and being a wife and a good homemaker as not very important.[40]

The association between symptoms of disordered eating (often at levels less than those characteristic of clinical eating disorders) and intellectual or professional aspirations may result in part because high-achieving women are most likely to associate curvaceous, stereotypically feminine bodies with lack of achievement. The slimmer woman portrayed in Figure 2 was rated as more successful than the more curvaceous woman by less than one-third of female college students without symptoms of disordered eating, compared to almost half of those women with those symptoms. Only about one in ten nondisordered women rated the slimmer woman as more intelligent than the curvier woman, compared to over one-quarter of the women with symptoms of disordered eating.[41] Finally, eating disordered women are more likely than nondisordered women to indicate that they feel that being female is disadvantageous by agreeing with such statements as "If I were not a woman, I would have planned my life differently," "My professional advancement is controlled by the fact that I am a woman," and "Men simply have more possibilities than women."[42]

We would suggest that disordered eating (along with depression and the other symptoms discussed in later chapters) occurs among women who strive to achieve in areas not traditionally associated with femininity, but who come to feel that various aspects of being female place them at an unfair disadvantage in these pursuits. If these women blame the obstacles they face on their gender and, therefore, on their bodies, which, after all, are what define them as female, they may come to be dissatisfied with those bodies and strive (consciously or not) to make them less stereotypically feminine. One way to accomplish this—to combat the development of breasts, curves, and menstruation marking them as female—is through disordered eating.

Our focus on issues of female identity has much in common with others who have written about disordered eating, including Hilde Bruch, Richard Gordon, and Harvey Schwartz.[43] However, we place greater emphasis than these other writers on the response of the huge number of "nontraditional" women living during periods of "women's liberation" to the gender biases that continue to confront them even during these "liberating" periods. (From time to time, we use "nontraditional" as a shorthand to describe those women pursuing traditionally "masculine" roles. Obviously, by calling them "nontraditional," we in no way wish to reinforce the stereotypes we hope to expose.)

What About "Traditional" Women?

Figure 1 demonstrates that an increase in the proportion of women graduating from college is accompanied by a slim standard of attractiveness. But how do these women's preferences translate into noncurvaceous models in women's magazines? One answer is hinted at in the business and fashion media.

As far back as 1922, M. A. Hopkins wrote in *The New Republic* that the "girl with the pay envelope sets the style for the women who dressmake at home." More recently, Rene Bartos advised marketers of fashions and cosmetics that "women who work set the standard for grooming." [44] From the inception of a mass-market fashion industry with its attendant fashion magazines, professional women have exerted influence on fashion beyond their numbers in the general population because they are overrepresented among the magazine readership, they spend more money on fashions, and many other women follow the fashion lead set by the professional women. In the words of a 1935 *Fortune* magazine article on "Women in Business",

> As the nineteen twenties drew to a close, the impact of women upon business was obvious . . . whole new industries began to revolve about the new buying power of women. . . . The cosmetic industry boomed, and in its wake other beautifying trades all centering around the new purchasing power of women. . . . The whole nature of national advertising changed: women's magazines flourished, supported by advertisements addressed to women. . . . The new trades serving the new woman with money.[45]

One ironic and disturbing implication of the relationship between female roles and standards of beauty is that the same stereotyping that exacts a price from nontraditional women also exacts an indirect price from even those women who strive for success in areas traditionally thought of as feminine. One of the criteria by which women traditionally have been judged is physical attractiveness, as a rule defined by how well their appearance matches current cultural norms. When the standard of beauty is slim, even women seeking success in traditional roles strive to be slim. When the standard is noncurvaceous, many women who are not naturally thin and noncurvaceous may feel compelled to force their bodies into a form that does not come naturally, often through dieting and extreme exercise. Women who attempt to achieve and maintain this fashionable figure must often exert constant vigilance regarding the foods they eat and each ounce of fat they add to their bodies. Often these attempts to maintain artificially low weights backfire, leading many women to periodically fall off the diet wagon with a vengeance by going on eating binges.

Many authorities on disordered eating have noticed that the increase in anorexia and bulimia over the past few decades occurred at the same time that the standard of beauty became thin and many women became very involved with dieting, exercise workouts, and other means of weight control. This temporal overlap led these authorities (including ourselves several years ago) to assume that anorexia and bulimia were more extreme versions of the dieting and weight obsession exhibited by so many women. Our more recent research leads us to believe that the process actually works in reverse. That is, it appears that nontraditional women, who are most prone to dissatisfaction with their own curves and to symptoms of disordered eating, are the ones influencing the standard of attractiveness set by the media. When societal opportunities for female intellectual and professional success increase (resulting in increased numbers of "nontraditional" women), anorexia, bulimia, and symptoms of disordered eating at levels below those considered to define a clinical diagnosis of disordered eating also become more prevalent and the standard of attractiveness influenced by these women becomes thinner. This thin standard, in turn, influences large numbers of more traditional women who want to be considered attractive to develop poor body image, chronic dieting, and obsessions with weight and food. Thus, the forces that produce anorexia precede, rather than follow, the forces producing the Scarsdale diet.

So women with traditional aspirations pay the price of the curves = competence equation in pressures to live up to unrealistic standards of beauty, leading to the yo-yo pattern of chronic dieting alternated with periodic bingeing. Nontraditional women also pay with symptoms of disordered eating, and possibly a wide range of other symptoms reported to accompany disordered eating in recent research that include depression, anxiety, somatic symptoms such as headaches, insomnia, and amenorrhea, feelings of low self-esteem and sexual indifference, and difficulty concentrating.[46]

But throughout history many women must have desired to achieve in areas not traditionally open to them and must have come to feel that being female placed them at a serious disadvantage. Why didn't those women develop these symptoms? When we attempted to answer this question, we learned to our surprise that they did.

2

The Disease of Young Women

During the 1970s, psychologists, psychiatrists, and the general public became increasingly aware of forms of disordered eating that appeared new. Obesity and overeating had been well known for many years, but not until the late 1960s, or so it seemed, did significant numbers of women exhibit the self-starvation of anorexia. A few more years had to pass before the syndrome of bingeing alternating with purgeing, referred to as bulimarexia, or bulimia for short, was recognized. Mental health professionals were intrigued—and perhaps even a little bit shocked—by what seemed to be the sudden increase in cases of what had been considered a "curiosity and a rarity."[1]

Modern industrial societies place a great deal of emphasis on novelty, newness, originality. This is particularly true of the United States, the center of much recent medical research, with its short history and its pride in not being tainted by the old-fashioned, feudal roots of Europe and Asia. To most of the general public, and to many professionals involved in studying or treating eating disorders, anorexia and bulimia were new phenomena. This is true despite the outbreak of self-starvation among young women that occurred during the 1920s, a period experienced by millions of Americans alive today. When we first became aware of this earlier outbreak, we were not only somewhat surprised that it had existed but also a bit chagrined at our short cultural memory. Realizing that the disorders are not new, we searched the medical literature of past centuries to determine when they first appeared.

Since the earliest large body of medical work available to modern researchers is comprised of texts of ancient Greece written by Hippocrates and several of his followers, we began our search there. One of these texts has been translated as "On the diseases of young women," sometimes as "On the diseases of virgins." Another is almost never referred to by modern researchers, perhaps because it has not yet been translated into English, but the French title, "De la Superfetation," has been translated as "On Overeating."[2] Together, these texts describe a syndrome afflicting females at adolescence that includes symptoms of disordered eating and depression, along with several other symptoms we will discuss more fully in later chapters. Focusing on the amenorrhea that has been found to be associated with both depression and disordered eating, these texts attributed many symptoms to the lack of menstruation among pubescent females, including the wasting away of bodies, later termed "consumption" (referred to as phthisis), great hunger, vomiting, difficulty breathing, aches and pains, feeling "afraid and fearful," hearing voices ordering them to drown themselves, and loving death. The treatment of the disorder recommended in the Hippocratic texts focused on the connections with sexuality, and childbearing, which we discuss later:

> My prescription is that when virgins experience this trouble, they should cohabit with a man as quickly as possible. If they become pregnant, they will be cured. If they don't do this, either they will succumb at the onset of puberty or a little later, unless they catch another disease. Among married women, those who are sterile are more likely to suffer what I have described.[3]

The linkage in the medical literature between disordered eating, amenorrhea, and consumption continued for many centuries after Hippocrates. In the fifteenth century, Antonio Benivieni, one of the founders of pathological anatomy, left records of several cases linking amenorrhea and disordered eating, including one in which a woman "whose monthly courses were held back for a whole year was reduced to complete emaciation" causing her to suffer from "wasting and consumption."[4]

In 1694, in his *Phtisiologia or a Treatise on Consumption*, Dr. Richard Morton described the case of Mr. Duke's daughter, a consumptive woman who in "the Eighteenth Year of her Age . . . fell into a total suppression of Her Monthly Courses . . . from which time her appetite began to abate and her Digestion to be bad, her Flesh also began to be flaccid and loose." Eventually, the young woman was subject to fainting fits and came to look like "a Skeleton only clad with skin." She had "no fever . . . no cough or difficulty of breathing. . . . Only her appetite was diminished, and her Digestion was uneasy, with fainting fits."[5]

Morton went on to describe other cases of consumption in which young women stopped menstruating and became emaciated. In a chapter entitled "Of a Consumption proceeding from the Green Sickness, and a suppression of the Monthly Purgations in Women," he wrote: "This [i.e., amenorrhea] is most commonly the Original of Women's Consumptions and I have very seldom seen any Woman that was capable of the Monthly Purgations, either Virgin, married Woman or Widdow, who ever fell into a consumption without an Obstruction of these Purgations coming upon it."[6]

These descriptions contain several themes that we see repeated in later centuries. One is the emphasis on the cessation of menstruation. But many authorities would conclude that the authors of these earlier descriptions reversed the causal connection between amenorrhea and emaciation: Nowadays the amenorrhea is usually thought to result when females become too thin or when they become anxious and depressed. But to Morton, Benivieni, and Hippocrates the most striking symptom of the disorders was the cessation of the menses and its associated fertility problems.

"Consumption" (or phthisis) was the term of choice for Hippocrates, Morton, and Benivieni in describing the wasting away associated with this disorder. As discussed in Chapter 1, several twentieth-century authorities related tuberculosis to the anorexia exhibited by many young women. These authorities used the term "tuberculosis" and were primarily discussing a lung disease. They believed that anorexia led to poor nutrition, which in turn increased susceptibility to tuberculosis.

Many people now consider consumption synonymous with tuberculosis. But note that, in the seventeenth century, Morton diagnosed consumption in the case of Mr. Duke's daughter, whose only symptoms were diminished appetite and amenorrhea. Like Morton, the ancient Greeks may have given the name consumption to the symptom of wasting away. In Chapter 4, we will demonstrate that the syndrome discussed in this book sometimes involves not only the wasting away associated with anorexia, but also hyperventilation and other difficulties in breathing. It may be that, throughout history, the labels "phthisis" and "consumption" have been used

to describe symptoms of the lung disease we now call "tuberculosis" as well as the syndrome discussed here that sometimes involves both wasting away and difficulty breathing. Other authors
who have studied the medical literature of previous centuries provide additional evidence linking what was sometimes called "nervous consumption" to the disorder now thought of as anorexia.[7]
Unfortunately, because modern methods for the collection of epidemiologic statistics were not used in previous centuries, we cannot estimate how many other cases of consumption, "the wasting
disease," may really have been instances of the syndrome we discuss here.

Hysteria, Neurasthenia, and Chlorosis: The Disease of Young Women by Other Names?

The medical literature of the seventeenth, eighteenth, and nineteenth centuries continued to describe disorders that afflicted
young, unmarried women at adolescence with depression, disordered eating, and several other physical and psychological symptoms. In 1796, Dr. Ebenezer Sibly wrote that the "sallow and inani-
mate female, by coition often becomes plump and robust."[8]
Sibley's description, so reminiscent of Hippocrates' prescription
that females suffering from the disease of young women should
cohabit with a man, dealt with a disease known at the time as
chlorosis. Chlorosis, the "green sickness" mentioned by Morton,
was frequently diagnosed among adolescent women prior to the
twentieth century. Common symptoms were depression, nervousness, amenorrhea, headaches, breathing difficulties, heart
clicks and murmurs, and insomnia, as well as anorexia, bulimia,
and vomiting.[9] In a 1901 description that sounds strikingly modern, Dr. Thomas C. Allbutt noted that "Chlorosis is a malady of
puberty. . . . Many young women, as their frames develop fall
into a panic fear of obesity and not only cut down their food but
swallow . . . alleged antidotes to fatness." Chlorotic women also
felt "gloom, despondency, ennui . . . giving up all for lost they
indulge in depression and despair."[10]

Another name given to a disease of young women involving
depression, disordered eating, and other somatic symptoms was
"hysteria." Today, most people who could list the symptoms of
hysteria would probably mention fits, fainting, or paralyzed limbs.
As recently as 1953, however, psychiatrist Judd Marmor wrote that

"vomiting, anorexia, and bulemia are by-words in the symptom-atology of hysteria." In 1951, over 60 percent of a sample of hysteric women were found to exhibit anorexia, vomiting, variations in weight, nervousness, symptoms of depression, headaches, breathing difficulties, and sexual indifference.[11]

These results confirmed what had been reported by physicians for many years. In 1840, Dr. Thomas Laycock discussed the anorexia, bulimia, and vomiting of hysteric women, and Dr. Leonard Corning in 1888 noted that hysteria was frequently complicated with melancholia and attempted suicide.[12] Many of the hysteric female patients Freud treated as he first developed his principles of psychoanalysis exhibited symptoms of depression and disordered eating. In describing the case of Frau Emmy von N., the woman with whom he developed the technique of catharsis, Freud wrote:

> I called on her one day at lunch-time and surprised her in the act of throwing something wrapped up in paper into the garden, where it was caught by the children of the house-porter. In reply to my question, she admitted that it was her (dry) pudding, and that this went the same way every day. This led me to investigate what remained of the other courses and I found that there was more than half left on the plates. When I asked her why she ate so little she answered that she was not in the habit of eating more and that it would be bad for her if she did. . . . When on my next visit I ordered some alkaline water and forbade her usual way of dealing with her pudding, she showed considerable agitation. . . . Next day the nurse reported that she had eaten the whole of her helpings and had drunk a glass of the alkaline water. But I found Frau Emmy herself lying in a profoundly depressed state. . . . she said . . . "I've ruined my digestion, as always happens if I eat more or drink water, and I have to starve myself entirely for five days to a week before I can tolerate anything." . . . I assured her that . . . her pains were only due to the anxiety over eating.[13]

The famous Anna O., who was treated by Freud's colleague Breuer and helped to develop the "talking cure" on which psychoanalytic treatment is based, also suffered from depression and anorexia, accompanied by severe headaches. On the death of her beloved father, she stopped eating. She would go for days without nourishment and for long periods subsisting on a bit of fruit. Dora, the other well-known hysteric patient of Freud's who is discussed in Chapter 6, also appeared to be depressed as well as anorexic. In fact, in 1893, Breuer and Freud concluded that among the symptoms that were "idiopathic products of hysteria" were chronic vomiting and "anorexia, carried to the pitch of rejection of all nourishment."[14]

Neurasthenia was yet another late nineteenth-century disease characterized by symptoms of depressed mood and disordered eating. While the most widely discussed symptom of this ailment was nervous exhaustion, others included dyspepsia, insomnia, asthma, headaches, and emaciation. Physician George Savage described a typical case of neurasthenia as follows:

> A woman, generally single, or in some way not in a condition for performing her reproductive function . . . becomes bed-ridden, often refuses her food, or is capricious about it, taking strange things at odd times, or pretending to starve. . . . The body wastes, and the face has the thin, anxious look not unlike that represented by Rosetti in many of his pictures of women.[15]

As in other quotes already cited, the woman is described as "not in a condition for performing her reproductive function," and we return to this point later not only because it is central in this disorder but because it is salient to the doctors treating these women. Misogynists, perhaps; and clearly the conveyors of societal values.

In 1894, two physicians included nervous depression, headaches, insomnia, nausea, and vomiting in a list of common symptoms of neurasthenia in young women and noted that "the line of demarcation in this disease between hysteria on the one hand and melancholia on the other is indeed a fine one. Some would consider both as phases of it."[16] They pointed out that neurasthenia often afflicted young, unmarried, slender women.

Saints and Fasting Girls

Not all women who exhibited similar symptoms were diagnosed as ill. In a recent book, *Holy Anorexia*, Rudolph Bell concluded that over half the Italian women officially recognized by the Roman Catholic church from 1200 A.D. onward as saints, blesseds, venerables, or servants of God displayed clear signs of anorexia, including fasting, vomiting, bingeing, and amenorrhea. Many also felt "deeply depressed."[17]

The women Bell studied were treated as holy figures. But, as described by historian Joan Jacobs Brumberg, by the nineteenth century, young women who went for very long periods seemingly without eating were beginning to be viewed as curiosities and termed "fasting girls." One woman, Mollie Fancher of Brooklyn, New York, in 1864 refused to eat and began to waste away. In 1866, the *Brooklyn Daily Eagle* reported that she had gone for seven weeks without food and looked "more like parchment than flesh and blood."[18] Like the fasts of the holy women studied by Bell, Fancher's apparent ability to survive without food was treated by many people as a miracle. But, living during a period when the explanations offered by science had come to vie with those offered by religion, she was also labeled by many physicians as "hysteric."

Were All the Disorders Identical?

Thus, the Hippocratic "disease of young women," chlorosis, hysteria, and neurasthenia are all names given over the years to syndromes that were said to afflict women at adolescence and that involved depression, anxiety, disordered eating, headache, and several other symptoms we will discuss. We do not believe that all these disorders were identical. Further research is needed to determine whether individual differences between women in, for example, genetic predispositions, family constellations, societal influences, or the age at which they begin to experience problems may lead to different forms of this disorder. For now, we wish to emphasize that all these disorders were characterized by a wide range of symptoms, allowing physicians throughout history to use the diagnostic categories popular in their own day in describing women whom we believe suffered from one or another variant of what we call anxious somatic depression.

While a large number of similar symptoms were reported as being exhibited by adolescent women diagnosed as suffering from hysteria, neurasthenia, chlorosis, and the disease described in the Hippocratic texts, much less is known about the range of "symptoms" exhibited by consumptive women, holy anorexics, and fasting girls. At present, we must treat the notion that these women exhibited the complete syndrome discussed in this book as only an intriguing hypothesis.

We will sometimes use the term "forgotten syndrome" as a convenient way to refer to the collection of symptoms on which we focus. We chose the term "syndrome" to emphasize that we are not simply referring to a single currently recognized disorder such as anorexia or depression, but to a combination of symptoms. We use the word "forgotten" to acknowledge that the idea that several of these symptoms often tend to coexist among particular individuals is not a new creation of ours, but is based on the writings of many authorities over the centuries.

A single term like "anxious somatic depression" or "forgotten syndrome" allows us to minimize the somewhat boring repetition of the list of symptoms to which we must refer so often. On the other hand, the act of naming something, particularly using a medical term like "syndrome," may seem to imply scientific certainty about its existence. In this book and in a series of articles in recent professional journals, we present evidence for the continuing existence of a single disorder or a nearly identical series of disorders. By giving the disorder a name, we do not mean to imply that our hypothesis is proven beyond the shadow of a doubt or that the existence of this syndrome is already widely accepted in the fields of psychology and psychiatry.

Discontent with Traditional Gender Roles

Our historical research indicated that, over the centuries, women who suffered from the symptoms under the various names it was given were nontraditional females discontent with societal limitations placed on them.

For example, anthropologists and historians who have studied holy women, like those discussed by Bell, have noted that women who entered convents after growing up in the outside world tended to view females as weak and vulnerable, and that they saw joining a monastery as a way to rebel against social constraints placed on them and as a means of achieving autonomy and self-sufficiency. Historians have also found that many medieval holy women dressed as males. Several have offered the explanation that "because male was in Western culture superior to female, women had to take on symbolic maleness (or, at the very least, abandonment of femaleness) in order to signify spiritual advance."[19]

The most famous Italian holy woman described by Bell may have done just this. Saint Catherine of Sienna, co-patron of Italy with Francis of Assisi, was born Catherine Benincasa around 1347. After the death of her father, she could not eat. According to the priest assigned by the Pope to be her confessor, "Not only did she not need food, but she could not even eat without pain. If she forced herself to eat, her body suffered greatly, she could not digest and she had to vomit."[20] She lost half of her body weight and bound an iron chain around her hips. She also suffered from depression.

Catherine's "symptoms" first started after her beloved sister died in childbirth. At this point, Catherine's mother began to prepare her for marriage, teaching her to put on makeup and how to dye and curl her hair. She rebelled, cutting her hair very short. Her angry mother reacted by forcing her to do additional housework and telling her she would be compelled to marry. Catherine's self-starvation eventually forced her family to relent, allowing her to remain unmarried and enter a convent. Her neighbors called her "Euphrosyne" because she idolized this character from a legend who, as a young girl, escaped an unwanted marriage by changing into men's attire and retiring to a monastery. Catherine escaped an unwanted marriage not only by shedding her female attire, but also her female physique.

Another famous holy woman also appeared to exhibit disordered eating. Several authorities have speculated that Joan of Arc, who led the army of France, tonsured and garbed as a male, was also anorexic.[21] Marina Warner based her conclusion on Joan's abstemious eating and frequent fasting, evidence that Joan did not menstruate, and descriptions of Joan vomiting when forced to eat.

In some of the literature we have examined, the connection between an urge to achieve and the development of this syndrome was explicitly noted, though the correlation was explained differently. Morton attributed the consumption suffered by Mr. Duke's daughter to the "Injuries of the Air" the girl was exposed to as a result of her "studying at Night and continual poring upon books." The *Brooklyn Daily Eagle* noted how "fasting girl" Molly Fancher's "vitality gradually ebbed" as a result of her interest in education: "Her books were her delight . . . she neglected all for them and would arise late in the morning . . . hasten away to school without breakfast, fearful of being tardy, and then at evening, in her anxiety to learn her lessons, again neglect a meal for which she felt no inclination."[22] The newspaper also attributed Fancher's disorder to the overstimulation of mental faculties resulting from too much education.

Anxious Somatic Depression Among America's First College Women

The argument that problems resulted from mental overstimulation among young women seeking higher education was common in the nineteenth century, a period of major advances in higher education for women. Prior to then, women received no formal edu-

cation after high school. By the early part of the century, semi-
naries for females were established, offering training in some
advanced topics, but it was not until 1839 that the first college for
women, the Georgia Female College, opened its doors to students.
Several other women's colleges began in the 1840s and 1850s, but
these were, for the most part, small, financially troubled institu-
tions, and few survived. By the time Vassar opened in 1861, however, the idea of higher education for at least some women was
firmly established, and by 1875, when Smith and Wellesley opened,
significant numbers of females aspired to become college graduates.[23]

But the idea of higher education for women engendered tremendous resistance. Intellectual arguments against educating
women took two forms. The more straightforward attacks were
based on social and psychological arguments regarding women's
proper functions: Educated women would have smaller families,
experience "a dropping out of maternal instincts," and become less
feminine, "analogous to the sexless class of termites," or "eunuchs
of Oriental civilization."[24]

In the words of one authority writing in the *Popular Science
Monthly* in 1904:

> Not only does wifehood and motherhood not require an extraordinary
> development of brain but the latter is a decided barrier against the
> performance of these duties. Any family physician could give innu-
> merable cases out of his experience of failures of marriage directly due
> to too great a cultivation of the female intellect, which results in the
> scorning to perform those duties which are cheerfully performed and
> even desired by the uneducated wife.[25]

Yet most arguments made against higher education for women
were not so overtly self-interested. They were couched in concern
for the women and usually based on medical reports regarding the
effects of education on women's health. To choose only one example: "As for training young ladies through a long intellectual
course, as we do young men, it can never be done. They will die
in the process."[26] Too much education for women was said to be
responsible for ailments ranging from headaches and insomnia to
depression and indigestion.

Once again, we could ignore these arguments solely for their
obvious biases and the offensive form they took. Doing so, however, leads us to overlook the reasons why these arguments took
that particular form.

We find when we examine the medical advice closely that much of it focused on the development of a relatively small number of symptoms that physicians detected among women seeking higher education, symptoms including depressed mood, anxiety, amenorrhea, and other somatic symptoms such as disordered eating, headache, breathing difficulty, insomnia and heart palpitations. For example, in 1873, in his widely read book summarizing the medical problems of females seeking higher education, Harvard professor Dr. Edward Clarke included the following maladies: anemia, angular, puny bodies, small breasts, abnormally weak digestion, depression, nervousness, headache, sleep disturbance, and hysteria. Other physicians, such as Charles Meigs, a professor at the Jefferson Medical College in Philadelphia, also discussed the thinness and loss of appetite afflicting females who attended school.[27]

Perhaps the mistake of these physicians was not that, because of some bias, they imagined a connection between women going to college and the development of these symptoms, for they apparently found these symptoms in many patients, but that they misconstrued its cause. As we will continue to explicate, particularly in Part III, we believe that it was obviously not the expenditure of intellectual energy that damaged the health of so many first-generation college women, but instead the conflicting role aspirations and emotional turmoil experienced by ambitious women in the context of a society that discredited and placed obstacles in their paths toward achievement. This emotional turmoil was expressed in the symptoms described by the physicians.

Many physicians posited that the ill effects on women's health caused by too much learning resulted from damage done to the women's reproductive systems. These experts expressed particular concern about women expending energy on education just at a time when their complex reproductive systems were rapidly developing. The most obvious sign of this supposed misexpenditure of energy was the development of amenorrhea, the symptom Hippocrates, Benivieni, and Morton had focused so much attention on. As Dr. Meigs noted in 1859, "It is very common for me to find young women who have grown up admirably . . . to lose, in five or six weeks, the habit of menstruation, upon being brought to town and set on the school form and compelled to undergo the fatiguing labor of mental and educational discipline and culture."[28]

Mental Strain

The effect of too much education on the women was usually referred to as "mental strain," which was reputed to be implicated in the development of a wide range of problems, including chlorosis, neurasthenia, and hysteria.[29] In 1894, for example, physicians Henry B. Deale and S. S. Adams attributed the symptoms of neurasthenia to "the natural nervous tendency of a young girl or woman harassed by the ambitions of school life . . . or annoyed with household and family chores." Dr. S. W. Hammond of Rutland, Vermont, went so far as to cite neurasthenia as "a positive argument against higher education of women."[30]

Another authority on neurasthenia was Margaret Cleaves, M.D., one of the relatively few women physicians in the nineteenth century. In 1910, toward the end of her career, she wrote an autobiography, aptly titled *The Autobiography of a Neurasthene*, in which she admitted to suffering from the disease. Her self-description clearly indicates her nontraditional aspirations and her anorexia, and hints at the connection between her disorder and the reactions of others to her gender:

> As a child . . . I ate well. . . . At the age of fifteen I began teaching country schools in order to pay for the education I wanted . . . I could not eat. . . . At college . . . food interested me less than books . . . to have eaten more meant such physical distress that I could not. Had my father lived these things would not have been. My education would have been provided. . . . He always called me his boy; my only brother succumbed at the age of seven months to pneumonia . . . and I was his [her father's] constant companion.[31]

In his book *A Treatise on the Nervous Diseases of Women*, Laycock wrote in 1840: "The relations of hysteria to the present modes of education are of great importance. The anxiety to render a young lady accomplished at all hazards, has originated a system of forced mental training, which greatly increases the irritability of the BRAIN. . . . The consequence of all this is that the young female returns from school to her home a hysterical . . . girl."[32] In yet another echo of Hippocrates, Laycock recommended marriage as a treatment for women suffering from hysteria.

Here again, we see the symptoms being blamed on the schooling. It was not mental strain that caused the hysteria, we contend, but the discontent of these women with the limitations they experienced as they sought avenues of higher education. For example, Anna O. was described by Breuer and Freud in the *Studies on Hys-*

teria as "markedly intelligent," and possessing a "powerful intellect." She resented that she was not allowed to attend college although she was brighter than her brother, who was sent to the University of Vienna, which was closed to women. Because she was female, she remained at home "engaged on her household duties." According to Breuer, "This girl, who was bubbling over with intellectual vitality, led an extremely monotonous existence in her puritanically-minded family." He noted: "She possessed a powerful intellect which would have been capable of digesting solid mental pabulum and which stood in need of it—though without receiving it after she had left school."[33]

Anna, whose real name was Bertha Pappenheim, went on to a distinguished career as an influential social worker and leader of the Jewish women's movement. She wrote a play entitled *Women's Rights* dealing with women's powerlessness and exploitation by men and translated Mary Wollstonecraft's *A Vindication of the Rights of Women*, which argued for equal educational opportunity. She believed that, to men, women were mere "beasts of burden" and found her lack of formal education a "defective spiritual nourishment." One description of the characteristics of hysteric patients made by Breuer and Freud appears to suggest that parental belief in mental strain may have increased the barriers placed in the paths of bright women, perhaps bringing on the development of hysteria. They wrote: "Adolescents who are later to become hysterical are for the most part lively, gifted and full of intellectual interests before they fall ill. . . . They include girls who get out of bed at night so as secretly to carry on some study that their parents have forbidden from fear of their overworking." Freud even noted that intellectual effort not only did not cause neurasthenia, but was helpful in protecting against it.[34]

Thus, the observations of Breuer and Freud, viewed from a social roles perspective, lead us to conclude that the adolescent hysteric symptoms experienced by Anna O., including her depression, her anorexia, and her headaches, were rooted not in the overstimulation of her mind but in the opposite problem—understimulation, anger, and low self-esteem felt by very intelligent women like herself not allowed to exercise their abilities.

Historical Commonalities and Differences

It appears to us that for millennia, young women have been afflicted with a syndrome that involves not only the symptoms of disordered eating, but also depression, anxiety, headaches, breathing difficulties, and several other psychological and somatic symptoms. Although abundant evidence is scattered throughout recent research in psychology and psychiatry that a similar syndrome continues to afflict young women, possibly in very large numbers, science and society have lost sight of its existence. In this book we argue that a disorder that may have been recognized in antiquity, widely diagnosed as hysteria, neurasthenia, or chlorosis for centuries, and causing great suffering among contemporary women has been forgotten by modern science and goes undetected in examining rooms and guidance offices.

Some historians, notably Joan Jacobs Brumberg, Caroline Walker Bynum, and Rudolph Bell,[35] have recognized that many women living during earlier centuries exhibited eating problems. But Brumberg has argued that these women confronted historical conditions vastly different from those facing modern women and that their problems resulted from different causes. She concludes that earlier examples of disordered eating were not the same as modern anorexia nervosa.

Along with Bell, we see the commonalities as being more important than the differences, particularly among women of the past two centuries. Undoubtedly, women who lived during each historical period faced conditions that were in many respects unique. Perhaps this is why some symptoms exhibited by women suffering from forms of this syndrome during earlier periods, such as the paralyzed limbs reported in hysterical women, were no longer common during later periods. We must take seriously the historians' caution that among people living during different historical periods, behaviors and symptoms that superficially appear to be similar may not be identical in their causes or their meaning. But when we found not only the symptoms of disordered eating on which Bell and Brumberg focused, but also depression, anxiety, headaches, breathing difficulties, and other somatic symptoms, which were described as occurring together beginning at adolescence among women living during several different periods, and when we read strikingly similar descriptions of the educational aspirations of these women and their discontent with traditional gender roles, we came to believe that a nearly identical syndrome has afflicted young women over the ages.

Cross-cultural Comparisons

Similarly, when psychiatrists Michael B. King and Dinesh Bhugra found young women in India who obtained high scores on questionnaire measures of eating disorders traditionally used in Western nations, they warned that the questions included in such measures may often be interpreted differently in other cultures.[36] They concluded that few of the Indian women actually exhibited eating disorders. We must take seriously the warning that among people living in different cultures, behaviors and symptoms that superficially appear to be similar may not be identical in their causes or their meaning. But, once again, our search of the cross-cultural literature has led us to believe that the syndrome we have been discussing is not limited to the United States or to Western developed nations.

The past is not the only blind spot of science in modern, industrialized nations. Most people living in nations like ours know very little about what goes on in developing countries. Except for some brief attention to sensationalized media treatments of famines or coups, events in those nations go unnoticed even by most social and behavioral scientists. The body of knowledge that we call the sciences of psychology and psychiatry is in some respects limited to an understanding of the behaviors and problems of people living in Western nations in the late twentieth century. Attention to whether these problems look the same in developing nations is generally kept isolated in the books and journals of anthropology and cross-cultural psychology and psychiatry, disciplines that specialize in studying other cultures. The literature of these disciplines contains many contemporary reports of women at adolescence beginning to exhibit afflictions involving depression in combination with disordered eating and other somatic symptoms. As we found in the literature and documents of earlier centuries, these afflictions go under a variety of names. Authorities writing about one form seldom refer to any others. And as we saw in the incarnations of these symptoms over the ages, under any name it takes among cultures throughout the world, this syndrome afflicts women who are experiencing rapid changes in gender roles and come to feel disadvantaged by their femininity.

Arab women in Qatar, for example, suffer from what has been called "culture-bound syndrome," which is characterized by nausea, poor appetite, breathing difficulties, palpitations, faintness, and fatigue. Like those with the Hippocratic "disease of young women," these modern women are likely to be unmarried or to have fertility problems. El Islam, who studied these Arab women, noted that the culture-bound syndrome is rooted in the notion that the value of women is based on their husbands and the children they have, which has become more problematic now that these women are receiving more education and are exposed to radio and television, which depict different male-female relationships of the more developed nations. Thus, women experiencing culture-bound syndrome are not successful as measured by traditional standards of their culture, but are still influenced by them; they have not yet been able to "trade in" traditional values for the newer values and role expectations of women they are being exposed to.[37]

Medieval Roman Catholics were not the only religious women whose rituals included behaviors associated with disordered eating. Zar cults, for example, in which people are possessed by spirits called "Zars," are common in North Africa and parts of Asia. In Northern Sudan, typical symptoms of Zar possession include anorexia, nausea, depression, anxiety, headaches, and fertility problems. Over 40 percent of women over the age of 15 in one region of Sudan said that they had been possessed at some time by Zar. Some scholars have argued that Zar possession is a strategy women use to redress gender inequality because they observed that women possessed by Zar are clearly those who have been subjected to unfair treatment as a result of being female.

We do not suggest that the complex religious rituals of medieval Catholic nuns or of the Hofriyati women of the Northern Sudan can be reduced entirely to a set of symptoms of a single disease. Clearly, these rituals occur within a complex cultural context and take on multiple layers of meaning. At least some of those layers, however, may be related to the gender issues we discuss here. For example, Janice Boddy described one Zar ceremony lasting several days in which women possessed by the Zar spirits would enter trances and behave in ways not at all typical for Hofriyati women. Some women wore male clothing. One woman was possessed by the spirits of a doctor, a lawyer, and a military officer. Another strutted around "mandarinlike," wielding a walking stick symbolic of authority, and puffing on a cigarette. These two then staged a sword fight closely resembling the men's dance of a nearby tribe. A third threatened a man with a sword. In Boddy's words:

> Smoking, wanton dancing, flailing about, burping and hiccuping, drinking blood and alcohol, wearing male clothing, publicly threatening men with swords, speaking loudly lacking due regard for etiquette, these are hardly the behaviors of Hofriyati women for whom dignity and propriety are leading concerns.[38]

We would suggest that, while these are hardly the behaviors of proper Hofriyati women, they may mimic the behaviors of Hofriyati men. Thus, within the complex rituals brought on by possession by alien spirits, we find both enactment of male roles traditionally closed off to these women as well as several symptoms of anxious somatic depression.

Nerves

In many nations, this syndrome is simply called "nerves." Spiritualist healers in Mexico, for example, have been observed to diagnose nerves among women exhibiting amenorrhea, "emptiness" in the stomach, and nausea, as well as headaches, insomnia, and excessive crying. Symptoms of nerves reported by Setha M. Low in Guatemala include headache, despair, anxiety, stomach pain, insomnia, difficulty breathing, and nausea. As we might expect, nerves tends to be much more common among females than among males, and is often found to be particularly frequent among women exhibiting problems in reproduction.[39]

Several anthropologists have noted that nerves is likely to occur among women who are experiencing a transition from a traditional society to a modern one.[40] Once again, with changing gender roles, we see the symptoms of anxious somatic depression. Case histories of women afflicted with nerves exhibit the discontent with traditional female roles that we believe plays such a large part in the development of the syndrome. For example, Toula was a 19-year-old woman living in a village in Greece, which had recently experienced dramatic increases in women's rights and opportunities when the Socialists took over from the military dictatorship. Although she lived for several years in the United States, where she was exposed to less traditional views of women, Toula was not allowed to attend secondary school when her parents brought her back to Greece. Her twin brother, however, was able to pursue his education. Like Anna O., she was envious of the advantages accorded her brother simply because he was male. In what we interpret as a wish to be masculine in order to reap those advantages for herself, she said that when he died, she would take over her brother's spirit. Toula also had a poor body image clearly associated with her discomfort over her developing femininity. Although slim and attractive, she felt "fat and ugly," a term she applied to a neighbor, too, because of what she called the neighbor's "huge breasts."[41]

In many cultures, the syndrome may sometimes simply be called depression, which may manifest itself somewhat differently in non-Western nations. Researchers and clinicians in these nations observe less guilt and hopelessness than in the West, and find somatic symptoms predominating. Nigerian psychiatrist T. Adeoye Lambo observed much confusion in his country between the diagnosis of depression and that of neurasthenia because the typical depressed patient "is invariably preoccupied with vague somatic complaints." In one international survey, the primary symptoms of depression found in non-Western nations were "fatigue, anorexia, weight loss, and loss of libido."[42]

Just as when it is called culture-bound syndrome or nerves, when this constellation of symptoms is called depression it is often related to changing gender roles. For example, Helen E. Ullrich conducted interviews in a village in India in which women recently experienced a high rate of depression as well as dramatic increases in educational opportunities. Of the 23 women age 40 or older interviewed by Ullrich, none had attended high school. Of the 22 women less than 40 years old, 20 had graduated from high school and 7 of these had even more education. Like American women in the late nineteenth century, these Brahmin Indian women were pioneers in their culture in attempting to seek higher education. Several women expressed discontent with the traditional female roles of wife and homemaker and wanted more education than they were allowed. They became depressed when they realized the full extent of the disadvantages of being female.

For example, Vani, a 24-year-old woman, was married at age 20 but "wanted to continue her education and still regrets her parents' insistence on marriage." Ullrich adds: "Vani openly discusses the misfortunes of being female." During her first year of marriage, she had a major depressive episode, "she ate little, had no appetite, lost weight, lost interest in everything, just sat in one position, refused to talk, cried a lot, and could not sleep." When her weight loss continued, a physician was consulted. "The depression resolved when she had a son," a pattern that we discuss in a later chapter. In Ullrich's words: "Vani . . . may have conflicts with the traditional female role and with parents' values that a woman should have primarily a domestic identity."[43]

Thus, like physicians of previous centuries, contemporary anthropologists have described a syndrome afflicting women at adolescence or early adulthood that involves depression, anxiety, disordered eating, and several other somatic symptoms. The one difference between the descriptions made by anthropologists in recent years and those made by physicians in past centuries is that the cross-cultural observations were made primarily by investigators quite knowledgeable about the workings of gender roles. As described in fascinating detail in the historical treatments of hysteria and neurasthenia written by such scholars as Carol Smith Rosenberg and Elaine Showalter, physicians of earlier centuries for the most part ignored the role played by gender inequality in the etiology of earlier versions of the syndrome.[44] In contrast, connections made by contemporary anthropologists between the changing status of women, particularly in the form of increased education, and the development of the depressive and somatic symptoms associated with nerves, Zar cults, culture-bound syndrome, and depression focus on gender roles, not mental strain. Most of the experts who study manifestations of this syndrome cross-culturally, however, seem unaware of the commonalities they exhibit with each other, with our culture, and with past cultures. As with the differences between hysteria, neurasthenia, and chlorosis, the factors leading to differences between these various forms of the syndrome found in contemporary developing nations need to be investigated further. But these differences should not be allowed to obscure the many commonalities.

During the past three decades, millions of women living in the United States and other industrialized nations have grown up in cultures that have socialized them to aspire to achievements historically reserved for men, and have confronted myriad barriers. The women of their mothers' generation did not, for the most part, achieve outside of the home. If such experiences lead to the development of the syndrome we have been discussing, we should be seeing evidence of this syndrome in high-school guidance offices, college infirmaries, mental health clinics, and hospitals throughout the developed world. To look for such evidence, we now turn our attention to contemporary research dealing with the various symptoms constituting the syndrome. We begin with depression.

3

Depression

At age 19, future political philosopher Hannah Arendt described in her journal the depression she suffered with these words: "Madness, joylessness, disaster, annihilation" and the desire that "the end, long and fervently hoped for . . . puts an end to this needless and futile life." Harriet Beecher Stowe, author of the widely read *Uncle Tom's Cabin*, also described a "great depression," one in which she felt "scarcely alive" half the time; the other half a "slave of morbid feeling." At age 16, she wrote to her sister, "I . . . wish to die young."[1] The diaries and journals of most of the renowned women whose lives we studied detail the thoughts and emotions that characterize depression: The feeling that nothing gives pleasure, the sense that each moment is to be dreaded, the fear that life is now, and will always be, made up only of suffering, the longing for death to end it all.

The pain evident in these descriptions falls disproportionately on female shoulders, for, like disordered eating, depression is much more common among females. Women have more symptoms of depression than men do, are more likely to be diagnosed as depressed, are more frequently hospitalized for depression, and are more likely to attempt suicide. Male suicide attemptors more often complete the act, with one notable exception: Professional women exhibit rates of successful suicide comparable to males. The estimate usually given in the psychiatric literature is that women are twice as likely as men to be depressed.[2]

Another striking parallel between depression and disordered eating is the importance of the adolescent years. Depression in children is relatively rare. But as children, particularly girls, pass through adolescence, more and more begin to feel sad, hopeless, worthless, or inert. In a recent study of over 900 Dutch students, males and females reported about the same low level of depressed mood until age 14. During the next four years of adolescence, the proportion feeling unhappy, sad, or depressed rose twice as much among females as among males, until by age 18, about one in three Dutch females reported feeling depressed compared to only about one in eight males.[3] Adolescence is the period in which signs of depression first appear, primarily among females.

Adolescent Sadness Becomes Midlife Depression

But while teenage girls are much more likely than teenage boys to show some symptoms of depression, relatively few are diagnosed as suffering from the psychiatric disorder called major depression. In adulthood, however, dozens of studies report high rates of major depression among women, rates much greater than those exhibited by men.[4] It appears that the depressive symptoms experienced by female adolescents often do not develop into full-blown cases of clinical depression until later in life.

In support of this notion, a recent survey of five U.S. communities found that the greatest number of females first reported symptoms of depression between ages 15 and 19. Other surveys, however, indicated that the greatest number of females first develop a full clinical depressive disorder later in life.[5] This pattern has also been found in other cultures. In Peru, younger women are said to suffer from "nervios" (Spanish for nerves), with a lowercase "n," which are feelings of depression. Older women, however, suffer from "Nervios," with a capital "N," which is similar to a clinical diagnosis of depression.[6]

This pattern is important because it tells us that depression may develop in stages. In childhood, some women may develop attitudes and personality traits predisposing them to develop disordered eating, depressed mood, and other psychological and somatic symptoms when they reach adolescence. Later they progress from depressed mood to full-blown clinical depression. Looking at the development in this way has powerful implications for understanding what causes depression, why women are so likely to suffer from it, and what can be done to treat, or—even better—prevent the disease. Perhaps most obvious is that we are drawn to study the childhoods of depressed women. As we describe in detail in Chapters 6 and 7, many of these women have told us that as children they developed a self-image as high-achieving, bright girls at the same time they began to notice that in certain highly valued areas of achievement their mothers and many other women were limited by being female. Because sex roles are somewhat less rigid early on, many of these girls were allowed in childhood to pursue nontraditional goals.

The realization of a step-by-step development of depression also leads us to ask what it is about the experience of adolescence that causes so many females to begin to feel depressed. As we will elaborate in Chapter 8, when girls undergo the physical changes of puberty and adolescence, other people begin to respond differently to them and the girls begin to think differently about themselves. As their bodies develop breasts and curves, the impact of their social and sexual status as women is experienced for the first time. For girls who have come to view womanhood as having a status lower than that attributed to manhood, this change engenders conflict and appears all too often to precipitate depressed mood and low self-esteem.

We speculate that the connection between anatomy and gender role is the reason why depressed women, like those with disordered eating, have very poor body image. Discomfort with their own bodies plagues not only hospitalized patients suffering from severe depression, but also college women with symptoms of depression. Depressed people view their appearance more negatively than nondepressed people, even when they are not rated by observers as being less attractive. It is telling that, beginning at adolescence, depression is more highly related to poor body image among females than among males, and that in one group of adolescent women whose body image was related to symptoms of depression, the statistical relationship disappeared when the women's self-esteem was mathematically taken into account.[7] That is, it seems that the poor body image of these depressed adolescents resulted because their feelings about their bodies were highly indicative of how they felt about themselves, and, we would suggest, about their identities as women. We contend that depression begins for most girls at adolescence, because that is when they become women, and that depressed girls have poor body image because it is their bodies that define them as women.

If depression really starts in adolescence, we would expect that the people who show signs of depression as teenagers are the ones who develop more serious indications of clinical depression later in life. And indeed, for females, depressive symptoms in adolescence are particularly likely to signify future problems. Girls who reported symptoms of depression in high school were more likely nine years later to have sought the help of a mental health professional, to have been hospitalized for a mental illness, to report health problems, and to have dropped out of high school. Among males, in contrast, reports of depressive symptoms in adolescence did not predict any of these problems during early adulthood.[8] Again, adolescence appears to be a crucial period for the development of what will eventually become more serious depression among females, but not so clearly among males.

Disordered Eating, Depression, and Development

Disordered eating among women is often accompanied by symptoms of depression, but researchers have trouble explaining why. The importance of adolescence in the development of depression and the finding that depression is more highly related to disordered eating among females than among males suggest that the conflicts over gender that may cause adolescent women to have eating problems may also cause depressed mood that later becomes clinical depression.[9]

Sharing the hubris of contemporary science, we thought that the role of adolescence in the development of later depression had only recently drawn the attention of psychologists and psychiatrists. We were quite surprised to learn that the relationship between the symptoms of the forgotten syndrome and the later development of depression (formerly called melancholia) had been recognized for over a century. In writing of the nervous disorders in which disturbances of appetite play a central role, one author noted in 1878: "Hysterical women . . . are especially prone to eat irregularly; to take food, if possible, when unnoticed; to eat altogether a very inadequate quantity, and to eke it out by an inordinate proportion of stimulants. . . . Often they are miserably thin . . . they may be fat . . . taking more than is necessary for a person in health." This observer then added, "While young they are termed hysterical, especially if they are women; when older . . . their nervousness then takes for the most part the form of depression and anxiety." In letters written to his confidante Wilhelm Fliess, Freud observed that "Melancholia develops as an intensification of neurasthenia," and that the "neurosis concerned with eating, parallel to melancholia, is anorexia. The famous anorexia nervosa of young girls seems to me (on careful observation) to be a melancholia where sexuality is underdeveloped."[10]

What causes the depressed mood and disordered eating of adolescent females, once diagnosed as neurasthenia or hysteria, to flower into the disease melancholia, now called major depression? We have much to say about childhood and adolescent experiences reported by female high school and college students suffering from anxious somatic depression. Only recently have we begun to comprehend the importance of the third stage of young adulthood and midlife and to survey women of these ages. At this juncture, our evidence as to what happens after adolescence to bring on major depression is based primarily on case histories and the research of others, and must be laced with a healthy dose of speculation.

For example, psychiatrist Charles Brenner recently described the case of a 33-year-old woman who at the onset of puberty became uncomfortable with her body and later became depressed. Brenner noted that it was clear that "this patient's conflicts centered about the fact that she was a girl, not a boy, and that they had done so since her brother's birth." He added that her "conviction that she was a second-class citizen in a man's world" had begun early in life and crystallized into poor body image when she reached puberty and began to menstruate, which meant the end of any possibility of being a man. The onset of her depression began in young adulthood, coinciding with her brother's entry into the family business. "Until that time the patient had been her father's right hand in the business. When her brother, who was five years her junior and her only sibling, came into the business, it soon became clear to the patient that it was not she, but her brother, who was destined to be her father's close associate and eventual successor."[11]

It appears that in the decades after adolescence, many nontraditional women face obstacles that keep them from living up to the aspirations they developed in childhood. These include the extra career hurdles in terms of promotion, prestige, and partnerships they confront in most workplaces, even in businesses run by their fathers, as Brenner's patient learned to her dismay. They also include issues of childbearing and raising a family while pursuing a career. If women do not have children, many people view them as failures. If they have them but continue to put in the time needed for a successful career, many people regard them as inadequate, selfish mothers—they may even view themselves this way. Surveys have found that women employed in professional careers spend more time in childcare than their husbands and that professional women with children are more likely than their husbands to feel that they are not the kind of spouses and parents they would like to be. If they devote time to childrearing, women must often give up hopes of major achievements outside the home. In the words of one woman with a doctorate in the social sciences, a part-time job at a teaching hospital, and two toddlers: "There is no good solution. You have to give something up either way." Another mother of two preschoolers who had two graduate degrees and a four-day-a-week job in an accounting firm confided, "I have a lot of latitude because I've been there for a long time and I'm respected. But I would never be considered for promotion working the hours I do." As we discuss in Chapter 5, many high-achieving women experience the symptoms of anxious somatic depression after the birth of their first child. Women are also more likely than men to take on the added burden of caring for infirm relatives, a burden that entails great costs—physically, psychologically, and professionally—but receives relatively little recognition.[12]

By midlife, many women come to feel that they will probably never reach their once-treasured goals, never win the respect they have worked for. If their marriages end in divorce and they have chosen to forego careers and devote their twenties and thirties to childrearing and homemaking, they may find themselves without the financial and emotional support of marriage or a satisfying means of earning a living. As one recently divorced suburban housewife put it, "In my twenties, I was somebody in my field. I had a high-paying job and was on my way up. Then I let it go when I got married and had a child. I was known as X's wife. Now I wish I had kept at it because the field has left me behind. I can't even get a job as a secretary."

Even women who have continued to work experience depression, anxiety, and somatic symptoms that make achieving more difficult. Many of the women we studied went for long periods suffering from loss of concentration, which resulted from the distraction of depressed mood, headaches, anxiety, and feelings of failure. One woman who had made partner in a major law firm but left her job when her husband's business relocated to a different state had frequent bouts of depression accompanied by migraine headaches and feelings of failure, interfering with her ability to find new work. When she was contacted by a prestigious law firm regarding an opening, she was unable to respond for months, convinced she had accomplished nothing and that the firm would find her as inadequate as she believed herself to be. Indeed, one study reported that in adolescence depressed females tended to feel that others viewed them as inadequate, but in adulthood depressed females tended to view themselves as failures.[13]

Childhood is thus a time of great potential and some flexibility regarding gender roles, a time when aspirations toward academic and professional success may become integral aspects of a girls' self-image. Adolescence, however, brings with it a sense of the limitations these young girls face as they begin to view themselves and be treated by others as women. Adulthood is a time when many women see that their childhood dreams of overcoming the limitations placed on their mothers will never completely come true, particularly if they are hindered by depressed mood, anxiety, low self-esteem, and somatic symptoms. For far too many women, serious depression may confront them in their adult years.

Historical Changes in Gender Differences in Depression

One hint that depression and disordered eating may both be aspects of a single syndrome comes from historical similarities exhibited by both disorders. The 1920s and the past few decades apparently shared not just similar standards of female beauty and outbreaks of disordered eating, as we previously discussed, but also similarities in the depression experienced by women. We found evidence of these similarities in case histories as well as in quantitative epidemiologic studies. For example, Brenner's 1991 conclusion that issues of discontent with being female frequently underlie depressive affect was also drawn by earlier therapists about women who reached adolescence during the 1920s, and exhibited depression combined with disordered eating and poor body image. Otto Fenichel cited a 1932 discussion of a disorder described as "not infrequent in women," in which women experienced periods of depression during which they stuffed themselves and felt fat, alternating with periods in which they "behaved ascetically," a reference perhaps to what we know as anorexia. These women supposedly exhibited "an intense unconscious hatred against their mothers and against femininity. To them being fat means getting breasts." In 1925, Feigenbaum described a case of what was called "hysterical depression." The female patient had suffered, starting at puberty, from depression, loss of appetite, "pseudo-hunger," and nausea. Feigenbaum attributed hysterical depression to "primary sex envy" and identification with men.[14] In cases that we discuss later, described in the works of eminent psychiatrists Ludwig Binswanger and Peter Blos, similar symptoms were attributed to the patient's discontent with traditional female roles.

These cases from the 1920s suggest that the outbreak of disordered eating recognized by the American Medical Association in 1926 may have been an outbreak of a syndrome that involved depression as well as disordered eating. If so, we might expect the pattern of women's depression over the course of the twentieth century to resemble the pattern of disordered eating. That is exactly what we found when we reanalyzed a major study on depression.

Based on interviews in which people were asked about the symptoms they had experienced throughout their lives, psychiatrist Gerald Klerman and his colleagues determined which males and females might have been diagnosed as depressed earlier in life and the age at which they became depressed. The people interviewed greatly ranged in age, allowing us to compare gender differences in rates of depression exhibited by males and females born during several different periods over the twentieth century. For our purpose of analyzing historical fluctuations in gender differences in depression, it is fortunate that all the people interviewed were first-degree relatives of patients who were diagnosed as depressed. As a result, genetic influences, which have also been found to play an important role in the development of depression, were roughly equivalent for those in the study, allowing a particularly powerful test of the influences of historical change.[15]

We might recall the pattern that disordered eating among women has exhibited over the course of this century. Anorexia and bulimia appear to have been rare at the turn of the century, when the fleshiness of Lillian Russell reigned supreme. By the mid-1920s, however, the "New Woman" born in the 1910s and 1920s began to exhibit symptoms of disordered eating, as described in our first chapter. This was followed by a period in which eating disorders became uncommon, which is why they were treated as a new disease when they began reappearing in the 1960s and 1970s among large numbers of women born after World War II. Support for the conclusion that the prevalence of disordered eating was relatively high among women born in the two decades prior to the 1930s, began to decrease among women born in the 1930s, and then increased once again among those born in the late 1940s and the 1950s comes not only from the anecdotal evidence already cited, but also from a statistical study of the cases of women retrospectively diagnosed as anorexic based on records of physicians who practiced in Rochester, Minnesota, between 1935 and 1984.[16]

The pattern we found of historical fluctuations in gender differences in depression mimicked the pattern in disordered eating. For readers who prefer to examine data visually, Figure 3 depicts the ratio of females to males among people born during each decade who were retrospectively diagnosed as having been depressed at age 40. Points near the dark horizontal line across the figure indicate birth cohorts in which females did not exhibit more depression than males and points near the top indicate cohorts in which

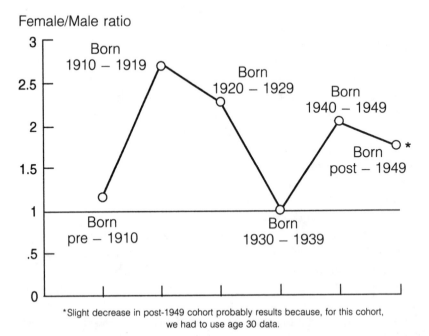

*Slight decrease in post-1949 cohort probably results because, for this cohort, we had to use age 30 data.

Figure 3 Female/male ratios of rates of diagnosed major depression by age 40 among cohorts organized according to birth decade.

females exhibited markedly more depression than males. Women born around the turn of the century were not more likely to be depressed than comparable men. But among people who were born in the 1910s and 1920s, women were two to three times as likely as men to be depressed at age 40. This was the same generation of women about whose thinness and self-starvation the American Medical Association was so concerned. Continuing to parallel disordered eating, gender differences in depression disappeared among people born in the 1930s only to resurface among those born after the 1930s. It appears that generations in which adolescent women had eating disorders were the same generations in which women were more likely than men to be depressed at age 40.

But, with one exception, major depression was not more likely among females than among males before the age of 40.[17] Thus, while major depression and disordered eating appear to afflict the same generations of women, the disordered eating and early symptoms of depression occur in adolescence, while major depression develops later on. Freud and others seem to have been correct in their observations that melancholia developed later in life among women who earlier exhibited disorders associated with problem eating and depressed mood, such as anorexia, hysteria, or neurasthenia.

Changing Gender Roles and Depression

The patterns of generational fluctuations in disordered eating and depression over the course of this century allow us not only to connect the two disorders, but also to relate both to changing gender roles. Each case described in this book is that of an ambitious, nontraditional woman whose mother did not wish, or was not able, to achieve outside the home. But it may be possible to select case histories that prove almost anything. In our attempt to investigate statistically whether trying to achieve academically and professionally when one's mother did not could produce a combination of depression, disordered eating, and somatic symptoms in women, we adapted the method used to create the bar graph in Chapter 1 (Figure 1) so we could measure generational changes in women's academic achievement. Using U.S. Census statistics, we calculated the rate of college graduation among American women over the course of this century. To create an index of generational change in opportunities for women, we subtracted the rate twenty years earlier from each measure of the female college graduation rate.

That is, high scores on this index occur during years when a much larger proportion of females graduated from college than had graduated during their mother's generation.[18]

Using this method, we found that two groups of women reached adolescence during periods in which changes in female college graduation were actually negative—they did not have much greater opportunity for educational achievement than the women of their mothers' generation. These are the women born at the very beginning of the century and those born in the 1930s. They also did not evidence much disordered eating and were the only groups of women who did not exhibit a greater incidence of depression than men born in the same period.

In contrast, some generations of women reached adolescence during periods when they had greater opportunities than their mothers. These are the women who reached adolescence in the mid-1920s and in the mid-1960s and thereafter. These are also the generations in which eating disorders became very prevalent and those who exhibited more depression than males. Figure 4 graphically presents this index of generational change in rates of female college graduation.

Thus, statistical studies of American women born over the course of the twentieth century, like the historical and cross-

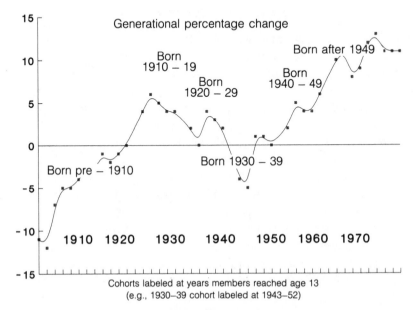

Figure 4　Female college graduation rates.

cultural evidence cited previously, suggest that women who mature during periods of changing gender roles develop preferences for slimness along with symptoms of disordered eating and depressed mood at adolescence, which often develops into major depression by midlife.

The interrelationship between several of these symptoms has been found cross-culturally as well as historically. Mandy McCarthy recently reported that women exhibit higher rates of depression than men only in nations that are industrialized (and thus probably undergoing changes in women's roles), have thin standards of female beauty, and in which reports of disordered eating among females appear.[19]

As we will discuss in greater detail later, during periods of changing gender roles many young girls are brought up to feel that educational and professional achievements—areas historically reserved for males—are much more valuable than the domestic achievements of their mothers and most other women. As these girls mature, however, many find that overt and covert gender biases continue to forestall the success of women in these pursuits. Confronted with traditional female roles that are devalued and traditional male pursuits for which they are placed at a disadvantage, many women who grow up during these periods come to feel like failures.

The notion that these feelings of failure may have played a role in developing symptoms of anxious somatic depression agrees with reports that low levels of self-esteem have been found to accompany weight concerns and eating problems among females but not males, and that concerns about competence have been reported to be more highly related to depression among females than males. For example, one study that followed children from age 3 through adolescence found that the level of concern regarding personal adequacy exhibited by 14-year-old boys was not related to their depressive symptoms at age 18. In contrast, 14-year-old girls worried about their personal adequacy were likely to be the ones who felt depressed four years later. Perhaps even more telling were the gender differences in the direction of the relationship between intelligence and subsequent depressive symptoms. For boys, higher intelligence predicted less depression, whereas for girls, those who became depressed at age 18 were the most likely to have been the more intelligent as children. Level of education also seems to have an unexpected relationship to depression among females and males. Among those who exhibited no psychiatric disorder at the beginning of one study, the males who had attended college were less likely to develop depression over a six-year period than men who had not attended college. Among females, however, those who had attended college were more likely to develop depression than those who had not. Similarly, depressed men who were found to exhibit high achievement orientation have been reported to respond well to treatment, whereas depressed women exhibiting high achievement orientation were found to be the ones most likely to respond poorly. There may be no clearer connection between depression and issues of female achievement than these indications—high intelligence, education, and the desire to achieve serve to protect males somewhat from depression but render females more vulnerable.[20]

4

Anxious Somatic Depression

Depression is not the only disorder for which high achievement appears to protect males but puts females at greater risk. Boys who exhibit such somatic symptoms as headache and breathing difficulties tend to do poorly in high school, whereas girls who report these symptoms are the ones who do well. Readers may recall from the vignettes of Chapter 2 that headache, breathing difficulty, insomnia, heart palpitations, and menstrual dysfunction were frequently included in the descriptions of the "disease of young women," hysteria, neurasthenia, chlorosis, and nerves.[1] Most of these symptoms were very common among our patients and among the eminent women whose biographies we studied.

We examined the lives of five women—India's Indira Gandhi, Britain's Queen Elizabeth I and Queen Victoria, Russia's Catherine the Great, and Israel's Golda Meir—all of whom belonged in one of the smallest occupational categories for women: rulers of nations. Each appeared to have suffered from the constellation of symptoms we call anxious somatic depression, with the possible exception of Indira Gandhi. We say "possible" because Gandhi was described as being ill throughout much of her life, but the details of her illness have not yet been revealed in the biographies so far published. We did find some indications, however, that she may have exhibited breathing difficulties and disordered eating.

We do know that, at adolescence, Indira Gandhi fell ill and

that, at age 20, she was sent to Switzerland to convalesce. Some books refer to possible lung problems, and her mother was also often ill and died of an alleged lung disease. So it is possible that Indira Gandhi may have inherited a predilection toward pleurisy. On the other hand, as we discussed in Chapter 2, women suffering from anxious somatic depression have sometimes been called consumptive because of the wasting away associated with anorexia. Indirect evidence exists that this may have been the case with Indira Gandhi. Many letters written by and to her father, Jawaharlal Nehru, contained references to her weight. In some, Nehru would write with concern that his daughter had lost weight. In others, friends would try to cheer him with news of a weight gain, as when Mohandas (Mahatma) Gandhi, imprisoned for revolutionary activities, thought it important enough to telegraph Nehru, who was in a different prison, that he had seen Indira looking "happy and in possession of more flesh." Between ages 16 and 23, she was described as "frail," "thin," "delicate," "wiry," and "almost ethereal."[2]

Perhaps because, unlike Indira Gandhi, England's Queen Elizabeth I did not reign in recent years, the details of her lifelong illness have reached print. At age 14, Elizabeth developed "pains in the head . . . which reduced her capacity for concentrated study." At 15, she suffered a "breakdown of the nervous system," lost her appetite, refused to eat, lost much weight, and exhibited insomnia and crying spells. By age 26, she was described by her ladies in waiting as "quite melancholy" and had trouble sleeping. She was said to be a "very light eater," to have a "spare appetite," and to eat "smally or nothing." By age 36, she was experiencing "episodes of mild hysteria," including fainting, and pains in the stomach, legs, and head. A physician called in to examine her the next year claimed that the queen was so thin "that her bones may be counted." She was described as "frail," "fleshless," and "thin and emaciated."[3]

Beginning in adolescence, Britain's Queen Victoria was overweight, unable to stay on a diet, and suffered from "indigestion," loss of appetite, and nervous vomiting. It is possible that some of these symptoms may have been associated with her recurrent migraine headaches or her depression but we cannot be sure. At age 20, she was so depressed that she could not get out of bed, and even brushing her teeth was a struggle. Victoria told a confidante that she often wished the time would come when she could go to that world where the "weary are at rest."[4]

Catherine the Great, Empress of all the Russias, and Golda Meir, the only female ever elected Premier of Israel, did not suffer, to the best of our knowledge, from disordered eating, but both had chronic headaches as well as depression, possibly to the point of attempting or contemplating suicide. A biographer reported that Catherine the Great regularly "fell prey to depression," particularly when she was menstruating, and may have attempted suicide. She was also an insomniac who had recurrent headaches. Golda Meir was described by a biographer as a "depressed housewife" in the period before she entered politics. Later she experienced "grinding despair" and a close friend felt certain that she was "entertaining a suicidal impulse." She, too, had severe headaches.

Although these five women are not necessarily representative of any woman who might attain power, it is distressing that common among even these very powerful and successful women were the symptoms of depression, disordered eating, and physical problems such as headaches and insomnia.[5]

When we began to look for evidence of the existence of a syndrome involving depression, anxiety, disordered eating, and somatic symptoms among contemporary women, we found that current authorities do not usually write of a single syndrome. Because of modern specialization, a separate research literature deals with each of the symptoms or disorders once grouped under the names we have already identified: "the disease of young women," consumption, chlorosis, neurasthenia, and hysteria. With some notable exceptions in the field of psychosomatic medicine, experts writing about any one of these disorders today do not refer to the striking patterns we found common among all of these symptoms when we compared the separate research literatures. These shared patterns include higher prevalence as well as greater comorbidity (i.e., the co-occurence of two or more disorders) among females than among males, greater increase during adolescence among females than among males, and similar patterns of fluctuation in prevalence over the course of the twentieth century.

Gender Differences in Disorders

Most recent studies report that contemporary women continue to be more likely than men to suffer from all the symptoms described in the past as characterizing what we call anxious somatic depression, which includes not only depression and eating disorders such as anorexia, bulimia, and obesity, but also body image disturbances, anxiety disorders, headache, some types of asthma, insomnia, sexual indifference, and mitral valve prolapse, the modern name given to the heart clicks and murmurs that were characteristic of women with chlorosis.[6]

From the time of the ancient Greeks, the syndrome was described as first striking females at adolescence. As we might expect if the same syndrome continues to afflict large numbers of women, contemporary researchers have reported that only at adolescence and in early adulthood do the individual disorders constituting the syndrome become much more common among females. Before adolescence, males often exhibit equal or greater rates of the disorders, but after adolescence the prevalence among females is much greater. For example, a recent study of Dutch students found that 11-year-old boys and girls were equally likely to have headaches. But, among males, headaches do not increase in frequency during the teenage years, whereas reports of headaches more than double among females, with approximately half of 17- and 18-year-old females reporting headaches. Similar patterns have been reported for insomnia and mitral valve prolapse (MVP), a common disorder of the valve separating the left atrium from the left ventricle of the heart, which causes heart clicks, murmurs, and palpitations. MVP is very rare among children under 15 but becomes particularly prevalent at adolescence and in early adulthood among females, but not among males.[7]

The pattern for asthma is complicated by the existence of two forms of the disorder. Extrinsic asthma is associated with allergies that can be measured with skin tests. This form of asthma develops in childhood, is not associated with neurotic symptoms, and is more prevalent among males. Extrinsic, allergic asthma is not part of the syndrome we are discussing here. Intrinsic asthma, however, is characterized by breathing difficulties that cannot be attributed to any measurable allergy. This form develops after childhood, has been found to be related to neuroses, anxiety, and introversion, and is much more prevalent among females.[8] These are the breathing difficulties we believe to be part of the syndrome, and they may have played a role in labeling women with the syndrome as consumptive.

Recently we have become aware that the research literature on fatigue reports a pattern quite similar to those of the symptoms already described. Fatigue is more common among women than men. Prior to adolescence, however, chronic fatigue is rare. During adolescence, reports of feeling overtired become much more prevalent among females. Fatigue has been found to be associated with other symptoms of anxious somatic depression, such as disordered eating and mitral valve prolapse. And, like the other symptoms we discuss, fatigue has been shown to be more common among depressed females than males. Fatigue was the defining symptom of neurasthenia and was also cited in descriptions of what we believe are other versions of anxious somatic depression, such as chlorosis and culture-bound syndrome. These findings suggest that fatigue should be included in future research on anxious somatic depression. They also imply the intriguing, but unproven, hypothesis that some women who have recently been diagnosed as suffering from chronic fatigue syndrome may actually be exhibiting anxious somatic depression.[9]

The Hippocratic texts and later writings on the syndrome describe it as appearing around the onset of puberty. Paralleling this, several individual disorders have been reported in the contemporary research literature to begin in females around the time of onset of puberty.[10] For example, a wide range of somatic symptoms including loss of appetite, nausea or vomiting, headache, sleep difficulty, breathlessness, and palpitations were found to increase greatly when Finnish girls entered adolescence and to develop earliest among the girls who reached puberty first. Thus, females exhibit higher prevalence than males of depression, disordered eating, headache, breathing difficulty, and insomnia but only after they reach adolescence. This pattern is exactly what we would expect to find if contemporary women, like those earlier, develop a syndrome involving these symptoms at adolescence.

Changes in Prevalence over the Twentieth Century

If the somatic symptoms are actually part of a syndrome involving depression and disordered eating, they should show similar patterns of historical fluctuation related to changes in women's roles. To date, we have found information on differences between people born over the course of the twentieth century in rates of headache and mitral valve prolapse.

We calculated fluctuations in gender differences in rates of frequent headache among people born over the course of the century reported in three surveys of headache prevalence: one done in 1962, one in 1969–71, and one in 1981.[11] We found that among people born at the turn of the century, who were surveyed only in the 1962 study, females were actually less likely than males to report "frequent unexplained" headaches. Recall that the people born at the turn of the century also exhibited no gender differences in depression, and there was little evidence that young women of the period preferred thinness or suffered from disordered eating. In all three studies, among people born between 1905 and the mid-1920s, females reported higher rates than males of frequent headaches. Females in these groups were also much more likely than males to be depressed, and this is the same generation of women about whose anorexia and quest for thinness the American Medical Association was so concerned. Among people born in the 1930s, gender differences in headache frequency were small. In fact, in two studies, females born in the 1930s actually reported lower rates of frequent headache than males. Gender differences in depression appeared neglible in this generation, standards of female beauty were curvaceous, and the prevalence of disordered eating diminished in comparison to previous generations. This difference reversed once again, with females born in or after the 1940s more likely than males born the same time to report frequent headaches—just as they were more likely to be depressed, prefer thin figures, and exhibit a high prevalence of anorexia.

To facilitate visual comparison of the gender differences in these studies, we included data on the percentage of females and males reporting frequent headaches in all three studies on the same graph, Figure 5, with the left-hand vertical axis used for the 1962 and 1981 surveys and the right-hand axis for the 1969–71 study.

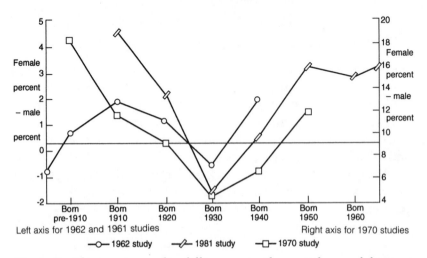

Figure 5 Changes in gender differences in the prevalence of frequent headaches over the course of the twentieth century.

Thus, in three separate studies, the pattern of gender differences in reported rates of frequent headache among people born over the course of the twentieth century resembled the pattern of fluctuations in depression, anorexia, standards of female beauty, and changing rates of female college graduation. The three headache surveys were performed over a period of twenty years, allowing us to determine whether the findings were due to the age of the people surveyed or their year of birth. For example, in the study done in 1962, among people in their early thirties, men reported higher rates of frequent headache than women, whereas in the study done in 1981, among people in their early thirties, the rate of frequent headache reported by women was twice as high as that reported by men. What appears to be crucial is not their age but their years of birth, or, as we believe, the conditions affecting females as they mature into adult women.

These studies on gender differences in headache prevalence were done in England, New Zealand, and Israel (primarily with respondents who had emigrated to Israel from Europe), not in the United States where we obtained the data used to calculate the index of generational change in rates of female college graduation. It is striking how closely historical fluctuations in headache prevalence among respondents from these nations appeared to track the college graduation data from the United States. One possible explanation is that historical economic forces influencing U.S. rates of female college graduation, such as the Great Depression and the two world wars, were widespread enough to influence the conditions of women in the British Commonwealth and Europe; however, further research is needed before conclusions can be drawn on this point.

We performed a similar analysis of gender differences in mitral valve prolapse with strikingly similar results.[12] Thus, gender differences in the prevalence of headache and mitral valve prolapse appear to exhibit the same historical patterns as gender differences in depression and disordered eating as well as thin standards of female beauty, becoming high among generations who reached adolescence during periods of great change in educational opportunities for women.

When Do the Disorders Coexist?

We believe that depression, disordered eating, preference for thinness, headaches, and mitral valve prolapse all exhibit similar generational fluctuations because they are all symptoms of a single syndrome. The very different types of evidence we have studied appear to indicate that the symptoms in this book often tend to occur together. Many of the eminent women we studied did in fact exhibit a mix of these same symptoms. For example, throughout her adult life, Louisa May Alcott, author of the ever-popular *Little Women*, was frequently depressed. At age 25, "she walked over the mildam in Boston and thought of throwing herself in the water." Later, complaints of poor health punctuated her letters. She suffered from "blinding neuralgic headaches," rheumatism, indigestion, bronchial catarrh, hoarseness, and insomnia, all of which she summed up as "nervous prostration." She described herself as living "the life of an invalid."

Alcott was born in 1833, a period when great writers were supposed to be men. Although her father never quite attained the success he hoped for as a philosopher/teacher, he certainly achieved some notoriety, much more than Alcott's mother, who was quite bright and ambitious and resented the limitations placed on her because she was female. After one unsuccessful attempt to supplement the money earned by her husband with an outside job of her own, Alcott's mother wrote: "This shows the incompetent wages paid to all female labor and proves the greater value of intellectual labor over manual or any service performed by women." And, in turn, her daughter, Louisa May Alcott, was never fully content being female. She wrote: "I was born with a boy's spirit under my bib and tucker. I can't wait when I can work." When asked about marriage she responded, "I'd rather be a free spinster and paddle my own canoe." [13]

Writers and artists are often thought of by the public as a little mad, but, as we have seen, the syndrome is not confined to women who achieved in the arts. Because of her arduous and dangerous labors nursing British troops during the Crimean War, Florence Nightingale has come to symbolize courage and tireless devotion. Nightingale exhibited not only those qualities but also, unfortunately, the syndrome we have described.

Florence Nightingale was born in 1820 to an upper-middle-class family in England. Her father had inherited money from his mother's uncle because the uncle's direct descendants had produced no male heirs and females were not viewed as suitable for inheriting large estates. Subsequently, because Florence had no brothers, her family also lost their inheritance, reinforcing her awareness of the greater value placed on males. Her mother wanted

Nightingale and her sister to take on the marital and social responsibilities expected of women of their background, but Nightingale was never content with what she perceived were the superficial duties accorded women. At age 17, she heard voices urging her to great accomplishments, and, by age 24, she decided on nursing as her career. Meeting tremendous resistance from her family, particularly her mother who viewed working women as lower class, it took Florence eight years to achieve her goal of having a profession. Eventually, she wrote to her parents, "You must look at me as your vagabond son."

Nightingale's chronic health problems began with a "nervous breakdown" at adolescence. The symptoms of what has been described as her "neurasthenia" included chronic cough, difficulty breathing, migraine headaches, nausea at the sight of food, and depression so strong that she felt that she was "going out of her mind." She wrote at age 25: "I cannot live—forgive me, oh Lord, let me die, this day, let me die." Indeed, she spent many years as an invalid.[14]

The evidence for a single syndrome composed of several symptoms is not limited to anecdotal descriptions that appeared before this century. If this syndrome continues to afflict large numbers of women, we would also expect to find that many contemporary women, but fewer men, suffer from a combination of these symptoms. Indeed, several such findings have appeared. For example, like disordered eating, such somatic symptoms as headache, asthma, insomnia, and menstrual dysfunction have been reported to be associated with depression in some manner that has not yet been satisfactorily explained by researchers. Of particular interest here is that clinical depression has often been found to be more likely to be accompanied by somatic problems in women than in men.[15]

This gender difference is not limited to studies of patients. One analysis of a National Institute for Mental Health (NIMH) survey of a large number of people living in North Carolina found that many women reported having a combination of lost appetite, fluctuation in weight, depression, nervousness, headache, and sexual indifference. The combination of depression and somatic symptoms was not found to be common among males. About one in ten female high school students we surveyed had high scores on the Center for Epidemiologic Studies Depression Scale combined with at least two of the following: symptoms of disordered eating, frequent headaches, frequent unexplained breathing difficulties, or frequent insomnia.[16] It would thus seem that many contemporary women do suffer from combined symptoms of depression, disordered eating, and somatic problems.

One indication that the historical patterns shown by depression and headaches result from fluctuations in the prevalence of a single syndrome comes from a survey asking people about both symptoms. People suffering from a syndrome involving severe headaches as well as depression should exhibit high levels of both symptoms. Our reanalysis of the survey showed that frequent severe headaches and depression went together (i.e., were significantly correlated) among all groups of females who reached adolescence when the proportion of women who graduated college was larger than that of their mothers' generation. By contrast, among the two groups that included large numbers of women born at the beginning of the century and during the early 1930s, who reached adolescence during periods when the proportion of women graduating from college was not larger than the proportion who graduated during their mothers' generation, the women who reported high levels of depression were not those who reported frequent severe headaches (i.e., level of depression was not significantly correlated with frequency of severe headaches). We recently repeated this study, administering different measures of headache and depression to women born in the 1920s and afterward, obtaining identical results depicted in Figure 6.[17] Because our research was done about fifteen years after the earlier study, the ages of the women in the groups who exhibited a relationship between depression and headache differed. The striking similarity between the two studies for women exhibiting a strong relationship between depression and headache was in their having reached adolescence during years of changing gender roles, not in their age.

Mixed Anxiety and Depression

Much attention has recently been focused on the possible existence of a disorder composed of depression combined with anxiety. The pattern of research findings on mixed anxiety and depression quite closely resembles the patterns we have previously described. Several studies found that somatic symptoms such as appetite disturbance, insomnia, and breathing difficulty are common among people with mixed anxious-depressive symptoms. In one NIMH study, the mixture of symptoms of anxiety, depression, and somatization was most common in younger people, primarily women. Among

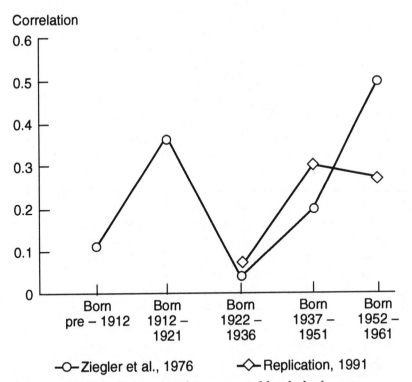

Correlation

−O−Ziegler et al., 1976   −◇−Replication, 1991

Figure 6 Correlation between depression and headache frequency among females divided into corresponding cohorts in two surveys.

people in middle to late life, the symptoms of major depression were prevalent, again primarily among women. Several other studies have found that females who suffer from symptoms of anxiety, depression, and somatization early in life are likely to develop clinical depression later on. The relationship reported in these studies between the symptoms of adolescence or early adulthood and subsequent clinical depression is much weaker for males. These findings agree with our hypothesis that many women who suffer from anxious somatic depression during adolescence and early adulthood may develop major depression later in life.[18]

W. Edward Craighead has found that, among adolescents, several subtypes of depression and anxiety are common. Equal numbers of male and female adolescents exhibit "pure" depression or "pure" anxiety—that is, high levels of one of these symptoms and low levels of the other. But the group of adolescents who exhibits high levels of both anxiety and depression includes mainly females, and shows a different pattern of responses from the "pure" groups on psychological measures, suggesting that those with the combination of anxiety and depression may be suffering from a different disorder than those who exhibit either symptom alone.[19]

In data we just recently collected from a sample of seniors attending two high schools, we defined anxious somatic depression as scoring high on a depression scale and an anxiety scale, along with reporting at least three of the following: (1) frequent severe headaches; (2) frequent unexplained difficulty breathing; (3) frequent insomnia; (4) appetite disturbance; (5) poor body image or preference for thinness. Following Craighead, we defined "pure" depression as scoring high on the depression scale but not meeting these criteria for anxious somatic depression. Female students were over ten times as likely as males to report the combined symptoms of anxious somatic depression, but the prevalence of pure depression among males and females was almost identical. It appears that the greater prevalence of depressive symptomatology among females than among males may result because many women, but very few men, exhibit a specific form of depression that is mixed with anxiety and somatic symptoms. (Because these data were collected too recently to have been published in a professional journal we describe details of the methods and results of this study in Appendix C.)

Why Is the Syndrome Not Studied or Treated?

If the syndrome described so often in the medical literature of previous centuries continues to afflict large numbers of women, why has it gone unrecognized? There are several answers. One is that the syndrome involves a combination of psychological symptoms, such as depression, anxiety, poor body image, and sexual indifference, along with several somatic symptoms, such as headaches, breathing difficulties, insomnia, disordered eating, and menstrual dysfunction. Many women who suffer from the syndrome visit a physician. If somatic symptoms, like headaches or breathing difficulties, are severe enough, physicians will often treat them, without focusing much attention on the other symptoms, particularly psychological problems. Studies show that physicians often overlook the depression of patients who present with somatic symptoms.[20] In addition, even in the 1990s, most people remain uncomfortable about psychological problems. People who are quite willing to admit they saw a physician often find it embarrassing to seek out treatment for a psychological disorder or admit to seeing a psychotherapist. Physicians, young women, and their parents may feel most comfortable when the women's problems are treated as a physical illness instead of as a psychological disorder.

We have already alluded to the role played by specialization. From the time of Hippocrates until fairly recently, most doctors treated a wide range of disorders and research was not very specialized. Today, for both treatment and research, specialized subdisciplines exist that deal with headaches, asthma, eating disorders, and depression. The specialized attention focused on each area has resulted in tremendous advances in the scientific understanding of their causes as well as their treatment. But this specialization also has its costs. A specialist in studying eating disorders may not ask research subjects about headaches or hyperventilation. Findings that appear in the journal *Headache* and those that appear in the *International Journal of Eating Disorders* are not very likely to be read by the same people.

In searching recent medical books and journals, however, we did find that some researchers, particularly those working with, or influenced by, Dr. Samuel Guze at Washington University in St. Louis, had recognized a syndrome related to what used to be called hysteria that afflicted young women and involved possible depression along with other somatic symptoms. They named it "Briquet's syndrome" after a physician who had written about it in 1859.[21] Unfortunately, neither Briquet's syndrome nor any other disorder involving the combination of symptoms we discuss was included in the most recent versions of the official manual used by psychologists and psychiatrists in making diagnoses. That manual, published by the American Psychiatric Association, offers guidelines regarding the symptoms that should be present in order to justify a particular diagnosis in a particular case. This manual, usually referred to as DSM (short for *Diagnostic and Statistical Manual*), is updated periodically to keep abreast of scientific advances and changes in thinking in the field.[22] Both neurasthenia and hysteria were included in the first two versions of the DSM. But they were both dropped from the third version, called DSM-III.

In their place was a series of disorders involving somatic symptoms. One, somatization disorder, was based on Briquet's syndrome. But of our list of symptoms common among women diagnosed as suffering from hysteria, chlorosis, and so forth, only vomiting, breathing difficulty, menstrual dysfunction, and sexual indifference are included in the criteria for somatization disorder.

(Headache has been added in DSM-IV, the latest edition of the *Diagnostic and Statistical Manual* of the American Psychiatric Association.) Other symptoms, such as depression, disordered eating, and anxiety, are incorporated into separate diagnostic categories. While the rationale for modifications was to more precisely identify and diagnose apparently separate disorders that should be a focus of treatment, this strategy has also obscured a combination of symptoms that may be a single syndrome, which is why we sometimes refer to it as "the forgotten syndrome."[23]

The history of medicine is rife with examples in which women's experience is described as pathologic, and this response is then attributed to some weakness in the women themselves. We feel that our description of anxious somatic depression does not fall into this pattern, in part because all the symptoms we have discussed are already acknowledged as being much more prevalent among women than among men beginning at adolescence. In suggesting that the gender differences in the prevalence of all these problems may result from a single disorder, we are simply reorganizing these findings under one name. And, as we will continue to explore in the remainder of this book, we attribute the high rate of this disorder among women not to some peculiar female weakness but to the gender biases that permeate most societies, gender biases that produce problems in many aspects of life related to gender, such as marriage, childbearing, and sexuality, toward which we now turn our attention.

5

Tying the Knot: Marriage, Childbearing, and Sexuality

If ever a woman had good reason to marry and have children, it was Queen Elizabeth I. She received enormous pressure to cement a political alliance with some powerful foreign nation or influential English family and bear a child who would be heir to the English throne. Her unwillingness to do either, leaving the nation with no obvious claimant to the throne, was much more than disappointing to the English people—it was perilous.

Elizabeth's avoidance of childbearing contrasts sharply with the drastic attempts of her father King Henry VIII to father a son. Yet Henry's dynastic aspirations must have greatly affected Elizabeth, perhaps even her attitudes toward marriage and childbearing. Henry married eight wives. Elizabeth's mother, Anne Boleyn, was executed because of her inability to produce a male heir. Thus, we might assume that Elizabeth saw her mother in a much less powerful position than Henry VIII, a position resulting in her death when Elizabeth was not born a male. Elizabeth surely had powerful reasons for feeling ambivalent about her femaleness. We speculate that in addition to the psychological and somatic symptoms described previously, Elizabeth may have responded to this ambivalence with an aversion toward marriage, childbearing, and sexuality.

Aversion to marriage is common among the cases we have studied, but what are we to make of it? As we discussed in Chapter

2, the Hippocratic "disease of young women" was said to afflict "virgins who do not take a husband at the appropriate time for marriage." Such women were urged to action: "When virgins experience this trouble, they should cohabit with a man as quickly as possible. If they become pregnant, they will be cured." This recommendation was repeated for those suffering from chlorosis in the eighteenth century and for hysteric women in the nineteenth century.[1]

Although marriage was often prescribed as the cure, quite often it was the pressure to marry that appears to have brought on the symptoms in the first place. When the holy anorexics studied by Bell were encouraged by their families to find a husband, the girls often responded by saying that they were married to Christ, and, with this decision, began to fast. Recall the case of St. Catherine of Sienna who thought of herself as a character from legend who avoided an unwanted marriage by changing into men's clothing and entering a monastery. When Catherine's married sister died, the pressure on Catherine to find a husband in order to supplement the business connections of her merchant family became intense. She resisted, consecrating her virginity to Jesus and Mary, cutting her hair short, fasting, and flagellating herself, until her family finally relented. They ceased the pressure and allowed her to enter religious life.[2] Several of the Haavik Brahmin women discussed in Chapter 2 also became depressed and stopped eating when forced into unwanted marriages. The attitudes of these women are probably best summed up in Freud's description of one of his hysteric female patients, Elizabeth Von R.: "She wanted to study . . . and she was indignant at the idea of having to sacrifice her inclinations and her freedom of judgement by marriage." The sentiment is echoed by Florence Nightingale: "There are women of intellectual or actively moral natures for whom marriage . . . means the sacrifice of their higher capacities."[3]

For most ambitious women throughout history, marriage has traditionally signified a sacrifice of inclinations and freedom of judgment. Young females who have been proud of their intellect have often been told at adolescence to play down this strength and find a husband to whom they would be subservient. In earlier centuries and in non-Western cultures, the pressure to marry at adolescence may have been the most common concrete form in which the lesser status of adult females was experienced by intelligent, ambitious, nontraditional women. In fact, in a nineteenth-century description of anorexia nervosa now cited as one of the earliest to recognize the disease as a distinct entity, Lasegue described the causes of anorexia as follows: "A young girl, between fifteen and twenty years of age, suffers from some emotion which she avows or conceals. Generally it relates to some real or imaginary marriage project."[4]

The oft-repeated prescription of marriage as a cure for the disease of young women, chlorosis, and hysteria may have sprung from a misinterpretation of the emotional and political issues grappled with by the women most likely to develop these disorders. In a possible case of post hoc ergo propter hoc reasoning, physicians may have noted the conspicuous, for the times, absence of matrimony among women suffering from the syndrome and so recommended matrimony as its cure.

To investigate if the desire, or at least the tendency, of women to remain unmarried mirrors other aspects of the syndrome we have been discussing, we looked at the pattern of marriage rates over the twentieth century. We based our analysis on the census taken each decade of the number of married, divorced, widowed, and single males and females of various ages, using the ratio of unmarried females to unmarried males aged 25 to 29 as an indicator of the tendency for women to remain unmarried.[5]

The pattern we found is familiar. Among people born at the beginning of the century, the proportion of unmarried females was moderate, increasing to its high point among people born between 1911 and 1915, reversing to a low point among those born during the early 1930s, and rising once again to its second highest point among those born in the early 1940s. The only differences between this curve and those presented in earlier chapters are that women born at the beginning of the century are slightly more likely than we might have expected to remain unmarried, at least until age 30, while those born between 1921 and 1925 are somewhat less likely to remain unmarried. But the low-then high-then low-then high pattern over the course of the century that characterized generational changes in female college graduation and the pattern of fluctuation in so many other symptoms discussed in earlier chapters also describes the tendency among females to remain unmarried, as Figure 7 depicts.

Because marriage rates may be influenced by many factors, we cannot attribute these fluctuations with certainty to the gender issues we believe are related to the development of the other symptoms. Nonetheless, when she likened married women to "flies preserved in Baltic amber," it is likely that the French novelist and

Female/Male ratio

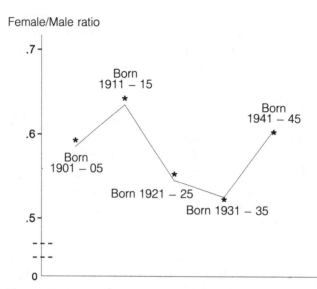

Figure 7 Ratio of never married females to never married males (age 25–29).

intellectual Simone de Beauvoir, who suffered from lifelong depression and migraine headaches, may have been expressing feelings shared by many women who matured during periods of changing gender roles.[6]

Childbearing

De Beauvoir also expressed aversion toward childrearing: "Babies filled me with horror. The sight of a mother with a child sucking the life from her breast, or women changing soiled diapers—it all filled me with disgust. I had no desire to be drained, to be the slave of such a creature."[7] In almost every previous chapter, issues of childbearing also play a role in this constellation of symptoms. The females afflicted with the "disease of young women" were not only virgins, but "among married women, those who are sterile." Savage described the typical neurasthenic as a woman who was "not in a condition for performing her reproductive function."[8] Fertility problems also plagued Sudanese women possessed by Zar, the Arab women suffering from culture-bound syndrome in Qatar, and Guatemalan women suffering from nervios.[9] Menstrual and reproductive difficulties, with their supposed attendant threat to the survival of the human race, have been among the most remarked on aspects of the syndrome throughout history.

But as we investigated the relationship between anxious somatic depression and childbearing, many complexities emerged. We found that while many women aspired to have children of their own, awareness of the limitations placed on females made some women reluctant, or ambivalent, toward this most concrete expression of the female role. Women with differing developmental histories appeared to resolve this conflict in different ways.

The complex relationship between conflicted feelings toward traditional femininity, which we believe underlie anxious somatic depression, and pregnancy and childrearing is exemplified in the lives of the two women perhaps most closely associated with applying psychoanalysis to the psychology of women—Karen Horney and Helene Deutsch. Karen Horney was the daughter of a stern, religious father whose profession, ship's captain, kept him away from home much of the time, and a mother, much younger than the father, who was quite close to Horney. The father held traditional views of women and gave preferential treatment to Horney's older brother, yet the mother, better educated and more cultured, supported Horney's desire for higher education. Horney called her mother "my great childhood love." At the same time, however, Horney saw that her educated mother was forced into a subservient role without "gratification." At age 15, she wrote in her diary, "Mother is ill and unhappy." She reported that even "as a child I wanted for a long time to be a boy." At age 12, she cut off her long hair to the neckline to be, in her later words, "the curly-haired prince once again." Subsequently, during her adolescence, she began to experience bouts of depression, often profound, that plagued her throughout her life. A biographer noted, "It seems clear she was depressed, often to a point that made it impossible for her to function," while she wrote of her own "inclination to passivity that increases to a longing for . . . death." Experiences like these led her to be one of the first major proponents for a psychology of women that took account of women's position in society.

Her experience with pregnancy and childrearing perhaps best epitomized her conflicted feelings about gender. Before becoming pregnant, she reported a dislike of children and childrearing and felt trapped for much of her first pregnancy. In her words: "I found myself inferior, being a feminine creature, and in consequence tried to be masculine, a situation [i.e., pregnancy] that like no other keeps my femininity before my eyes and others' must be painful to me." Yet after the death of her mother, about eight months into Horney's pregnancy, she began to express excitement and pleasure about carrying a child. This newfound pride and pleasure in giving birth lasted through her two other pregnancies. These feelings led her to recall how much she had enjoyed playing with dolls as a girl and brought to consciousness the importance she placed on her femininity. They also spurred her to include in her theories of gender the envy felt by men toward women because of their ability to bear children.[10] Thus, Karen Horney's attitudes toward childbearing exemplify a dilemma. Pregnancy and childrearing keep a woman's femininity before her eyes and others, which may be discomforting to women dissatisfied with the limitations placed on their achievements by their gender. But carrying and giving birth to another human being are also powerfully positive experiences— experiences, and achievements, open only to women.

The case of Helene Deutsch exhibits several striking differences from that of Karen Horney as well as some distinct similarities. Deutsch was born to a father who was a successful lawyer and a homemaker mother (although servants did the housework) whom she described as a superficial social climber. Her parents were disappointed in their only son, and Helene felt that they were very dissatisfied she was not a boy. She later wrote of the type of father who wants the daughter to replace the son he never had or the son who was a failure. A biographer noted, "Intellectually she was so bright that . . . people called her 'the old Rosenbach' [her father's name,] a chip off the old block."[11] She reported that she was never jealous of her brother because her father treated her like a worthy successor and heir from the time she was very young. Yet, although Deutsch's father was much more supportive of her desire for education than her mother (reversing the pattern experienced by Horney), she wrote of how hard it was for her father "to acknowledge that a full-fledged feminine creature could have talents and interests his society ascribed only to boys."

The conflict Deutsch experienced between "femininity" and "masculinity" is clear in her autobiography written late in her life. She described the complexities caused by "my hate of my mother and horror of identification with her . . . and the difficulties of identifying with [my father]." Of her analysis with Freud, she wrote: "I can recall one of the dreams I had during this period, in which I have a masculine and a feminine organ. . . . Freud told me only that it indicated my desire to be both a boy and a girl. It was only after my analysis that it became clear to me how much my whole personality was determined by the childhood wish to be simultaneously my father's prettiest daughter and cleverest son."

Although, unlike Horney, Deutsch was not plagued by deep depression throughout her life, at adolescence she became so depressed that she was sent to a sanatorium for treatment.

Regarding her pregnancy, Deutsch reported "joy and happy expectations . . . mixed with panic." She recalled that when her son was born "my happiness was without bounds," but added, "I of course remembered the saying of the Talmud: 'A woman becomes a woman only when she has given birth to a boy.' "[12] This echoes the case of Vani, the Indian villager discussed in Chapter 2, whose depression and fasting resolved when she gave birth to a son.

The Male Heir

As implied in Deutsch's Talmudic citation, even women who have gone the traditional route of having children and trying to be good wives and mothers have been regarded as failures if they cannot produce male offspring. Just as Indira Gandhi's mother was experiencing the exaltation of the successful delivery of her child, Indira's grandmother was heard to lament, "It should have been a boy."[13] After the mother of Princess Diana of England had given birth to three daughters, she was actually sent to a clinic to determine what was wrong with her since she had not yet had a son. Thus, mothers have been devalued not only for their own gender but for the "inferiority" of their female offspring. Indira Gandhi's mother responded by becoming an ardent feminist, but she was also overtaken by bouts of depression. As we explore further in our next chapter, this preference for boys has also had devastating effects on many girls who have been made to feel inferior just because they were born the "wrong" gender. Princess Di was not given a name until she was a week old because her parents had neglected to consider any girl's names. She subsequently said, "I was supposed to be a boy." By now, most of the world knows that she developed depression, migraine headaches, and bulimia.[14]

Although we have not studied the process, we speculate that the relationships of many boys to their mothers must also be distorted by the importance placed on delivering male offspring. In particular, the feelings toward their sons of many ambitious mothers who themselves were prevented from achieving their aspirations may be influenced by the preferences given to boys. The love, pride, and caring for their sons may be mixed with the resentment of a talented adult who realizes that her major role in life is to prepare a child to take his valued place in the world; with jealousy as she sees all the advantages she so sorely missed heaped at the feet of her young boy; with pressure she exerts on him to succeed so that she too will be deemed a success; with disappointment she may not hide if, like Helene Deutsch's brother, he is unwilling or unable to supply the glory in whose reflection she can bask; with guilt she may induce because he represents, in some ill-defined way, those who place her in such an untenable situation. She may never put her hostile feelings into words or even be fully aware of them. In fact, many women, rather than confront such feelings, may bend over backwards to give their sons the best of everything.

Being a child, the son may be even less likely than the mother to understand what is happening. But he may grow up with the vague feeling that his achievements don't belong to him, that he must choose between inciting disappointment through failure or resentment through success, that his unchosen maleness renders him simultaneously both savior and villain. In rare instances, as with the brothers of some of the eminent women we studied, he may bear the added shame of achieving "less than a girl." Helene Deutsch's brother, who so disappointed his parents, changed his name and his religion, moved away from home, and ceased communicating with them. Branwell Brontë, brother of renowned novelists Emily and Charlotte, failed as a teacher, a painter, and in every other occupation he attempted. He eventually turned to alcoholism and, after a long period of dissipation, died of consumption.[15] Thus, while we have no research evidence, we believe that boys may not escape unscathed from families in which women are devalued.

But being the siblings in their family who were acknowledged as successful did not save Helene Deutsch from the need for treatment in a sanatorium or Charlotte and Emily Brontë from the ravages of depression and disordered eating. Although the symptoms of Charlotte Brontë, author of *Jane Eyre*, and of Emily Brontë, who wrote *Wuthering Heights*, were quite similar, biographers of the two sisters have emphasized somewhat different aspects. Perhaps as a result of her recurrent migraine headaches, Charlotte suffered from nausea and periodic loss of appetite. But her biographers have focused primarily on her depression. She wrote in letters that "earth and heaven are dreary and empty to me," and was described by others as frequently "deeply" depressed. A reading of any biography of Emily Brontë gives one the impression that she too was often melancholy. But because Emily fasted for long periods and began wasting away at adolescence, two biographers have concluded that she died of anorexia nervosa.[16] Branwell Brontë may have suffered from having successful sisters, but the suffering of those sisters was at least as great.

As we will touch upon again in future chapters, relationships between husbands and wives may also become distorted in such families. A bright, ambitious woman who has given up her chance for success in a career in order to take care of her home and family may come to feel resentful. Without fully acknowledging it, she may place some of the blame for her failure to live up to her aspirations on her husband, who obviously bears half the responsibility for existence of the marriage and the children. Even if she does not blame him, she may be jealous of the ease with which he appears to be able to "have his cake and eat it too" by having both a family and a busy career. If he makes some obnoxious remark about the lateness of dinner or the messiness of the home, or insensitively wonders aloud about what she does with her time, she may become enraged. At the very least, when he comes home after a long day and complains about how tough it is taking part in the "rat race," she may not feel or act completely sympathetic, leading him to feel unloved, unsupported, or underappreciated.

Contemporary Evidence on Childbearing

Among contemporary women, the relationship between childbearing and the symptoms of anxious somatic depression continues in its complexity. Pregnancy has in some instances alleviated symptoms of modern women suffering from eating disorders. These women may experience elation over their success in the feminine role of mother and gratification in expressing their nurturant strivings, both overshadowing their negative feelings regarding the limitations placed on them by their gender. On the other hand, S. Louis Mogul reported three cases in which women became anorexic during pregnancy.[17] In each case, the women reported difficult childhood relationships with their mothers, who were described as "depressed, bitter, limited people," resentful at not having been given the opportunity for educational and professional advancement. In these and other similar cases, pregnancy may heighten the women's awareness of their femaleness and the similarity between their lives and those of their mothers.

And childrearing is obviously much more than just a symbol of a woman's gender; it is a time-consuming job. But it is a job that is simultaneously highly valued and devalued in contemporary societies. To understand why, we need to look at childrearing in a historical context.

For by far the greatest part of our time on earth, we humans have earned our living hunting wild animals and gathering wild plants. In hunter-gathering cultures, death rates—from accidents, disease, malnutrition—are very high, so many children need to be born just to keep the population stable. Because the average woman in such a society has a short life expectancy, she has to spend all of her adult life bearing and raising children.

With the development of agriculture in human society, other social changes take place. The moderate-sized family farm needs a great deal of labor, so from a fairly early age, children living on a farm contribute labor, which is as valuable as the resources they consume. In agricultural societies then and now, children become a form of social security. When people are too old or too sick to continue to work the land, their children take over. In other words, if you are a farmer, it makes economic sense to have a large family.

With the transition to industrialism, however, new social influences shape the family. In industrial societies, people commute to a factory or office. Workplaces and homes change, for the most part, from generation to generation, and sometimes from year to year. And while children need many years of education and do not become economically productive until they are adults, new forms of social security and retirement income emerge. Thus, the transition to industrialism increases the economic productivity of children and decreases the reliance on one's kids in old age. As a result, in industrial economies large families are very costly and women have fewer kids.

Women in agricultural societies obviously have full-time jobs raising, clothing, feeding, educating, and nursing large families. Compared to these women, it may seem that many modern homemakers who have two or three children, and who purchase from others much of the food, clothing, medical care, and education needed by their families, have it relatively easy. But as anyone who has been in charge of shopping, chauffeuring, making appointments, preparing meals, and managing the household knows quite well, these tasks can take an enormous amount of time, even if you can afford to hire some help. The need to be available to take care of kids at various times during the day, sometimes on the spur of the moment, also makes pursuing active careers difficult.

Thus, contemporary mothers are placed in a bind. Their accomplishments at home are demeaned, and it is anything but easy for them to raise a family and attain some measure of a career. To us it seems inaccurate and somewhat offensive when authorities call some modern women "superwomen," as if they are unrealistically ambitious and selfishly want to have it all, when they are actually caught in a bind that makes it difficult to achieve in the traditional "feminine" sphere or the traditional "masculine" sphere, a bind brought on by having children.

The Case of Ellen West

The case of Ellen West tragically illustrates what may happen when women are unable to achieve in either sphere. First described in 1944, it was widely cited as a forerunner of the many cases of anorexia nervosa that appeared in industrialized nations in the 1960s and 1970s. Beginning at age 20, Ellen West exhibited an obsession with thinness, fear of fat, anorexia, bingeing, vomiting, and laxative abuse—all the symptoms now associated with eating disorders. She was diagnosed by two world-famous diagnostic authorities, Ludwig Binswanger and Emil Kraepelin, as suffering from melancholia that she depicted as "dread," a feeling she began to experience at age 32 that eventuated two years later in suicide.

Ellen West was described as "extremely intelligent," a good student who was very ambitious. The connection between gender roles and her obsession with thinness is made clear in her therapist's report that "for her, being thin was equated with a higher intellectual type, and being fat with a bourgeois . . . type." This is reminiscent of the studies we described in Chapter 1, in which a curvaceous woman was selected as less intelligent and less successful than a noncurvaceous woman by many college women with symptoms of disordered eating. In his analysis of the case, Binswanger focused on Ellen West's discomfort with feminine gender roles and her dismay at being "thrown" into the role of an adult female.

When she was young, West was a high achiever, having managed to arrange the establishment of children's reading rooms in the city where she lived. But, because she was female, great achievements in the outside world were closed off. With much reluctance, she decided in early adulthood to marry. At this point, she concentrated her ambition on more traditional pursuits, setting her sights on becoming a great wife, mother, and homemaker. Unfortunately, even great achievements in traditional female pursuits were denied her when she discovered that she could not bear children. In the words of her therapist, "When she learned from a statement of the gynecologist that she would have no success along the womanly-motherly-line, despite her renunciation of higher intellectuallity . . . she now resolved 'to live for her idea' [being thin] without any inhibitions and began to take large daily doses of laxatives."[18]

Thus, childbearing may allow some women to feel that they have made great success "along the womanly-motherly line." But if women are infertile, they may feel that not even traditional avenues of success are open to them. The resulting sense of failure and low self-esteem may lead to the symptoms of anxious somatic depression. This may help to explain the frequently mentioned connection between descriptions of the syndrome and female reproductive difficulties.

Sexuality

That issues of both matrimony and maternity seem linked to conflicting feelings about gender is no surprise. Nor is it unusual that these issues relate to conflicts regarding sexuality. The resistance of Queen Elizabeth I to matrimony and maternity may have been accompanied, as Elizabeth's well-known nickname "The Virgin Queen" implies, by the avoidance of sex. Some English translations of the Hippocratic texts use the phrase "the disease of virgins" because it afflicted women who were not engaging in sexual relations. For the same reason, several authorities attributed chlorosis to the lack of sexual experience. Sexual indifference was also one of the symptoms used to diagnose Briquet's syndrome. In light of the finding in 1953 that almost nine out of ten hysteric women were found to exhibit sexual indifference, we might speculate as to whether Freud's emphasis on the role of the repression of sexuality was influenced to some extent by the fact that many of his early patients were hysteric women. Breuer, for example, described the sexuality of Anna O. as "astonishingly undeveloped." In 1918, years after his work on hysteria, Freud observed: "It is well known that there is a neurosis in girls which occurs . . . at the time of puberty or soon afterwards and which expresses aversion to sexuality by means of anorexia."[19] Even today, contemporary research on inhibited sexual desire indicates that it is more common among females than males and more common among professional women than other women.[20]

Some avoidance of sexual activity shown by these women has undoubtedly been related to fear of pregnancy, particularly before effective methods of birth control were developed. But it may also result because the conflict over femininity underlying anxious somatic depression, which we refer to as "gender ambivalence," entails issues of identity and gender, both heightened during sexual encounters. Erik Erikson has noted that, from a developmental framework, issues of intimacy are built on issues of identity, and that to a person experiencing confusion over identity (which we argue in Chapter 9 is related to gender ambivalence), "fusion with another becomes identity loss."[21] Sexual intercourse might also fit Horney's description of pregnancy as "a situation that like no other keeps my femininity before my eyes and others." To acknowledge one's sexuality is usually tantamount to acknowledging one's gender. A woman who is sexually aroused by, or active with, a man is likely to be quite aware of her femaleness. To a woman who is thinking about, or active with, another woman, the mere fact that the object of her desire is not male is likely, given traditional social mores, to heighten her own and other's awareness of her gender.

Sexual Abuse

The role of sexual abuse in anxious somatic depression also deserves mention. The experience of sexual abuse, particularly incest, has been linked to the development of just about every symptom of the syndrome as well as to conflicts regarding gender identity.[22] Like women unable to fulfill their intellectual and professional ambitions, those who have been sexually abused may come to feel that it might not have happened if only they had not been born female. After all, increased exposure to sexual abuse is one of the worst disadvantages of being female. In addition to several other reactions to the horrors of sexual abuse, we speculate that women who have been sexually abused may come to feel ambivalence regarding their gender and this may play a role in the development of their physical and psychological symptoms. We are just beginning to test this hypothesis and, until more research is done, offer it as only an unproven speculation.

Not having done much research on sexual abuse, we do not discuss it here. Nonetheless, one important reason for the apparently high prevalence of anxious somatic depression among women may be that many traditional women who might not otherwise have developed the syndrome may have done so after being sexually abused. Of course, many high-achieving, nontraditional women have also been abused sexually, as Virginia Woolf was. In part because of the explicit feminist attitudes expressed by Woolf in several of her novels, she is a particular favorite among many contemporary readers. As a young girl, she was sexually abused by her much older half-brother. (The details of the abuse are not clear.) At age 22, she began to hear voices telling her to starve her hateful body, and throughout the rest of her life she ate as little as possible. At the same time she fasted, Woolf attempted suicide. She also suffered severe headaches, insomnia, and great anxiety. After years of severe depression, she finally ended her own life by walking into the river Ouse.

The case of Virginia Woolf exemplifies the difficulties in drawing firm conclusions regarding underlying causes of symptomatology based on a single biographical study. Woolf exhibited almost every symptom discussed in this book, including depression, anxiety, disordered eating, poor body image, headaches, insomnia, low self-esteem, difficulty concentrating, and (according to several biographers) aversion to sex. She was diagnosed as suffering from neurasthenia by Dr. George Savage, an expert on the disease whom we cited in Chapter 2. Yet while Louise DeSalvo makes a strong case for the important role played by sexual abuse in the etiology of her symptoms, Thomas Caramagno makes an equally strong one that Woolf suffered from manic depression and came from a family that may have exhibited a biological predisposition toward this disorder. There is no way of knowing whether Virginia Woolf's suffering was rooted in her genes, in her exposure to the horrors of incestuous sexual abuse, or in some combination of the two.

To further complicate matters, Virginia Woolf was clearly aware of, and bothered by, the fact that the lives of women, including her own, had been limited by societal biases against women. She had a father who was a writer of some renown who held very traditional views of women, and Woolf noted that, because he was male, her father occupied an "extraordinarily privileged position." Her mother was very subservient to Woolf's father and may have worked herself into an early grave catering to his needs and those of her own parents. Nonetheless, she also held very traditional views of women, advocating "the sanctity of separate spheres and the futility of votes, careers, or university education for women." Given the traditional views of these parents, it is no surprise that the boys in the family were obviously preferred by both parents, accorded more privileges, and treated as superior to the girls.

So, in addition to her genetic predisposition and her exposure to abuse, Virginia Woolf was an extremely bright, talented woman who aspired to achieve intellectually but grew up in a family in which females were treated as inferior. As we discuss in the next two chapters, this constellation of privileged fathers and brothers and unhappy, restricted mothers and daughters is typical of the families of women who develop anxious somatic depression.[23]

Part II

FEMALES, FAMILIES, AND ACHIEVEMENT

6

Daughters and Sons

We have argued that anxious somatic depression afflicts women who aspire to achieve in areas historically reserved for males, particularly during periods of changing gender roles. If these women confront societal prejudices against "acting like men" that serve as barriers toward achieving in these areas, they may develop ambivalent feelings about themselves and their femininity that lead to other psychological and physical symptoms. But to fully understand this ambivalence, it is not enough for us to point to some general societal attitudes regarding female inferiority. We must learn how those attitudes become integrated into women's self-concepts, how some women come to experience such mixed feelings about something so central as their femininity and the bodies that define them as female.

Every society disseminates attitudes that are negative toward particular groups of people, with results ranging from inconvenient to devastating. Gender bias, racism, ethnic or religious prejudice can cause economic hardship, promote violence, and almost certainly lead to minor putdowns and major disappointments on a regular basis. Clearly, great suffering can be entailed in being a member of a group that is the subject of bias. The response to such suffering, however, is not preordained and varies greatly from person to person. Some people become angry, actively, even violently, rebeling against the strictures placed on them due to their member-

ship in a devalued group, while others may simply become resentful.

Ambivalent feelings spawned by gender bias represent a deeper,
more subtle, response than these, for several reasons. One is the
centrality of gender. Although some authors have envisioned un-
gendered societies, to date no status, no group membership has
been so defining as one's gender. When asked to describe a person
to someone who knows nothing about that person, most of us will
indicate the person's gender within the first few words. From birth,
perhaps even from conception, in the musings of prospective parents about pretty daughters pirouetting in dance class or athletic
sons starring in little league, gender defines the responses of other
people toward us.

The second crucial aspect of this gender ambivalence is that it
internalizes the prejudices of society. At least in part, it entails
applying to oneself the devaluation of femininity promulgated by
one's culture. In Chapter 9, we will argue that this is only part of
the story; that it is erroneous, offensive, and even dangerous to
reduce these complex emotions to statements like "women hate
themselves." For now, however, it is important to emphasize that
many of the women discussed in this book have, in some respects,
been placed in the position of regretting that they are what they
are—namely, female.

Many women over the centuries have experienced this regret
and, as we will continue to demonstrate, even those who have been
the most successful outside the home and those extremely aware
of society's unfairness to women have not been immune. To understand this process by which women internalize a devalued image
of their own sex, we must look to their families.

It is primarily through the family that the values of society are
mediated. In large part, by reflecting the attitudes of her parents
toward her, a girl comes to build a basic sense of self—of who she
is and the value of being who she is. Through observation, imitation, and identification with adults, again initially and most often
primarily family members, a girl first develops a conception of
what it is to be a person, an adult, a woman. The primary role
model for most people is the parent of their own gender. And so
we now turn our attention to the families of women suffering from
gender ambivalence and the symptoms of anxious somatic depression associated with it.

In this part of the book, we discuss the attitudes and actions of
family members that lead girls to develop ambivalent feelings to-

ward their femininity. Chapter 6 focuses primarily on the preferential treatment given to boys with regard to academic, professional achievement, even in families with talented, very intelligent, ambitious girls. Chapter 7 shifts the focus slightly to the greater non-domestic opportunities offered, and respect accorded, in most families to fathers versus mothers. Our discussion of families is divided into two chapters to maximize clarity and readability, but the processes dealt with are so interrelated that each chapter can only be fully understood in the context of the other.

Freud's Hysteric Patients

We begin our discussion of family dynamics by reviewing what is perhaps the single most famous psychological case study of all time: Freud's hysteric patient Dora. This case was the first one described at length by Freud, and his first to use dream analysis. Several books have been written about the case as well as commentary by such noted psychoanalysts as Erik Erikson and Jacques Lacan. Because it involved hypocrisy, deception, adultery, and other sexual intrigue, it has also been treated as a literary work by critic Steven Marcus.[1] Since so much has been written, we will confine ourselves here to a discussion of the issues of gender it raises that are the focus of this book.

Dora, whose real name was Ina Bauer, was the adolescent daughter of a successful businessman who insisted she see Freud when he found a suicide note in her writing desk. Freud noted that hers was a very typical case of hysteria because she exhibited "the commonest of all somatic and mental symptoms: dyspnoea [i.e., breathing difficulty] . . . possibly migraines . . . depression" as well as "some disinclination for food." In our minds, there is little doubt that Dora displayed what we have been calling anxious somatic depression. There is also little doubt that hidden among all the issues of sex and intrigue are obvious issues regarding Dora's feelings about being female.

Freud described Dora's father as "a large manufacturer in very comfortable circumstances" who was a "dominating figure . . . owing to his intelligence and his character . . . a man of rather unusual activity and talents." This glowing tribute stands in fascinating contrast to Freud's description of Dora's mother:

> I never made her mother's acquaintance. From the accounts given me by the girl and her father I was led to imagine her as an uncultivated

woman and above all as a foolish one, who had concentrated all her interests upon domestic affairs. . . . She presented the picture, in fact, of what might be called the "housewife's psychosis." She had no understanding for her children's more active interests, and was occupied all day long in cleaning the house.

As a result, Dora "looked down on her mother" and modeled herself on a maiden aunt who mysteriously starved to death, possibly due to anorexia nervosa. In childhood, Dora had been very close to, and even idolized, her successful father, who returned her feelings, particularly in his pride over her "intellectual precocity." Freud wrote that Dora's father "had been so proud of the early growth of her intelligence that he had made her his confidante while she was still a child."

But, perhaps coincidentally, at about the time Dora reached adolescence and her body began to mature into that of an adult woman, her father took on a new confidante, the wife of his friend Herr K. Like Freud's other famous hysteric patient, Anna O., Dora was pressured by her parents to stay at home doing household chores. On her own, she attempted to obtain what higher education she could, "attending lectures for women" and carrying on "more or less serious studies," but her mother "was bent upon drawing her into taking a share in the work of the house."

And, like Anna O., Dora envied the educational advantages given to her brother. Freud wrote, "During the girl's earlier years, her only brother . . . had been the model which her ambitions had striven to follow." But while her brother was given the education that allowed him to become a leader of the Austrian Socialist Party, Dora was being pressured to clean the house. Particularly telling, we believe, is Freud's description of how Dora was feeling at the time she first became ill. Freud reported Dora's "declaration that she had been able to keep abreast with her brother up to the time of her illness, but that after that she had fallen behind him in her studies. It is as though she had been a boy up till that moment, and had then become girlish for the first time."[2]

That statement is particularly striking in light of Freud's discussion of the case of Elizabeth von R., the hysteric woman with whom he developed the technique of free association. Freud reported Elizabeth's description of her emotional state just prior to her first experience of the symptoms of hysteria: "despair of a lonely girl like her being able to . . . achieve anything. . . . Till then she had thought herself strong enough to be able to do without the help of a man; but she was now overcome by a sense of her weakness as a woman."

Like Dora, Elizabeth von R. was extremely bright. Her father was so proud of her intelligence that he "used to say that this daughter of his took the place of a son and a friend with whom he could exchange thoughts." But, Freud added, "Although the girl's mind found intellectual stimulation from this relationship with her father, he did not fail to observe that her mental constitution was on that account departing from the ideal which people like to see realized in a girl." As a result of such attitudes, Elizabeth von R. "was greatly discontented with being a girl. She was full of ambitious plans. She wanted to study . . . and she was indignant at the idea of having to sacrifice her inclinations and her freedom of judgement by marriage."[3]

Thus, several hysteric patients with whom Freud (and Breuer) developed the basic techniques of psychoanalysis had experiences that might lead them to feel ambivalent about being female. They were bright and aspired to achieve academically and professionally. During childhood, they were treated as intellectual confidantes by their fathers, but at adolescence they were pressured to live up to a more traditional female role. Anna O. and Dora saw their brothers being given educational opportunities kept from them because of their gender. Elizabeth von R. expressed her anger to Freud at the limitations placed on her because she was female, and Anna O. spent much of her life writing about and working against such limitations. Freud noted that both Dora and Elizabeth became ill when they first realized these limitations.

Breuer and Freud were aware of these issues of gender and achievement. They described the "features which one meets with so frequently in hysterical people" as including "giftedness," "ambition," and "the independence of . . . nature which went beyond the feminine ideal."[4]

Anorexics and Female Achievement

Other clinicians have recognized these same gender issues experienced by patients with symptoms associated with anxious somatic depression. Hilde Bruch was the clinician who probably exerted the most influence on contemporary views of anorexia nervosa. After discussing obesity in her 1973 book *Eating Disorders*, she described the workings of anorexia nervosa, which had not yet received much attention. Perhaps because she wrote of this disorder when very few other clinicians had, anorexics from throughout the country sought her out. In 1978, she published *The Golden Cage*, a collection of descriptive cases of women suffering from anorexia that is still the most complete, influential collection of its kind. In a review, one of us pointed out that Dr. Bruch did not use these scintillating histories to create a theory that apecifically addressed why anorexia afflicted females. Here we focus on just that issue.[5]

Looking at issues of gender and achievement, striking similarities exist between Freud's descriptions of the childhood experiences of hysterics and Bruch's descriptions of the childhoods of women suffering from eating disorders. Bruch portrayed anorexics as "outstanding students" and noted, "In [one] case the patient was convinced that not having a son had not been a problem for her father, that he took pride in his daughters, that he treated them intellectually as sons. . . . It is significant that the fathers value their daughters for their intellectual brilliance."

Bruch went on: "A conspicuous feature of these families was the paucity of sons." This fact, we believe, plays a large role in the family's dynamics, leading fathers to treat their daughters intellectually as sons. Those anorexics who did have brothers appear to have been very envious of their achievements. Bruch described one as remembering "her father's teasing as painful in his sarcastic remarks that she did not bring home as many prizes as her older brother had." About another anorexic, Bruch observed, "Her whole life was an endless competition with an older brother. . . . Only what her brother did was counted as worthwhile." Attitudes such as these appear to have led some of Bruch's anorexic patients to regret being female. "Though few express it openly, they had felt throughout their lives that being a female was an unjust disadvantage and they dreamed of doing well in areas considered more respectful and worthwhile because they were 'masculine.' "[6]

Thus, Hilde Bruch and Sigmund Freud used remarkably similar language in drawing very similar conclusions regarding the familial interactions of their patients around the issues of female achievement and the discontent experienced by these women regarding traditional gender roles. Both groups of patients were bright, high-achieving females who were valued as children for their intelligence, even though intelligence was not considered by their families as a feminine characteristic. The young women with brothers in both groups often felt envious of their brothers' achievements. Both groups resented the limitations placed on them because they were female.

This discovery of such striking similarities in descriptions of two groups of patients—Freud's and Bruch's—who were separated geographically, temporally by almost a century, and culturally, led us to several years of research. At first, the research was confined to our original focus of interest, disordered eating. But, over time, we became aware of the scope of anxious somatic depression and expanded our studies to include depression and later other psychological and somatic symptoms. Our goal was to use similarities in the case studies of Freud and Bruch (as well as others cited throughout this book) as a source of hypotheses about the social and psychological correlates of the symptoms of anxious somatic depression. To test these hypotheses, we distributed research questionnaires to large numbers of women. Respondents were asked to choose answers from numerical scales designed to measure their perceptions of attitudes and actions of members of their families, particularly regarding issues of female achievement. The questionnaires also included scales for determining the frequency and intensity with which respondents exhibited the symptoms of anxious somatic depression, allowing us to use statistical techniques to measure the relationship between symptom reports and family reports.

The methods used in the questionnaire studies on which we focus in this part of the book—sampling, statistics, psychometrics—are important if we want to draw scientific conclusions. But we assume many of our readers will not be very interested in statistics. To bring them alive, we illustrate the results of our questionnaire studies with concrete examples of the family interactions measured by each questionnaire item. Because the problems appeared to strike women who defined themselves nontraditionally, we studied the biographies of almost forty women who have been acknowledged to have made great achievements in areas traditionally reserved for men. (A listing of these women appears in Appendix A.)

What we found in doing these case studies was somewhat surprising but, on second look, took on features we had seen before. Symptoms of anxious somatic depression—particularly depression, disordered eating, or headache—were described in the biographies of most of these women, usually beginning at adolescence or early adulthood. The finding that many of history's most eminent women suffered these symptoms is not only disheartening but also quite startling in that many of the biographies were written in the tradition of "lessons to be learned" from the lives of great people.

These play up the hard work, courage, and talent exhibited by their subjects, ignoring weaknesses and personality flaws. Often, as in our study of the life of Clara Barton, the founder of the American Red Cross, we would read two or three biographies of a particular woman with no hint of any problems, only to learn in a fourth book that the woman suffered at adolescence and throughout her adult life from "nervous prostration," including insomnia, back pain, and, eventually, an inability to move or eat that was associated with chronic depression. Barton herself wrote that she had "lived over the years wishing myself dead."[7]

We found several biographies of Marie Curie, Nobel Prize winner in physics and chemistry for her work on radiation. All mentioned that after graduating from high school, Marie Curie spent a year in the Polish countryside. In her autobiography, she briefly mentioned that this time away from home and school was occasioned by "the fatigue of growth and study." The biography written by her daughter Eve offered an even more benign interpretation: "In the course of the mysterious passage called adolescence, while her body was transformed and her face grew finer, Manya [Marie's nickname] suddenly became lazy." Only when we read a biography written by a disinterested observer did we learn that Marie Curie had a history of anxiety, depression, and other nervous problems beginning at this time in her adolescence and that doctors diagnosed her as suffering a "nervous breakdown." It took a few more years before we came across a biography of Curie that described possible anorexia. It seems that when she began attending school in Paris, Curie was so uninterested in food that she would frequently faint from starvation. Later, a colleague was so shocked at her frailty that he wrote advising her husband Pierre not to let her use lack of hunger as an excuse not to eat. Like neurasthenic physician Margaret Cleaves and fasting girl Mollie Fancher, a few decades earlier, and Eleanor Roosevelt, a few decades later, people thought Marie Curie was too preoccupied with science to take time to eat.[8]

We do not treat our biographical investigations as a scientific study of a representative sample of eminent women because of obvious weaknesses inherent in anecdotal data. We hope biographies will add flavor and interest to the epidemiologic research done by us and by others reviewed in Chapters 3 and 4, to the historical and cross-cultural studies described in Chapters 1 and 2, and to the series of questionnaire studies among high school and college students discussed in Chapter 1 and in this part of the book. Using very different methods, our aim was to search for converging evidence of a link between the symptoms of anxious somatic depression and family interactions that centered on female achievement similar to those described by Freud and Bruch. We found a great deal of such evidence.

Gender Bias in Families

Bruch reported that many of her anorexic patients had no brothers. The college women we surveyed who reported frequent bingeing were almost twice as likely as nonbingers to come from families with no brothers.[9] This led us to believe that fathers who have no sons may treat their daughters as "substitutes" for boys. Hilda Bruch's anorexic patient felt that her father treated her intellectually like a son; to her father, Freud's hysteric patient Elizabeth Von R. took the place of a son, being someone with whom he could exchange ideas; and neurasthenic physician Margaret Cleaves felt that her education would have been supported by her father if he had lived because he treated her as his "boy" after her brother's death. One historian speculated that Florence Nightingale's father's unusually rigorous "educational endeavors with his daughters constituted in large part a working out of his desire for a son."[10] We found that high school girls who described their fathers treating them like boys were four times as likely as those who did not to report high levels of depression combined with at least two of the following: disordered eating, frequent headaches, frequent breathing difficulties, or frequent insomnia.[11]

Like Freud's and Bruch's patients, many eminent women were portrayed as their father's "confidantes." The father of noted English poet Elizabeth Barret Browning was depicted as her "intellectual companion." At age 15, the poet became mysteriously ill, eventually describing herself as "a recluse with nerves." When she met her future husband, poet Robert Browning, Elizabeth Barret was five feet tall and weighed only 87 pounds. Her domineering father frequently "railed at his daughter for eating so little" and often coerced her to eat more than she did. In a journal article, psychologist Carol R. Lewis concluded that Elizabeth Barrett Browning was an anorexic.[12]

We believe that girls treated as "boys" in childhood suffer from these problems because they develop childhood aspirations and self-concepts built around abilities that, in the words of Breuer and Freud, go "beyond the feminine ideal." Because they define themselves in ways not considered appropriate for females, they are never fully accepted—not even by their fathers. Furthermore, at adolescence, biological, psychological, and social changes place pressure on them to discard "masculine" aspirations and settle for feminine roles that the girls have been brought up to think of as inferior.

Women who have no brothers may also sense that their fathers would have really preferred them to be male. In our most recent study, we found that high school girls disagreeing with the statement "My father was pleased with the fact that I was a girl" were particularly likely to report depression combined with anxiety and symptoms of somatization, disordered eating, and poor body image.[13]

The father of Elizabeth Cady Stanton, one of the leaders of the U.S. movement for women's rights in the second half of the nineteenth century, was clearly not happy she was a girl. Stanton's mother "paid little attention to Elizabeth's love of learning, and was primarily interested that her daughters learn domestic arts and genteel skills." But on treasured visits to her father's law office, Elizabeth was allowed to read his law books and told that when she grew up she might work to change the laws that discriminated against women. She came to identify with her father. Nonetheless, the boys in her family were clearly given preferential treatment. Of 10 children born to her parents, however, only six survived childhood: Elizabeth, four sisters, and one older brother. Stanton's earliest memory was of friends commiserating with her parents on the birth of another daughter. When she was 11, her only surviving brother died, leaving her father disconsolate. She tried to comfort him, to replace her brother through intellectual achievement, and to become, in the words of a biographer, "in effect the male child." Stanton wrote, "I thought that the thing to be done in order to equal boys was to be learned," but her father told her that she could not make up for his loss because she was a girl. A few years later, at adolescence, she "fell into a depression so intense she thought she was going insane."[14]

Favorite Sons

The brothers of many of the women we studied received privileged treatment in their families. Sometimes that treatment took the form of access to, and resources for, higher education. This was true for both of Freud's most well-known hysteric patients, Anna

O. and Dora. In her diary, psychoanalyst Karen Horney wrote about her own father: "He, who has flung out thousands for my step-brother Enoch, who is both stupid and bad, first turns every additional penny he is to spend for me ten times in his fingers. . . . He would like me to stay at home now, so we could dismiss our maid and I could do her work. He brings me almost to the point of cursing my good gifts."[15]

In many cases, girls come to feel that their brothers are treated as if they are smarter or their intellectual achievements are more valuable. Among the college women we surveyed, those who reported that their fathers treated a brother as the brightest child in the family were over twice as likely as those who did not to binge frequently. In contrast, women who reported that their father treated a sister as the brightest child did not suffer from disordered eating.[16]

Alice James was the one daughter in a preeminent intellectual family that included psychologist/philosopher William and novelist Henry. Her life exemplifies the problems experienced by bright, talented girls whose brothers are allowed to achieve in areas closed to women. When her brothers were beginning their brilliant careers, Alice was limited to joining the sewing bee formed by several other young women in Cambridge, Massachusetts. She early came to realize that "matrimony seems the only successful occupation that a woman can undertake," and her self-esteem began to suffer. She wrote to brother William, "You must excuse the frivolity of this letter if you condescend to read it, on account of the frivolity and want of intelligence of the writer. You must remember that this mental baseness is not her own fault, and that as she is your sister her having so little mind may account for your having so much."

We suggest that Alice James's self-denigration and her realization of how limited her opportunities were may have caused her illness. Her symptoms included facial neuralgia, stomach pains, fainting spells, headaches, and difficulty concentrating, along with the anxiety, terror, and despair that led her to threaten suicide. She described herself as suffering from "convulsions—digestive, mental and sentimental." The letters written by her family when she was sent away for treatment at adolescence contain references to her weight, such as her mother exalting over the fact that Alice's cousin had seen her "looking fat as butter."

All her symptoms began during adolescence, when Alice James was, in the words of biographer Jean Strouse, "trying to find out whether she could engage in studious activities and assert her intellectual potential, or whether she must accept that she was not equipped with whatever made men capable of 'cerebration.' " She believed that her mind was not on a par with those of her famous brothers and felt that competing with men was not appropriate for a woman, constituting what she referred to as "spiritual snatching."[17]

The emphasis given to the intelligence of brothers takes place within the context of a devaluation of women's intelligence. Alice James may have felt less bright than her brothers not simply because they were so accomplished but also because her father "disapproved of equality for women in intellectual and political life." Similarly, in our surveys of contemporary college women, we found disordered eating to be common among women who reported that their fathers believed "a woman's place is in the home."[18]

The Attitudes of Fathers and Mothers

Several findings from our questionnaire studies appeared to indicate that the attitudes and actions of mothers and fathers may work somewhat differently to produce ambivalence about femininity and the symptoms we have been describing. For example, although we found that college students' reports of having a father who treated a boy as the most intelligent sibling in the family were related to frequent bingeing, the sibling in the family who was treated as most intelligent by mothers was not significantly related to reports of frequent bingeing.[19]

In traditional families where fathers have been the intellectual achievers, fathers seem to play the role of judges: Their opinions regarding the intellectual achievements of their offspring are particularly influential for their "nontraditional" daughters. As a result, the ambitious daughters of traditional fathers who consider women as inferior or as best suited for domesticity may come to feel that there is something wrong with, or lacking in, themselves. Mothers, on the other hand, appear to act as role models of adult femininity. To many daughters, mothers represent the model of what it is to be an adult woman. Their experiences of their mothers' lives may lay down a psychological template that colors their expectations regarding their own adult lives. One study found that the development of a high degree of femininity occurred among daughters whose fathers encouraged femininity and whose mothers exhibited high levels of self-acceptance.[20] The self-acceptance of the fathers and the mothers' encouragement of femininity were unrelated to the degree of femininity of the daughters. That is, what affected the daughters was how their fathers reacted to them and how their mothers viewed themselves. We cannot say whether this would continue to occur if the daughters were brought up to accord more respect to their mothers' intellectual opinions.

But, as we will see, being a model for a bright, ambitious woman is problematic for many mothers living in societies that place great limitations on females, particularly if daughters are very talented or grow up during periods of great change in women's roles.

7

Idealized Fathers, Devalued Mothers

"If I only were a man . . . I have read too much, seen too much, drunk too much. So I don't like myself anymore. I'd like to lose thirty pounds of weight. Please, doctor, send me to a plastic surgeon." The words were those of a 20-year-old woman who was, according to her therapist, preoccupied with her weight and obsessed with the shape of her breasts. Another woman described as obsessed with her breasts, also suffering from depression, was a 27-year-old unmarried Ph.D. with a "brilliant reputation" as a researcher. These women were the daughters of successful fathers, one a director of a factory, the other a well-known lawyer, and of mothers who were homemakers. The first woman spoke little of her mother but was "very attached" to her father, while the second woman, according to her therapist, strongly identified with her father, and not her mother, who was described as "below the father's level from an intellectual point of view."[1]

The pattern is one we have seen many times. Ambitious, nontraditional women who admire and identify intellectually with their successful fathers but not their traditional mothers develop the symptoms of anxious somatic depression when they reach adolescence. Clinicians Kim Chernin and Susan and Wayne Wooley have found that their female eating-disordered patients have trouble identifying with their mothers because of the devaluation of the mothers' roles and intellectual status by the society at large and, in many cases, by the daughters themselves.[2] In the two women described here, the poor body image took the form of an obsession with the shape of their breasts, which we would suggest was really discomfort with developing any breasts, a sign of ambivalence toward becoming women.

Our research questionnaires included several items measuring whether females attending high school or college looked down on their mothers or perceived them as being limited because they were female. To put flesh on and add detail to our descriptions of statistical findings regarding contemporary women who grow up in families whose fathers are esteemed for their achievements but whose mothers are relegated to lesser roles, we include anecdotal incidents from the lives of daughters of four men who have had great influence on modern thought: Freud, Marx, Darwin, and Einstein.

In our own work, we have found disordered eating is common among college students who reported that their mothers believed "a woman's place is in the home." This appears to have been the case with the daughter of Albert Einstein. Einstein had no biological daughters from his first marriage, but when he remarried, his second wife had two young girls whom he helped bring up. One, Margot, lived with him for many years. While Margot was described as sharing Einstein's attitudes, her mother was quite traditional, portrayed in one biography of Einstein as "housewifely, of no intellectual pretensions." Einstein's daughter was said to be ill throughout her life but her symptoms are nowhere specified. We were struck, however, by the similarity, in books written by different authors, of the rare descriptions of Margot, almost all referring to her extreme thinness. She was described as having an "extremely fragile appearance," looking "excessively slim," "too slender," "strangely like her [emaciated] dying sister," and as "frail," "very frail," "as frail as ever."[3]

One survey of college women found that those who reported frequent bingeing were more likely than those who did not to report that their fathers thought that their wives were unintelligent. Among the same women, however, no significant relationship was found between reports of frequent bingeing and of having mothers who thought that the women's fathers were unintelligent.[4] Once again, fathers appear to be acting as judges and mothers as models.

Martha, the wife of psychoanalyst Sigmund Freud, was, according to one biographer, the "complete bourgeoisie" with an "unremitting sense of her calling to domestic duty." Bearing six children in nine years, she led what Freud called a "tormented life" and was not treated by her husband as an intellectual equal. Like his hysteric patient Dora, Freud's renowned daughter Anna was intellectually precocious, served as her father's confidante, and was faced with a father who modeled success and a mother who modeled domesticity. Despite being the brightest of the Freud children, Anna envied her brothers. The most obvious statement of her conflict over gender appeared in a letter she wrote in response to a story: "But if one looks like . . . me, one only feels envy—in two directions: the one that shows how one might be achieving like a man, and the one that shows dancing and being generous like Mathilde [a female character in the story]. One would like to be able to do both, and does find oneself to be a little of both, but neither becomes real."

At adolescence, Anna Freud began to feel ashamed that her body was not slim like that of her sister Sophie and to suffer from an illness that included weight loss, back pains, and menstrual difficulties, causing her to be sent to Italy to recuperate. In letters he wrote to her in Italy, Anna's father advised her to relax and gain weight. In response, she "wrote almost every day, and reported eagerly to her father each time she put on half a kilogram of weight." Anna's biographer Elizabeth Young-Bruehl also observed that an illness "that was not physical kept irrupting making her feel exhausted and stupid," and concluded that Anna was suffering from "a mild eating disturbance of the kind Freud associated with hysteria."[5]

One symptom of disordered eating measured in one of our studies of college students was purging—that is, using laxatives, diuretics, or self-induced vomiting to control one's weight. Among the women in this study who reported that in childhood they considered their homemaking skills to be about as important as their academic achievement, purging was rare whether or not they reported having a father who considered his wife unintelligent. Purging was also rare among women who reported that in childhood they considered their academic achievement much more important than their homemaking skills, but also reported that their fathers considered their mothers at least moderately intelligent. In contrast, among women who reported that in childhood they placed much more importance on their own academic achievement than on their household skills and also reported that their fathers considered their mothers unintelligent, over one-third reported purging.[6] Girls who want to be seen as intelligent themselves are particularly devastated when their mothers are not viewed that way.

These findings resemble the contrast between the intellectual interests and aspirations of Henrietta Darwin, daughter of naturalist Charles Darwin, and the lack of those interests in her mother Emma, which was captured in the strikingly different descriptions of the two that appeared in biographies of Charles Darwin. For example, in 1938 Geoffrey West described Emma as "in no way intellectually comparable to her husband . . . despite her early resolves, she found it impossible to be interested in Charles's studies." Of the daughter West wrote, "Henrietta . . . exercised her bright intelligence [as editor] upon the work not only of her father but sometimes of [biologist Thomas] Huxley too."

Like Margot Einstein, Henrietta Darwin was ill throughout her life with symptoms that are nowhere fully delineated. She was the sickest member of a family that suffered from nervous ailments, a lifelong invalid afflicted with a variety of psychosomatic disturbances. Her niece pointed out that illness did not prevent Henrietta's brothers from leading active, productive lives and becoming quite eminent, but "unfortunately, Aunt Etty, being a lady, had no real work to do" so "ill health became her profession." At 14, she became "out of health," and from age 17 to 18, she suffered from "weakness" and "indigestion." The niece also provided a few other tidbits that hint at disordered eating, recounting stories of Henrietta calling down to the kitchen to ask the cook to count the number of pits on her plate to ascertain whether she had eaten three or four prunes for lunch. She described her Aunt Etty as having a "tiny form," and as being very "frail," the same word frequently used about Margot Einstein.[7]

Mothers Viewed as Limited by Gender

The problems go far beyond the alleged "intellectual deficiencies" of particular mothers. Most of the women we studied were acutely aware of and troubled by the lesser status of roles allotted to their mothers compared to their fathers. Women's rights activist Elizabeth Stanton "had a negative reaction toward a mother identified with domesticity," while French writer Simone de Beauvoir identified with her father, who was associated with "the mind," not with her mother, linked to "daily drudgery." We found that disordered eating is common among college women reporting that their mothers were not satisfied with their own career choices. In fascinating contrast, these women's reports of the extent to which their fathers were dissatisfied with their own careers were not related to disordered eating.[8] From the time they were young girls, these women confronted a model of adult femininity associated with limitations, low status, unhappiness, and lack of respect. At adolescence these girls were "thrown" (in the word used by Binswanger to describe Ellen West) into the role of woman that they had seen so devalued.

The prevalence of anxious somatic depression among women of talent results, in part, because the syndrome is not limited to nontraditional daughters of traditional mothers. Having a mother who is highly concerned with professional achievement and intellectual interests does not protect a nontraditional woman from the syndrome if her mother is barred from pursuing such interests. Contemporary high school students who told us that their mothers were often "fed up with playing the mommy role" were particularly likely to exhibit depression combined with disordered eating, headaches, breathing difficulties, or insomnia.[9]

Jenny Marx, wife of Karl Marx and mother of three daughters, including Eleanore Marx, was apparently fed up with playing the role of traditional homemaker. Living in an overcrowded residence, always short of money, and restricted to being wife and mother, Jenny Marx felt depressed and understood that her depression was related to the limitations placed on her as a woman. In a letter, she wrote, "while the men are invigorated by the fight in the world outside, strengthened by coming face to face with the enemy . . . we sit at home and darn stockings. It does not banish care and the little day-to-day worries slowly but surely sap one's vitality."

The attitudes of both her mother and father probably played a role in leading Eleanore to devalue femininity. Karl Marx had six children, but only three daughters survived childhood. On the birth of Eleanore, his youngest daughter, Marx expressed his disappointment that she was female. He wrote to his friend Friederich Engels that she was "unfortunately of the sexe par excellence . . . had it been a male the matter would be more acceptable."

At this point, it will probably come as no surprise to readers that Eleanore Marx became ill at adolescence. She suffered from back pains, insomnia, and depression that eventually led to suicide. Her father realized that her illness was related to her unfulfilled ambitions. To Engels, Marx wrote that he "was convinced that no medicine, no change of scene or air could cure her sickness . . . [her teacher] was the only doctor who could help her, since she was burning with the desire to find an opening for herself."

Eleanore Marx was also anorexic. Her mother described her as "emaciated." Her doctor concluded that nothing was wrong with her except derangement of the stomach due to fasting. Her father Karl was as befuddled by her anorexia as any father of a contemporary anorexic. He lamented in a letter that one of the features of women's ailments "in which hysteria plays a part was that one had to affect not to notice that the invalid lived on earthly sustenance."[10] If the problems we were studying were not so serious, we might find some amusement in the amount of correspondence exchanged by some of the greatest thinkers of the past two centuries—Sigmund and Anna Freud, Karl Marx and Friederich Engels, William and Henry James, Mahatma Gandhi and Jawaharlal Nehru—that contained references to the weight and eating of sisters or daughters.

Many women are simultaneously subjected to several familial attitudes regarding female inferiority—preferential treatment given to brothers over sisters, greater respect accorded to fathers over mothers, mothers who are dissatisfied with the choices available to them, and both mothers and fathers who believe women are best suited for domesticity. In one survey, college students reported whether the following four problems characterized their families: their mothers agreed that a woman's place is in the home, their mothers were dissatisfied with their own career choices, their fathers thought that the women's mothers were unintelligent, and their fathers considered a brother the brightest child in the family. About half the women surveyed reported that none of these attitudes were characteristic of their families. Of these women, only 15 percent reported frequent bingeing. About one-third of the women reported that only one of these gender biases characterized their families. Of these women, 21 percent reported frequent bingeing. About one in seven women reported that their families exhibited two of the four problems described above. Over one-third of these women reported frequent bingeing. And of the 4 percent of the sample who reported that their families exhibited at least three of the problems, about three-quarters reported frequent bingeing.[11]

Emily Dickinson was a woman subjected to several familial biases against female achievement. Her brother's ideas were doted on by her father and treated as more valuable than those of the noted poet. At the same time, her father thought that women were inferior to men and believed "a woman's place is in the home." Dickinson's mother was described by a biographer as the intellectual inferior of Dickinson's father, who clearly did not respect his wife. The poet wrote of her mother, she "does not care for thought [as I do]." But Emily Dickinson was noted not only as a great American poet but as a recluse. At adolescence she began to suffer from "prostrating depression," "almost unrelenting anxiety," "preoccupation with death," and phobias. The evidence we uncovered for her anorexia is indirect. In a letter to a friend, she wrote of herself: "Am told that fasting gives to food marvelous aroma, but by birth a Bachelor, disavow cuisine." With our emphasis on the relationship between achievement, ambivalence about gender, depression, and disordered eating, we were highly intrigued by a letter in which a noted female poet who was clearly depressed tells of fasting and disavowing food because she considered herself to have been born a "Bachelor." Other writers have also concluded that Dickinson had an eating disorder, based on references she made in her poetry. But with the wealth of very powerful evidence for disordered eating and depression among the eminent women we studied, we are loath to make too much of poetical allusions.[12]

Throughout history, most women, some completely willingly and others less so, have focused the bulk of their time and energy on tasks associated with home and family. Most daughters, socialized to value similar pursuits, have modeled themselves to a large extent on their mothers with relatively few problems. But daughters who, because of their talent or their times, aspired to achieve outside the home have had more difficulties. Daughters who noted the relative powerlessness and lack of respect accompanying the roles of wife and homemaker often devalued their mothers who were content to be traditional, and experienced difficulty identifying with the roles of adult women enacted by these mothers. At the same time, daughters of mothers not content with the roles allotted to them by a gender-biased society often observed, and in many cases shared, the suffering of their mothers. These daughters may have strongly identified with their mothers but not with the roles of adult women ascribed to them. While the two types of mothers may have been very different, the nontraditional daughters of both types viewed their mothers as being limited by their gender and experienced conflicts between their own aspirations and the social and psychological pressures placed on them to identify with their mothers.

About one of five college women we surveyed reported either that they felt that their mothers had been very limited by being a female, that they felt guilty over living better lives than their mothers, or that they minimized their own accomplishments so that their mothers would not feel bad about themselves. Women who reported any one of these problems were about 20 times as likely to list symptoms of disordered eating combined with frequent depressed mood. Female high school students who reported the same concerns about their mothers' limitations were more likely than those who did not report these concerns to exhibit depression combined with at least two of the following: disordered eating, headaches, breathing difficulties, or insomnia. These students were not more likely than others to report high levels of depression in the absence of somatic symptoms. And depression accompanied by somatic symptoms struck almost half the female high school students who reported not only that they felt at least one of these concerns regarding their mothers' limitations but also that they believed that their fathers often wished they were boys or agreed that a woman's place is in the home.[13]

In the data we recently collected in two high schools (described in detail in Appendix C), anxious somatic depression—the combination of high levels of depression and anxiety along with several somatic symptoms including disordered eating, poor body image, and preference for thinness—was exhibited by over one-quarter of females who scored high on a scale measuring whether they felt that their mothers had been limited by being female (for example, one question read: How limited was your mother by being female?) or on a scale that measured whether they themselves felt limited by being female (sample question: How much do you agree with the statement that more people would pay attention to your ideas if you were male?). Like the male students, very few female students who did not report feeling that they or their mothers were limited by being female exhibited anxious somatic depression. In contrast, the prevalence of "pure" depression (defined as scoring high on the depression scale but not meeting criteria for anxious somatic depression) was about the same among both groups of female students and among the males. So female students who did not report that they or their mothers were limited by their gender exhibited a pattern of depressive symptomatology quite similar to that exhibited by males—moderate prevalence of pure depression and very low prevalence of anxious somatic depression. Female students who reported feeling that they or their mothers were limited by their gender exhibited about the same prevalence of pure depression as other females or as males, but many also exhibited anxious somatic depression. That is, we found that females did not differ from males in the prevalence of pure depression. They did differ in the frequency of anxious somatic depression, and this difference resulted simply because anxious somatic depression was quite common among the subset of females who reported feeling that they or their mothers were limited by their gender.

These findings suggest the hypothesis that gender differences in the prevalence of depressive symptomatology may be due in large part to the high prevalence of a syndrome of depression combined with anxiety, physical problems, and disordered eating among a subset of females who report feeling that they or their mothers were limited by their gender. This hypothesis helps to explain two findings resulting from our reanalyses of data from a large study performed by the National Institute of Mental Health. The first finding, discussed in Chapter 3, was that females exhibit higher prevalence of clinical depression than males only in cohorts that reached adolescence during periods when females graduated from college at a greater rate than the women of their mothers' generation. These data allow for historical analyses, but do not provide information relating the educational attainment of individual males and females to the development of clinical depression. This information was included in a report that recently came out of the NIMH study. Our renalysis indicates that among people who exhibited no psychiatric disorder at the beginning of a longitudinal study, gender differences in the development of clinical depression over the subsequent six years occurred only among those who had attended college. Among the people who did not attend college, 11.6 percent of females and 11.5 percent of males had developed major depression six years later. In contrast, among those who had attended college, 19 percent of females and 4.6 percent of males developed major depression. Together, these reanalyses indicate that the gender difference in the prevalence of depression may result because females but not males develop a form of depression associated with psychological issues related to academic achievement, particularly in contexts wherein the previous generation of females was not able to achieve academically.[14]

We suggest that women who do not grow up during periods when females are much more likely to achieve academically than their mothers usually do not feel that their mothers were limited by their gender. Women who do not strive to achieve in areas traditionally considered more appropriate for men are not likely to feel that they have been limited by being female. Based on our recent findings, if these women develop depression, it is likely to be what we call here pure depression, and it is usually about as prevalent as the pure depression developed by men.

By contrast, women who strive to achieve academically, particularly during periods when their mothers were not likely to have graduated college, are probably the ones who report that their own achievements have been limited by their gender as were their mothers' achievements. Although these women will exhibit about the same prevalence of "pure" depression as other women and men, they will also exhibit a high frequency of anxious somatic depression. As a result, the total prevalence of depression among these women will be high, leading to gender differences in depression prevalence only among people who aspire to achieve academically and belong to generations who mature during periods of increased rates of female college graduation compared to their mothers' generation.

Overidealized Fathers

It appears that anxious somatic depression frequently occurs among women who admire and identify with their fathers but not their mothers. In some cases, fathers may be motivated to encourage their daughters to identify with them. Many men may crave admiration for their intellect and their accomplishments that is greater than what they receive outside their families. Such fathers may find in their intelligent daughters what seems like perfect intellectual companions: Ones with whom they can share ideas and who will provide them with praise and admiration that may not be forthcoming from their wives, particularly if the wives are resentful of the privileged treatment accorded their husbands simply because of their gender.

Clearly, these intellectual relationships are often accompanied by strong emotion on the part of daughters. Pioneering social worker Jane Addams, feminist activist Elizabeth Stanton, and nurse Clara Barton idolized their fathers, and Ellen West's "veneration for her father knew no bounds."[15] All of these women were also depressed. In the words of one eating-disordered patient, "When I think back, I can't remember her [mother] as being in my life when I was little . . . all my memories are with my father— sharing things like going to the science museum, eating a hamburg at Burger King, my building model ships while he built his model ships, being able to share a joke with him or an important conversation." Some psychologists would describe these reactions as an "overidealization" by the daughters of fathers who inappropriately treat these young girls as "confidantes."[16]

At the same time, the fathers may come to view their wives as very limited, unintellectual, interested in just those details perceived as mundane trivialities that were the center of the supposedly valued role they were socialized, or pressured, to take on just a few years before. The daughters may sense that their main advantage in the battle for their father's love and attention lies in being less traditionally feminine than their mothers who chose, or were forced into, a devalued role. Unfortunately, at adolescence these daughters often find that biology and society conspire to force them into just the role they have considered so inferior.

Part III

THE THEORY OF GENDER AMBIVALENCE

8

Adolescence

Adolescence is often portrayed as a period of turmoil. And whether or not that description is applicable to boys, it is certainly true for many girls. A recent study of Dutch adolescents found that between ages 11 and 18, the proportion of females who reported feeling unhappy, sad, or depressed increased almost five times as much as the proportion of males. During the same period, the proportion of females who reported that they felt fearful doubled, while that of males actually decreased. The same was true regarding reports of not eating well.[1] As discussed in Chapter 4, the prevalence of many other disorders—including headache, breathing difficulties, insomnia, and mitral valve prolapse—increase dramatically among females during adolescence.

Several other findings indicate that the transformation into adulthood is a much more negative and problematic experience for females than for males. For example, as adolescent boys mature, their ideal male physique becomes larger on average, approximating more nearly that of the men they are becoming. As girls progress through adolescence, however, their ideal physique tends to become slimmer on average and less like that of the women they are becoming. As a result, females at more advanced pubertal stages more frequently dislike their bodies than less mature females. Similarly, whereas early puberty has been found to have positive effects on males, developing early is much more problematic among females—boys appear much more eager to become men than girls to become women.[2]

Adolescence is also a time when self-esteem drops much more among females than among males. The number of females reporting that they are "happy the way I am" declines half again as much from elementary school to high school as the proportion of males, and those reporting feeling "good at lots of things" drops twice as much.[3] At adolescence, but not before, females who feel badly about themselves and their achievements are the ones who feel depressed and are concerned with their eating and the size and shape of their bodies. When we reanalyzed a study of male and female students, we found that, in elementary school, a low level of academic self-esteem (i.e., how the people studied felt about themselves as students) was no more strongly related to depression among females than among males. In junior high school, however, low academic self-esteem was more strongly associated with depression among females. In another study, low self-esteem was not found to be related to concern about weight among either preadolescent boys or girls, or among adolescent boys. Among adolescent girls, however, concern about weight went along with low self-esteem. Similarly, high levels of depression or somatic symptoms only accompany high levels of intelligence or scholastic achievement among adolescent females, not among adolescent males or among preadolescent males or females.[4] It seems that, as they become adults, large numbers of females, but not males, come to deprecate themselves, dislike their bodies, and feel depressed.

Gender Intensification

The problems of adolescence may be particularly great among females who aspire to achieve in areas traditionally reserved for males. One reason for this is that even people who take pride in a girl's intelligence when she is a child may come to treat her more traditionally when she begins to develop. This increasingly traditional response to female intelligence is one aspect of the process that has been labeled "gender intensification," described as follows.

> A number of authors have proposed that adolescence represents the first point in development when females receive intense social pressure to be feminine. Before they reach puberty many girls can happily be tomboys, not worry much about how they look or whether they are sweet, attractive, and feminine. Girls who prefer baseball to dolls

are tolerated during elementary school. With the onset of adolescence, however, comes a high premium on being socially successful, attractive to boys, and on giving up masculine activities and interests.[5]

Because of gender intensification, adolescence may actually be a time of decreased independence and increased limitation to some females. When asked to complete a task along with their daughters, traditional fathers were found to offer more help and allow less autonomy as their daughters progressed through puberty. Even in 1852, one physician, Dr. Edward J. Tilt, observed: "Puberty, which gives man the knowledge of greater power, gives to woman the conviction of her dependence."[6]

That fathers may exhibit gender intensification in response to talented daughters was quite clear in the lives of several eminent women. For example, George Eliot, the writer of such popular novels as *Middlemarch* and *The Mill in the Floss,* was said to have been her father's favorite child. But "as she grew into young womanhood, the relationship between them became increasingly strained and uneasy." One biographer wrote, "If even her father had been proud of Mary Ann's [Eliot's actual name] precocity, the pride was soon supplanted by hostile suspicion toward the large world of the mind she had opened for herself."

At about the same time, Eliot began to suffer from a wide range of psychosomatic symptoms that often kept her bedridden. She acknowledged that they were psychosomatic: "My troubles are purely psychical—self-dissatisfaction and despair of achieving anything worth doing." The symptoms, including "dreadful headaches," began in early adulthood. By age 30, she wrote in her journal of experiencing "despair that sucked away the sap of half the hours," which was described by a biographer as "dreadful nervousness and depression."[7]

French writer Simone de Beauvoir paid the same price at adolescence. De Beauvoir was known for her fiction, but even more for *The Second Sex,* the highly influential nonfiction work that outlined the tragedies of gender inequality. During her early childhood, she did not feel that her parents would have preferred her to be male. Only when her younger sister was born did their disappointment at not having a son become clear. As a child, de Beauvoir was her father's favorite because of her intelligence. She wrote that, to her father, "I was simply a mind." He even remarked one day: "Simone thinks more like a man." But her relationship with her father changed at adolescence. She wrote:

I did everything he told me to do at first. He took pride in my mind, so I embraced learning, I prepared myself for a profession from the moment he told me that was what I had to do. And then, after all that blind obedience on my part, it was he who rejected me. How shall I describe it? I suppose I should call it my "awkward years": I was an ugly, graceless adolescent, and he preferred my prettier sister because at heart he detested intellectuals. . . . It was never expressed in words, and we were always polite with each other, but whatever had been between us was completely broken off. Sometime around my eleventh year, from then on, we didn't get along at all.

During this rocky adolescence, de Beauvoir began to suffer from stomach problems and vomiting, probably associated with the intense migraine headaches afflicting her throughout her adult life. Also plaguing her in adulthood was the "extreme" depression that began at age 19. When walking through the streets, she would sometimes break into uncontrollable sobbing.[8]

To both Eliot and de Beauvoir, it must have been quite clear that their fathers' alleged distaste for intellectuals became focused on them only when they turned into young women. This process is obviously not limited to successful females. Peter Blos, noted authority on adolescence, described the case of Judy, an adolescent girl who was the only female in a group of triplets. Her mother "felt trapped by her children, defeated and sucked dry." As a child, Judy did extremely well in school, much better than her brothers. She was called "gifted" and a "genius" by her teachers. She was quite proud of her intelligence and "acted as if her life depended on her succeeding in her school work." At adolescence, she was determined to go to college, but her family argued that "sisters should renounce a college career in favor of brothers." Judy had no major problems as a child, but "with her entrance into puberty a change came over Judy. Her family and teachers noticed how troubled and worried she was. . . . With the onset of puberty she was possessed by feelings of rage and despair alternating with remorse and depressed moods. Headaches made her afraid she might have an illness of the brain. Thoughts of death and suicide filled her fantasy life," and "she felt ugly."[9]

We have already seen the case of a twin in Chapter 2—Toula, the Greek girl who suffered from nerves. She was not allowed to continue her education, while her twin brother was. She also felt ugly and fantasized that her brother would die and she would take over his masculine spirit. We wonder how many other bright, ambitious girls have suffered at adolescence on seeing advantages conferred on twin brothers, so similar to themselves save for their gender.

To some women, pursuits stereotypically considered "masculine"—the world of the mind, professional success, power—are more highly valued than the feminine pursuits they are expected to partake in. This attitude receives wide reinforcement from the larger society. If a girl is talented in these "masculine" areas, if she shows promise as a child of excelling in such widely respected pursuits, then being treated "like a girl" will seem a comedown. If she senses that "feminine" pursuits are not highly respected, being a female may seem limiting. And, if just as she is developing the frame and secondary sex characteristics of an adult woman, people begin to accord her less autonomy and pay less attention to the abilities she has come to value, and that others previously valued in her, she may develop a host of problems. Her self-esteem may falter. She may start to feel anxious and depressed. Psychosomatic symptoms may develop.

She may also begin to react negatively to her newly developing body, for, after all, it is that body that causes people to accord her less status than she has been accustomed to. One female Ph.D. told us of how, as a child, she often helped her father and brother with the yardwork. One hot summer day during her early adolescence, she found them stripped to the waist, hard at work on the lawn. Preparing to join in as always, she pulled off her shirt, exposing two developed breasts, at which point her father told her to put on her shirt, leave the yardwork to him and her brother, and go inside to help her mother with the housework.

Anxious Somatic Depression as a Temporary Reaction to Adolescence

Some problems exhibited by females at adolescence may be temporary. Among the contemporary women we have talked with and the eminent women whose biographies we studied, several seem to have ceased their symptoms of anxious somatic depression after adolescence or early adulthood. Psychoanalyst Helene Deutsch and feminist activists Susan B. Anthony and Elizabeth Cady Stanton reported little depression after what appear to be relatively severe depressive episodes during adolescence. Several contemporary women we interviewed had eating disorders during adolescence, including severely restricted food intake on weekdays accompanied by episodes of bingeing on weekends, moderate anorexia, and bulimia that lasted for a few years before disappearing. Scores on measures of depressive symptomatology are particularly high and diagnoses of eating disorders are particularly prevalent among adolescent females and decrease somewhat thereafter, suggesting that some girls may temporarily respond to puberty with these symptoms. Among some females, symptoms of anxious somatic depression may constitute a temporary reaction to the "shock" of becoming women. Given the widespread gender bias throughout history, many girls may experience at adolescence at least a brief period of ambivalence toward becoming adult women along with the symptoms of anxious somatic depression. In this context, it is interesting to note that in 1901 Dr. Thomas C. Allbutt wrote: "Perhaps every girl passes, as it were, through the outer court of chlorosis in her progress from youth to maturity." And in 1890, Dr. Charles Mercier wrote: "At [adolescence] more or less decided manifestations of hysteria are the rule."[10] Although these comments may betray some gender bias on the part of the physicians, they do suggest that the symptoms of the forgotten syndrome may be quite common among female adolescents.

Among some women, the entire syndrome may be temporary; among others, some symptoms may go away after early adulthood while others linger; among still others, the entire syndrome may continue throughout their adult lives. Our case studies suggest one hypothesis. Perhaps mothers who are discontent with limitations placed on them by traditional gender roles, as in the case of the mothers of Karen Horney, Louisa May Alcott, and Eleanore Marx, are more likely to have daughters who suffer from chronic severe depression, while mothers who may have been devalued by their families but appeared content with their traditional roles of wife and mother, as in the case of the mothers of Helene Deutsch, Anna Freud, and Elizabeth Cady Stanton, may have daughters who exhibit symptoms that are particularly severe at adolescence but become less severe later in life. That is, the pain of girls who share the suffering of their mothers may be more enduring than that of girls who grew up with mothers for whom they have little respect. This hypothesis must be tested with further research.

Identification

For nontraditional women, whether their mothers were traditional and devalued or nontraditional and discontent, adolescence is also problematic because it is a period in which the intertwined issues of identity and identification with the mother once again take center stage. The preoccupation with identity exhibited by adolescents, both female and male, is rooted, in part, in the tremendous changes they experience. Every aspect of life appears to alter at this time. It is not too great an exaggeration to say that adolescent bodies sometimes seem to be changing as rapidly as horror film depictions of werewolves hit by the first light of the full moon. Teenage boys and girls may be forgiven for wondering at night what their bodies may look like when they awaken. Social identity is also up for grabs. Friendships that were stable throughout childhood may change. New people and new groups of people become important. And notions of vocation, profession, and career assume much more importance in the self-images of children as they pass through adolescence. To the extent a preadolescent is asked about career plans, it is usually in the form of the question "What do you want to be when you grow up?" The typical clichéd, unrealistic responses of cowboy, fireman, actress, dancer, or astronaut are not taken seriously. But while adolescents may not be expected to have completely solidified their career plans, they are supposed to be thinking seriously along these lines. Expressed vocational plans of becoming a cowboy would be met with a grin when coming from a child, but would instill dismay if uttered by an adolescent.

These transformations in physique, social interactions, and self-image underlie the uncertain response of adolescents to the question "Who am I?" The discomfort engendered by doubt about such a basic issue pushes the typical adolescent toward actions that will help to resolve the uncertainty in his or her identity. For example, becoming a respected member of the right group or clique takes on great importance, along with the superficial trappings involved in such membership, like hanging out at the right places, wearing the right clothes, and, in general, looking the right way. Adolescents seeking a firmer sense of self identify not only with peer groups but with older individuals whom they admire and on whom they model aspects of themselves. This is the time of life when people may be most likely to put photographs of movie or sports stars on their bedroom walls. Wearing clothing like Madonna or shoes like Michael Jordan not only helps one fit into a social group, but enables one to try out different identities and mold one's adult roles by modeling those of others.

While teenagers create their identities through identification with peer groups and pop idols, the core of their identification is most often centered on their parents. Imitation and modeling of parents takes place throughout childhood. At adolescence, however, it assumes a new cast, because the child is now becoming an adult, much like her parent in the eyes of the world and in her own eyes. And the child's immature body is becoming like those of the parents or, more to the point, like that of one of the parents, the one sharing the child's gender. Thus, psychological and social forces emerging at adolescence push girls toward identifying with mothers.

With an understanding of ambivalence regarding adult femininity and the process of identification, it is not surprising that eating disorders and depression develop at adolescence and have been found to be particularly common among women who strive to excel, who fear maturing, who exhibit a distaste for curvaceous, stereotypically "feminine" bodies, bodies that resemble not the high-achieving fathers or the brothers who are encouraged to achieve, but instead the mothers who were not given those opportunities. In the words of one woman, a patient of pioneering psychiatrist Jean Charcot: "I prefer dying of hunger to becoming big as mama."[11]

If we incorporate into this equation an awareness of the devaluation of women's roles, we find some similarity between our hypotheses regarding identification with mothers and a classic psychoanalytic hypothesis about female development that has drawn the fire of many feminists. Some psychoanalysts have suggested that adolescence is stormier for females and that they have greater difficulty than males in accepting their developing physiques and relinquishing emotional ties with parents because they have been less successful at completing earlier developmental tasks. For example, females are said to be less successful in ending the intense attachment to the opposite sex parent by identifying with the same-sex parent at the resolution of the Oedipal phase at about age 5 or 6. One reason given for females being less likely to complete this developmental task is that they view themselves as "castrated" and blame this "castration" on their mothers.[12]

We would argue that the extent to which gender-ambivalent adolescent females may have had difficulty resolving attachments to fathers by identifying with mothers when they were younger depends on parental attitudes and behaviors that are rooted in the social and historical treatment of females. The spoken and unspoken messages about the differences between the sexes communicated to the young girl by her parents when she first becomes aware of anatomical differences will influence the attitude she adopts toward her gender, as will the nature of differential treatment accorded boys and girls in her family, in preschool, or in daycare settings, and any differences she observes in how happy, powerful, or respected her mother and her father are. In the words of noted psychoanalyst Roy Schafer, classical psychoanalytic theory

> was clearly not appreciating two factors, one being the part played in the girl's development by the example of the active, nurturant mother who has her own sources of pride and consolation, and the other being the part played by the great variety of positive environmental emphases concerning girls and women.[13]

From this perspective, 5- or 6-year old girls will have difficulty resolving Oedipal issues of attachment to fathers and competition with mothers through identification with the mothers if, because of environmental influences, they have come to view their mothers and the female role embodied by them as demeaned in some way.

Psychoanalysts have discussed several motivations that are thought to induce young girls to resolve Oedipal issues through identification with their mothers. One motivation is the desire to avoid the defeat they sense they will suffer if they continue to compete with their mothers for their fathers' love and attention; in the eyes of most daughters, the apparently powerful adult mother has many advantages in this competition. Another motivation is the daughters' sense that they might come to psychologically share some of their mothers' adult power and prestige through the process of identification.

Both inducements may be less powerful for the ambitious, nontraditional women discussed in this book, particularly those who mature during periods of changing gender roles. These girls, some of whom are treated as intellectual confidantes by their fathers, may not believe their mothers have such great advantages in competing for their fathers' attention. Furthermore, they may not view the mothers' status as adult females as something so valuable to share. That is, we might redefine "castration" in females to signify the historically rooted social process of females being assigned inferior positions to males and of being viewed as personally inferior to males. Using this sociocultural definition, it is possible that some girls experience difficulty in resolving Oedipal attachments to their fathers by identifying with their mothers during childhood, and in completing the process of identification during adolescence, because they perceive themselves and their mothers as "castrated."

This would most likely occur when the mother feels limited or inferior as a result of being female, and when, as discussed earlier, the father also devalues the mother's intellectual abilities while encouraging his daughter's overidealization. Consequently, these girls may confront extreme difficulties at adolescence in accepting their developing femininity.

For the nontraditional female it all comes together at adolescence: Maturing bodies that forever signify womanhood; issues of identification with mothers either dissatisfied themselves with their female roles or clearly of lesser status in the family and in the world; and the gender intensification that describes how other people seem to become particularly concerned that they now act "like girls." One study found that college women who observed a drop in parental concern with their academic achievement as they reached adolescence were likely to report symptoms of disordered eating, but only if the women's mothers were not highly educated. That is, college women who reported eating problems were those who experienced a double whammy—parents who demonstrated gender intensification by becoming less interested in their academic achievement and their own possible difficulties identifying with mothers who did not achieve academically.[14]

The combination of symptoms discussed in this book is particularly likely to strike at adolescence and to affect intellectually ambitious females who view their mothers, and the role of adult woman that they share with their mothers, as limited. Of course, some nontraditional women have had mothers who were successful in those very realms the daughters so value. Of all the eminent women, and daughters of eminent men, that we studied, only one, anthropologist Margaret Mead, apparently managed to escape all symptoms of the syndrome we have been describing. And of all the women we studied, Mead was the only one with a mother who not only greatly supported her quest for higher education, but managed herself to earn a graduate degree and carry on a fairly active research career.[15]

9

Gender Ambivalence

In Margaret Mead's family, intellectual achievement did not necessarily signify maleness. But Mead stands out as an exception among the eminent women we studied. More frequently, these women confronted familial and societal conditions summed up in the words of Susan B. Anthony: "Those who have worked out for themselves an individual destiny . . . are . . . hardly counted as women."[1]

As a result, many women who achieved great success outside the home labeled the ambitious, talented aspects of their own personalities as male. Of Ruth Benedict, widely acknowledged as one of the great anthropologists for her work on cultural patterns, one biographer wrote: "But the more she thought about her lack of fit to the female role, the more she seemed drawn to considering the maleness in herself. She noted her craving for achievement . . . and wondered whether she possessed too largely the traits her society defined as male." Novelist George Eliot took on a male pen name; Joan of Arc, male dress and haircut. The French novelist George Sand did both. At adolescence, Sand became deeply depressed and experienced a compulsion to commit suicide by drowning herself, a compulsion also mentioned in the Hippocratic description of the "disease of young women." Louisa May Alcott, another eminent novelist who nearly drowned herself at adolescence, declared: "I was born with a boy's spirit." Emily Dickinson referred to her childhood as the period when she was "a boy" and signed letters "Brother Emily." Recall that Florence Nightingale wrote to her parents regarding her choice to pursue a career: "You must look at me as your vagabond son."[2]

The conflicted feelings toward femininity exhibited by many women throughout history and exemplified in the above descriptions were first termed "ambivalence" by Peter Blos, the noted authority on adolescence, in his discussion of a young woman named Betty. Born in 1920, she was the daughter of a successful executive and homemaker mother. Betty had one very bright older brother, who was clearly the mother's favorite. Her mother had been quite proud of how pretty Betty looked until a childhood illness altered her appearance, at which point the mother no longer bought expensive clothing for Betty and stopped showing her off. As a child, Betty did well in school, but just before adolescence she failed to skip a grade as her mother had hoped, and so the mother focused her pride solely on the academic achievements of Betty's brother.

At adolescence, Betty began to exhibit fairly serious problems. Despite superior intellectual ability, she was not doing well in high school. She was anxious, depressed, and had trouble sleeping. Blos noted that, as she reached adolescence, Betty came to focus her fear and insecurity on aspects of her physical appearance, becoming overly concerned about a mole on her cheek and obsessed with her weight. Although not overweight, she was described as well developed and several teachers remarked on how much time and attention she spent trying to reduce her weight and keep a trim figure. Blos recognized that she had great difficulty in identifying with her mother, in part because Betty had a "deep-rooted conviction about the inferiority of women." He concluded that her concern with physical attractiveness was "closely related to the problem of accepting herself in the feminine role." Blos labeled Betty's "conflict in accepting the feminine role" as "ambivalence," based on the following formulation cited in his discussion of the case:

> Ambivalence denotes contradictory emotional attitudes toward the same object either arising alternately, or existing side by side without either one interfering necessarily with or inhibiting the expression of the other.[3]

To understand the development of contradictory emotional attitudes toward oneself as female that, following Blos, we will refer to as ambivalence toward one's femininity or, for sake of brevity, "gender ambivalence," we must delve deeper into the development of gender identity from early childhood to adolescence. Gender identity, the basic sense of oneself as female or male, has been found by such investigators as Robert Stoller, John Money, and Anke Ehrhardt to develop in early childhood and to constitute a core aspect of personality.[4] Gender identity is usually conceptually distinguished from the patterns of "feminine" or "masculine" behavior referred to as "sex roles": Sex roles are frequently described as developing later than gender identity and primarily influenced by social and cultural factors.

But social and cultural influences are present from birth or earlier; indeed, studies have demonstrated that parents respond differently to male and female children who are only a few months old.[5] We are in agreement with John Money who argues that the influences of gender identity and sex roles cannot be disentangled. He argues for a combined notion of gender-identity/role influenced by conditions ranging from genetic predispositions and the biochemical environment in the womb to early interactions with parents and social conditions confronting males and females as they mature.[6] Thus, genetic and prenatal biological influences create in most women a core feminine gender-identity/role that is further developed in preschool years through imitation of the mother.

A female gender-identity/role is also socially reinforced. Before girls are out of diapers, mothers delight in dressing their daughters in frilly party frocks and hair ribbons and doting grandparents give them "baby" dolls to play with. Cosmetics specially formulated for children are advertised as appropriate for 5-year-old girls and are widely available in toystores. In contrast, little boys are given cars and train sets, and even mothers who are career women can be heard to speak proudly of their son's "aggressive" play. How, then, do ambivalent feelings toward femininity develop at adolescence among girls who may have loved dressing up like mommy during their early childhood?

As we have already discussed, during childhood girls are often allowed some latitude, and sometimes even encouraged and rewarded for achieving intellectually and academically. Many take great pride in these accomplishments and begin to build self-concepts around their abilities. At the same time, through observations of their parents, television, movies, and even textooks, they learn that these abilities have traditionally been associated with being male and that traditional female roles do not receive nearly as much respect and approval.

For some, such as Simone de Beauvoir, whose father said she

"thinks more like a man," or Freud's hysteric patient Elizabeth Von R., whose father realized that her intellectual abilities were not those that people "like to see realized in a girl," the connection between their abilities and masculinity becomes very explicit and very personal. Yet even in less extreme instances, many young women come to realize that they have the ability to succeed in areas that are highly valued but often associated with maleness, and to attain greater success and respect outside the home than usually available to women, including in most cases their mothers.

Although most intelligent, ambitious, nontraditional women might not go as far as Louisa May Alcott, who described herself as being born with a "boy's spirit," many have come to associate their abilities and ambitions with masculine gender-identity/roles and to devalue, to some extent, feminine gender-identity/roles.

Beginning in many cases at adolescence, the biological, psychological, and social forces discussed earlier combine to exert pressure on young women to behave in a more feminine manner. This pressure may take the form of subtle hints to dress more fashionably and find a husband or may be manifested in the barriers particularly likely to face women trying to get into and pay for good colleges and do well in prestigious careers. In some cases, these barriers are not apparent to everyone. In other cases, they are far from subtle, such as those of Toula the Greek twin discussed in Chapter 2, who was not allowed to attend secondary school, and Judy, the triplet discussed in Chapter 8, who was not sent to college.

As the difference between Toula and Judy demonstrates, the timing of the development of limitations associated with femininity differs for females from different families, cultures, and historical periods. As a child, Elizabeth Cady Stanton was already unsuccesfully trying to "equal" boys in the eyes of her father through her pursuit of learning. In contrast, the intelligence of Freud's hysteric patient Dora was highly valued by her father until she reached early adolescence when she received pressure to take on more housework. In most cases we have studied, the talents and aspirations regarding nondomestic achievement around which girls may have developed a sense of positive self-identity as part of their continually developing gender-identity/role begins in adolescence to be clearly labeled "masculine" and subtly or overtly discouraged by late adolescence.

Thus, genetic, prenatal, and early childhood influences lead most women to develop a core feminine gender-identity/role. Yet childhood experiences of many women who aspire to achieve intellectually and professionally lead them to develop a self-definition that incorporates both "masculine" and "feminine" attributes and to devalue the exclusively feminine gender-identity/role. Then, at puberty and adolescence, biological changes and psychosocial influences overtly or covertly discourage the further development and expression of "masculine" traits, fostering a gender-identity/role that is labeled feminine. For many women, the result of these contradictory influences is the development of contradictory emotional attitudes, or "ambivalence," toward the feminine gender-identity/role associated with a confused, somewhat negative sense of self.

By the time they reach adolescence, many young women confronting such circumstances have both attraction toward and repulsion from the feminine gender-identity/role. This ambivalence toward femininity is sometimes consciously experienced as a wish to be a boy, as exemplified in Blos' discussion of the fantasies Betty had since childhood just before falling asleep. These fantasies demonstrate not only her ambivalence regarding her gender but also the increasing internal and external pressure to give up the fantasied male identity and acknowledge her femininity:

> *Betty:* Yes, you see, at first, when I was young I was a girl who was dressed like a boy and nobody knew I was a girl. Then I was a girl dressed like a boy, but only a certain few people knew I was a girl; finally I was a girl dressed like a boy and then half of the time I was a girl.
>
> *Interviewer:* When you were little, would you rather have been a boy than a girl?
>
> *Betty:* Yes. When I was a very little child, I wanted to be a boy.
>
> *Interviewer:* Why? Do you remember?
>
> *Betty:* Why, I just wanted to be a boy—I don't know—Now I like to be a girl because I like—because I hate the way boys dress.[7]

This last, obviously vague, response we believe represented a gut feeling of being attracted to feminine aspects of herself as well as aspects labeled by society as masculine that she found difficult to put into words.

Responses to Gender Ambivalence

Manifestations of gender ambivalence and responses to the often conflicting demands of fulfilling traditionally "feminine" and "masculine" role expectations take different forms among different women. At one extreme are those women who appear to wish they were not female, like Emily Dickinson, about whom a biographer wrote that she felt "loathing of herself as a woman." Anthropologist Ruth Benedict suffered in adolescence from stomachaches and "torturous" vomiting. Her biographer noted that at age 23, "In depression . . . Ruth turned inward and closed off the world." A few years later, Benedict lamented, "Oh, I want to stop! If there is any discomfort in the thought it's that there would be some left who would suffer." She observed, "So much of the trouble is because I am a woman. To me it seems a very terrible thing to be a woman." [8]

Other women find themselves wishing that they were both male and female. Psychoanalyst Helene Deutsch harbored the desire to be "simultaneously my father's prettiest daughter and cleverest son." British social researcher and reformer Beatrice Webb, who was depressed throughout her adult life, reported experiencing a strange "doubleness" of being both male and female. But in societies with definitions of sex roles that are discrete and that demonstrate little overlap between prescribed masculinity and femininity, such duality is never completely attainable, leaving many nontraditional women with less narrow role aspirations feeling caught between male and female roles. Such sentiments were expressed by Anna Freud in writing of her conflict between "achieving like a man, and . . . dancing and being generous like Mathilde [a female character in a story]. One would like to be able to do both, and does find oneself to be a little of both, but neither becomes real."

This feeling of being betwixt and between may lead to the experience of isolation from others. One woman told us of feeling that she never really belonged to any group in late elementary and high school. She viewed the girls as too preoccupied with superficial concerns, while she perceived the boys as intellectually superior. Similarly, Alice James did not want to "step down to the intellectual level" of her mother but felt that competing with males would be what she called "spiritual snatching" for a girl. [9]

Some women, even those extremely successful in traditionally "masculine" spheres, sometimes seem to wish that they could resolve the conflict by settling for traditional femininity. Georgia O'Keefe, the well-known painter whose work has received widespread acclaim, suffered from severe headaches, constricted breathing, and insomnia accompanied by depression so "deep" and "severe" that she was hospitalized. Her suffering caused her to feel "she might lose her mind." Recognizing the difficulties she experienced when trying to integrate the supposedly masculine and feminine aspects of her personality, O'Keefe wrote to a friend that she wanted to "be loved and laugh—and not think—be just a woman . . . it is this dull business of being a person that gets me all out of shape." [10]

Many women who harbor nondomestic aspirations decide to try to live up to the traditional female role expected of them. Some find great fulfillment as mothers, wives, and homemakers. But when their children mature, or if something goes wrong, such as a divorce that leaves them with insufficient resources or fertility problems that leave them without children (as discussed in Chapter 5), the doubts they had suppressed about their decision rise to the surface.

Yet other women seek resolution through their attempted denial of gender entirely. In the words of one anorexic, as she lay dying of starvation, "There it is, my problem. I want neither to get fatter nor thinner, to be neither boy nor girl, to have no more periods." [11]

Contemporary women with symptoms of anxious somatic depression also appear to experience a conflict around gender-identity/role. We administered to college students the Human Figure Drawing Test, a measure frequently used by psychologists for assessing conflicts regarding gender identity, in which people are simply asked to draw a picture of a person. Normative sex role behavior is indicated by drawing a figure of one's own gender, with readily discriminable features of gender differentiation such as hair length, attire, and body build. Conversely, drawing a figure of the opposite sex or one with few or no features of sexual differentiation is usually considered an indication of gender-identity conflict. We found that women with disordered eating are much more likely than other women to draw a picture of ambiguous gender, like those depicted in Figure 8, or an obvious picture of a male, like that depicted in Figure 9. [12]

Questions About Gender Ambivalence

One unresolved issue is whether women who suffer from what we refer to as gender ambivalence believe that females are inferior to males or if they think females are the equals of males but not accorded equal treatment. The case histories we have studied appear to indicate that both views are held by these women. Peter Blos's patient Betty held a "deep-rooted conviction about the inferiority of women." Elizabeth Barret Browning apparently agreed with this conviction, writing, "There is a natural inferiority of mind in women."[13] On the other hand, symptoms of anxious somatic depression clearly afflicted women such as Susan B. Anthony, Elizabeth Cady Stanton, and Simone de Beauvoir, whose achievements rested in large part on their awareness of the unequal treatment accorded women.

Some women may progress as they mature from believing that women are inferior by nature to seeing this as social inequality. While Simone de Beauvoir wrote *The Second Sex* as an adult, a classic analysis of gender bias, she grew up believing "girls were inferior to men."[14] De Beauvoir's lifelong depression and migraine

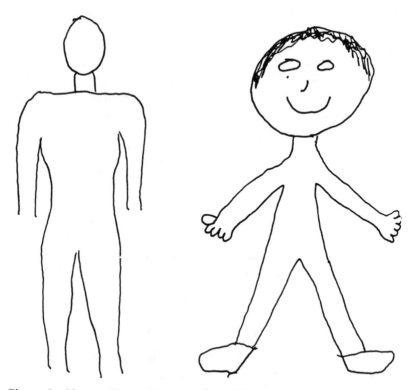

Figure 8   Human Figure Drawings by college women with symptoms of disordered eating. The gender of these figures is ambiguous.

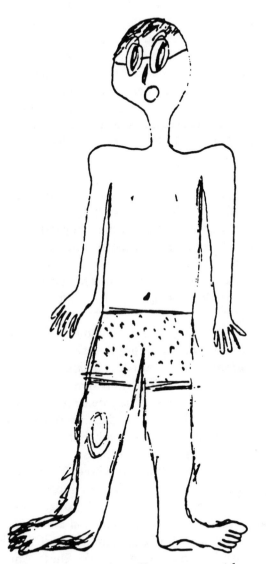

Figure 9 Human Figure Drawing by college woman with symptoms of disordered eating. The figure here is obviously male.

headaches suggest to us that her childhood belief in female inferiority, though consciously repudiated, may not have completely disappeared. Even the tough-minded intellectual and sophisticated feminist de Beauvoir may have carried with her throughout adulthood some haunting, perhaps not fully conscious, residue of her childhood belief that females are inferior.

The example of de Beauvoir raises another important question: To what extent is the development of anxious somatic depression rooted in conscious awareness of ambivalence toward femininity? Our historical case studies along with our contemporary questionnaire studies clearly indicate that many women are quite aware of some aspects of the ambivalence they feel toward being female. Reports of some contemporary women do indicate an awareness of the disadvantages of being female as clear as anything Ruth Benedicts had to say on the subject. For example, female students attending a suburban high school who reported that they often wished that they were males, or that they felt very limited by being female, were three times as likely as other female students in their high school to exhibit a combination of depression and at least two of the following: symptoms of disordered eating, frequent headache, frequent insomnia, and frequent unexplained difficulty breathing.[15]

On the other hand, recent psychological research has provided empirical support for the notion that humans may process important information without being aware of it.[16] It is therefore possible that aspects of gender ambivalence are not fully conscious. One intriguing hypothesis is that the belief that women are inferior and the belief that they are not but are treated as inferior can be differentiated on a conscious level, but that on the unconscious level the two beliefs may not be so easily separated. Thus, a woman like Simone de Beauvoir who evidences clearly formulated conscious awareness of gender bias in adulthood may continue to be influenced by the largely unconscious belief developed in childhood that "girls are inferior to men" and may continue to feel inferior herself. This would help explain the large number of outstandingly successful women like George Eliot, Anna Freud, Karen Horney, and Florence Nightingale who suffered from symptoms of anxious somatic depression and continued to feel that they were failures despite their great accomplishments.[17]

To say that these women "just wanted to be men" is not only to oversimplify, but to do them a great disservice. What they wanted was to be allowed to achieve goals that were important to them and be accorded the respect for their abilities and their work that they deserved. That they would have been more likely to attain this respect if they were male is true, given cultural biases. This sad fact initiated the developmental processes we have already described that culminated in gender ambivalence at adolescence. Even some of the most enlightened women in history—those quite aware of the vast amount of female talent going unrecognized—internalized some basic sense of inferiority that was not eliminated by their consciousness of gender bias.

To blame the problems of these women, and of the millions of others who suffered from anxious somatic depression and have not achieved renown, on the weakness of gender, or on their conflicts regarding their gender, is to accept the bias against women. The problem is not that they were female, or that some wished to be men. The problem is that the roles allotted to men have been accorded more respect than those allotted to women and that females with the talent to succeed at the more respected roles have either not been allowed to succeed or have been labeled "masculine." That many women have internalized these cultural biases, labeling themselves as masculine, or at least the part of themselves involved in the world of ideas or power, is a *result* of a terrible problem, not its cause. That is, Georgia O'Keefe's real problem was not that she yearned to "not think—be just a woman," but that she had been brought up to view the two as contradictory.

Gender Ambivalence as a Form of Identity Conflict

The problem centers around identity. Crucial questions for every human being are: Who am I? Where do I fit in? Am I valued? The answers constitute a person's sense of identity and accompanying feeling of self-esteem. Conflict about identity has for over a century been the focus of many scholarly considerations of psychological malaise, ranging from the philosophical to the empirical. In 1843, Danish philosopher Søren Kierkegaard wrote: "Can you think of anything more frightful than . . . your nature being resolved into a multiplicity, that you really might become many . . . and you thus would lose the inmost and holiest thing of all in a man, the unifying power of personality?" Six years later, he described "despair at not willing to be oneself" as the first form of "sickness unto death." Approximately a century later, based on his clinical experience, Erik Erikson formulated the concept of "identity diffusion." (He later wrote that perhaps "identity confusion" was a more appropriate term.) People suffering from identity diffusion experience "a split of self-images . . . a loss of centrality, a sense of dispersion and confusion." Twenty-five years later, two research psychologists concluded that many of the college students they interviewed exhibited identity diffusion and "were not satisfied with their parents' way of life, but neither could they become productively involved in fashioning one of their own."[18] These descriptions of losing the unity of one's personality, of despair at not "willing to be oneself," of split self-images, and of dissatisfaction with one's parents' way of life capture important aspects of the gender ambivalence experienced by many nontraditional women throughout the centuries, because gender ambivalence is a form of inner conflict over identity.

Modern Western industrialized societies promulgate an ideology of individualism in which a person's identity is rooted within the self. But many social scientists have discussed how people's supposedly "individual" identities are based in the society and culture within which they live and in the social groups in which they participate.[19]

This relationship between social interaction and identity takes several forms. First, as discussed earlier, people develop their identities through processes of imitation of and identification with others, including peers, movie stars, sports heroes, historical figures, teachers, and—particularly—parents. Second, the dimensions on which identity and self-esteem are measured and the standards used for these measurements usually come from other people. The notions that a lawyer is more successful than a midwife or that a woman who gives birth to a male child is more successful than one who bears a female are social standards. While it is possible for people to override these social standards and consider themselves successful when the rest of the society does not, it is neither easy nor common. In most cases, self-esteem is based on the opinions of others.

Third, the evaluations that others make of us usually include social categories. We are viewed as males or females, adults or children, black or white. The dimensions of these evaluations differ according to categories. A man may be evaluated based on the size and location of the house he can afford, while a woman may be judged by whether the rooms inside the house are clean and tastefully decorated. The standards used in evaluations also differ according to the social category of the person being judged. A sexually active person is a "stud" if male, a "slut" if female. A person who spends much time at work and so has little time for his or her children is viewed as an overworked breadwinner if male, but may be regarded as a selfish mother if female. As with other aspects of evaluations we receive from others, the social categories in which we are placed color our sense of identity. Whether we like it or not, and whether we admit it or not, we often experience ourselves in terms of gender, ethnic group, nationality, age, and other categories thought important in our society. If we belong in categories that are negatively evaluated, our own sense of identity and self-worth is likely to suffer. Erikson eloquently summarized the relationship between the social and individual aspects of identity as follows.

> It is this identity of something in the individual's core with an essential aspect of a group's inner coherence which is under consideration here: for the young individual must learn to be most himself where he means most to others—those others, to be sure, who have come to mean most to him. The term "identity" expresses such a mutual relation in that it connotes both a persistent sameness within oneself (selfsameness) and a persistent sharing of some kind of essential character with others.[20]

This process transcends gender. Kenneth and Mamie Clark, Frantz Fanon, Abraham Kardiner, and Lionel Ovesey have discussed how the sense of identity and self-esteem of black people can suffer if they are raised under conditions of racial prejudice. Particularly intriguing to us is Kardiner and Ovesey's observation in 1951 that common among black people who suffer from this sense of devalued social identity are low self-esteem, depression, anxiety, and somatic symptoms such as headaches.[21] It may be that the group of symptoms we have identified as anxious somatic depression afflicts people who develop ambivalence toward their identity because they are categorized as belonging to a devalued group.

Identity and Body Image

A symptom common to people who become ambivalent about their identity is poor body image. As we might expect, the body parts people in devalued groups tend to be uncomfortable with are those differentiating them from members of dominant groups. In 1951, Kardiner and Ovesey noted the discomfort experienced by some blacks with their curly hair, which was graphically illustrated by the black revolutionary Malcolm X in his description of the first time he used a combination of lye, eggs, potatoes, and vaseline to "conk" his hair in order to get rid of his "Negro" curls:

> This was my first really big step toward self-degradation: when I endured all of that pain, literally burning my flesh to have it look like a white man's hair. I had joined that multitude of Negro men and women in America who are brainwashed into believing that the black people are "inferior"—and that white people "superior"—that they will even violate and mutilate their God-created bodies to try to look "pretty" by white standards.[22]

Similarly, in 1946 Erikson discussed the case of a successful rancher who tried to hide the fact that he was Jewish. Erikson wrote:

> The patient in question sincerely felt that the only true savior for the Jews would be a plastic surgeon. In the body ego of such cases of morbid ego identity, those body parts which are supposed to be of strategic importance in the characterization of the race (in the last case, the nose . . .) play a role similar to that of the afflicted limb in a cripple. . . . The body part in question . . . is felt to be larger and heavier . . . seeming to loom dominantly in the center of the attention of others.[23]

This description captures quite well the feelings many women have about their breasts, hips, and thighs, which characterize them as female. Recall the words of the woman obsessed with the shape of her breasts described in Chapter 7: "If I only were a man . . . I have read too much, seen too much, drunk too much. So I don't like myself anymore. I'd like to lose thirty pounds of weight. Please, doctor, send me to a plastic surgeon." The social categories in which we are placed, the evaluations we receive from others, our sense of identity and self-worth, and our images of and emotional reactions to our bodies all are intimately related.

While the effects of gender resemble the effects of other social categories that are sometimes devalued, important differences remain between being female and being, say, black or Jewish. One difference is the developmental sequence summarized in the term "gender intensification" discussed earlier. These developmental changes are less evident for categories other than gender. Certainly, the reactions of one's parents to one's race or religion do not become particularly restrictive at adolescence. And the bodily parts that characterize one as belonging to a group that is treated by some as inferior, the hair of a black person or the nose of a Jewish person, do not become more salient at the same time as new limitations are experienced, as is the case for adolescent girls who discover new restrictions along with their feminine physiques. This developmental difference between femininity and other devalued categories may render adolescence more of a problem for women than for members of other groups. Erikson discussed the developmental processes of adolescence in this way: "The young adult gains an assured sense of inner continuity and social sameness which will bridge what he was as a child and what he is about to become, and will reconcile his conception of himself and his community's recognition of him."[24] This bridging and reconciliation are particularly distorted by the increasing limitations females experience at adolescence.

Another difference between gender and other social categories is that gender inequality is embodied within the families of the girls experiencing it. In most cases, parents and siblings of a Jewish or black child are Jewish or black. Most girls, however, are raised by both a male and a female parent and often have a male sibling. Seeing someone no more talented than you receive resources and encouragement not given to you because of your race, religion, or gender is a powerful experience. But the impression made by the inequality is likely to be magnified if the person is a brother whom you interact with every day and with whom you share a family history of competition over the attention, love, and approbation of your parents. Likewise, having a parent who is unhappy, or who seems to you to lead a limited life because of her or his race, religion, or gender is distressing. But the distress and conflict may be heightened if only one of the parents shares with you the limitations inherent in membership in a devalued social group. To the extent that identification with both parents is a powerful force in identity development, there is more room for ambivalence with regard to gender than with other characteristics.

Why Do Symptoms Develop?

Researchers interested in studying anxious somatic depression and clinicians interested in treating it may be interested in why the syndrome takes the particular form it does. For those readers, our model for the development of the symptoms of anxious somatic depression is discussed and depicted in Appendix B.

At present, many assertions made in this chapter and in Appendix B regarding the development, dynamics, and effects of gender ambivalence must be considered hypotheses in need of further testing. Other investigators may offer competing explanations for the patterns we have discussed. One such pattern that we have found again and again must, however, be incorporated within any theory of gender ambivalence and its connection with anxious somatic depression—the apparent paradox that both the ambivalence and the symptoms of anxious somatic depression appear to become most prevalent when conditions for women improve.

10

Anxious Somatic Depression During Periods of Changing Gender Roles

To some readers, the most surprising and controversial finding reported in this book may be that the physical and psychological symptoms associated with gender ambivalence are particularly likely to afflict women who have greater opportunity for educational and professional achievement than their mothers had. The eminent women we studied and many daughters of eminent men were able to achieve successes not possible for their mothers. The cross-cultural literature on depression in India, culture-bound syndrome, and nerves, and the medical writings on chlorosis, hysteria, and neurasthenia point to a high prevalence of the symptoms during periods of increased educational opportunity for women. Contemporary female high school and college students we surveyed who reported concerns about achieving more than their mothers were particularly likely to exhibit the combined symptoms of anxious somatic depression. And over the course of the twentieth century, the prevalence among females compared to males of depression, anorexia, headache, and mitral valve prolapse was greatest among people who matured during periods of large generational increase in rates of female college graduation.

On the face of it, we would expect gender biases to exert their greatest effects when women are most limited. But because the development of gender ambivalence is mediated by factors influencing identity development, the process is considerably more complex. As a result, familial interactions and attitudes regarding female achievement associated with the development of anxious somatic depression are more likely to present a problem for females who mature during periods of changing gender roles.

One reason may be that females growing up during such times are particularly likely to perceive their mothers as being unhappy or unsuccessful because they are women. Unhappy mothers who did not achieve professionally and academically have existed throughout history. But if their daughters mature at a time when young women are encouraged to achieve outside of the home, these daughters may be particularly likely to connect the unhappiness, dissatisfaction, and frustration their mothers evidenced to the limited opportunities they had because they were female. Such perceptions would tend to increase the daughters' dissatisfaction with feminine gender-identity/roles, resulting in increased gender ambivalence. This process may be exacerbated if the mothers feel or express ambivalence toward their daughters' increased potential for achievement relative to their own. Such mothers may view their daughters' nondomestic accomplishments with a mixture of pride and understandable envy. The daughters, sensing this ambivalence, might be prone to more problematic identification with their mothers.

In Chapter 7, we discussed the two forms of such problematic identification. Some women, like Eleanore Marx, Indira Gandhi, Karen Horney, and Louisa May Alcott, may have had intelligent, ambitious mothers discontent with the limitations placed on them by the societal response to their gender. During periods when younger females are encouraged to achieve outside the home and when the role of homemaker tends to be devalued, the mother, particularly if ambitious or talented, may feel extremely resentful of her weak position and the lack of respect accorded her. As a result, during these periods there may be an increase in the number of women reporting that their mothers were "dissatisfied with their own career choices," or were "fed up with the mommy role," as well as an increase in those reporting that they "felt guilty about leading better lives than their mothers," or that they often "minimized their own accomplishments so that their mothers would not feel bad about themselves."

Because these mothers are worn out, dissatisfied, or under stress, or because they resent their husbands' privileged positions, they may be inhibited from praising the husbands in their roles as achievers outside the home, increasing the likelihood that these men look to their bright daughters for this praise.

The other route toward the development of problematic identification and gender ambivalence, taken by such women as Anna Freud, Florence Nightingale, Eleanor Roosevelt, and Sigmund Freud's hysteric patient Dora, is to have a mother who is content with traditional female roles but is devalued by a daughter who views these roles as inferior to those offered to males. Periods of increased opportunity for women are those during which traditional female roles are most devalued. There is then likely to be an increase in the number of women who feel that their mothers were very "limited by being female" and in the number who are bothered by their mothers' beliefs that "a woman's place is in the home"; they would also be deeply affected by their fathers' beliefs that their mothers are unintelligent. If a female is socialized to value academic and professional success more than homemaking and childrearing, she may respond to her mother's unhappiness, lack of nondomestic achievement, and relative powerlessness with discomfort toward, and devaluation of, the feminine identity personified by the mother. This discomfort may cause problems if it makes it difficult for maturing women to integrate the valued "masculine" attributes with the "feminine" attributes of the self. Devaluation of the mother for her feminine attributes is at best a temporary compromise that ultimately serves to promote increased gender ambivalence and the symptoms associated with such ambivalence. Thus, both forms of problematic identification with mothers, and with the status of adult women as represented by mothers, are likely to be most prevalent during periods of increased educational and professional opportunities for women.

Aspirations Outpace Achievements

Another aspect of this apparently paradoxical relationship between increased opportunity, gender ambivalence, and anxious somatic depression can be understood by applying William James's equation "Self-Esteem = Success/Pretensions." Women growing up during times of increased opportunities are more likely to have high "pretensions" or aspirations toward nondomestic achievement instilled during childhood and to experience a narrowing window of opportunity for success in nontraditional arenas as they reach adolescence. These are the women who will most experience identity confusion when they confront the gender intensification and pressure toward identification with their mothers that take place at adolescence. They are also the ones to feel very "limited by being female," or bothered by having fathers who believe "a woman's place is in the home," or who treat a brother as "the most intelligent sibling in the family." Such women are likely to feel that the ratio of their successes to their pretensions is low and thus, according to James, suffer from low self-esteem.[1]

The Industrial Revolution, Gender Role Changes, and Anxious Somatic Depression

In the developed nations, the past century and a half has, for the most part, been an era of increased educational and professional opportunities for women. It has also been a period in which girls have been socialized to value nondomestic achievement. And it has been a period marked by an apparently high prevalence of anxious somatic depression. Although we have cited descriptions of the syndrome that appeared in earlier centuries, we are not certain that it was very common among women before the late nineteenth century. The Hippocratic texts of ancient Greece and the biographies of the medieval holy women studied by Bell, along with other sources cited in Chapter 2, indicate that among young women a syndrome of depression, anxiety, disordered eating, amenorrhea, sexual indifference, and other psychological and somatic symptoms has existed for millennia. None of these sources, however, describe the syndrome as occurring very often. But in the last half of the nineteenth century, the syndrome—under the names hysteria, neurasthenia, and chlorosis—began to be described as very prevalent among women seeking higher education, and during several periods of the twentieth century it has been portrayed as epidemic. Our analyses of generational fluctuations indicate that only among two cohorts of twentieth-century women were the symptoms not prevalent. These were the women who reached adolescence in the mid-to-late 1910s and in the mid-1940s, the two periods of world war during the century.

It is possible that the apparent increase in the syndrome in recent centuries is an artifact of changes in recognition of its symptoms, in classification methods, or in the range of historical sources available to us. We were struck, however, by the strength of the words that began to be used to describe its prevalence toward the end of the nineteenth century. As we discussed in Chapter 8, in 1901 chlorosis was seen as afflicting "perhaps every girl" and in 1890 the manifestations of hysteria among adolescent females were said to be "the rule." In Chapter 1, we reported that the Delaware

County Tuberculosis Association found that 18 percent of girls in later adolescence were "under the danger line" with regard to weight. And many writers have referred to the modern "epidemic" of eating disorders and have termed recent decades the "age of depression" among females.[2]

Such strong terms as these only began to appear, as far as we have found, during the past century and a quarter, suggesting that the existence of anxious somatic depression on a mass scale may be based on changes in the role of women that were engendered by the Industrial Revolution and accelerated, except for periods of depression and world war, during the later or "postindustrial" period. In the early industrial period, work traditionally done at home or for barter or in small shops was centralized in factories and transformed into work done for wages. This set the stage for the devaluation of homemaking, based on the notion that men went out to work to earn wages to support their families while women remained at home earning no wages. Not until the late nineteenth century did the same thing begin to happen to women's traditional work; "women's tasks"—teaching, nursing, many phases of food preparation, clothing production, and so forth—were suddenly transformed into paying jobs outside the home. At that time, women began to do for wages what they had done at home and then use those wages to purchase the products that they no longer had time to make themselves. Many of these jobs, such as teaching, nursing, and counseling, have been progressively professionalized with the attendant increase in educational prerequisites. Even care of young children is increasingly being done for pay, and recent movements have developed to professionalize this activity.[3]

Thus, the shift to an industrial capitalist economy, and eventually to a high-technology economy based on information, services, and consumerism, produced massive shifts in women's roles, first devaluing traditional homemaking and then producing pressure and incentives for wage labor, professionalization, and higher education—formerly the provinces of men. These changes have not all proceeded smoothly. They have progressed in fits and starts, engendering resistance among many people who feel more comfortable with traditional gender roles, developing unevenly among different sectors of the population, and being subject to temporary reversals caused by macroeconomic developments, such as widespread depression or war when limitations in professional jobs and places in college are felt disproportionately by women. Changes in roles and attitudes that accompanied economic changes have been experienced by some people as threatening and by others as liberating. But massive changes that take place on such a large scale—and that impact on something so deep-seated as what it means to be female—will bring in their wake many psychological repercussions. From this perspective, the epidemics of anxious somatic depression that have occurred in the last century and a half can be viewed as a symptomatic response to a long period of fairly rapid role transformation, punctuated by two brief periods of reversion to older roles.

Do Increased Opportunities Put Women at Risk of Developing Anxious Somatic Depression?

The increased prevalence of anxious somatic depression exhibited during periods of increased opportunities for women might lead some people, particularly those uncomfortable with changing gender roles, to suggest that women are put at risk by being given access to greater opportunities. For several reasons, we believe that conclusion to be misleading and oversimplified.

First, gender ambivalence and anxious somatic depression are rooted not simply in the increased opportunities available to women, but in the simultaneous devaluation of traditional women's roles. Periods when large numbers of women graduate college and work as professionals are those in which a homemaker attending a party is most likely to be embarrassed by the question "What do you do?" and her reply "I'm a housewife." As we have already mentioned, this attitude that a woman who works long hours each day shopping, sewing, cooking, cleaning, and caring for children is really not working is based on the changes wrought by industrial capitalism during the past two centuries. During the early industrial period, many wage laborers were women who worked in textile mills. But as wage labor rose to become the dominant form of employment, most paid jobs came to be taken by men. Only at this point in history did women's unpaid labor in the home come to be devalued. Although the teaching and nursing and production of food and clothing and cleaning, and so on, done by women contributed greatly to the welfare of their families, the women did not produce profits or wages and so came to be seen as unemployed.[4]

Thus, both short-term periodic fluctuations in nondomestic opportunities for women, as measured by our index of generational changes in rates of female college graduation, as well as the longer-term change that took place during the postindustrial period were accompanied by changes in our evaluation of the work and skills of traditional women. With increased opportunities for academic and professional achievement came decreased valuations of home-making. From this perspective, gender ambivalence is as much a response to the devaluation of traditional women as to the increased opportunities for nontraditional women.

Similarly, gender ambivalence and anxious somatic depression appear when possibilities of nondomestic achievement are better for women of one generation than for those of an earlier generation. In looking for the cause of the problems, we can equally focus on the decreased opportunities of the older generation as on the increased opportunities of the younger one.

For women, nontraditional aspirations, in and of themselves, do not cause the problems. Instead, women develop depression, disordered eating, and so on, when they try to achieve in areas traditionally considered the province of males and confront biases against women achieving in these areas. In one of our studies, the data on laxatives, diuretics, or self-induced vomiting as used by college women to control their weight demonstrate this point. Nontraditional women—those who reported that as children they had been much more concerned with their academic achievement than with their household skills—were no more likely than their more traditional peers to report such purging if they believed their fathers did not agree that "a woman's place is in the home." Among those who indicated that their fathers did believe that a woman's place is in the home, nontraditional women were twice as likely to purge as more traditional women.[5] Apparently, problems result when women who define themselves in terms of academic and professional achievement are told that such endeavors are not appropriate for them. Some argue that periods of increased opportunity for women can bring on problems because they assume that women's self-esteem during these periods is low precisely because their level of "pretensions"—their level of expectation—is high. But it is at least as fair to conclude that the low self-esteem results because the level of success allowed to women even during these periods of opportunity remains low.

These arguments also apply to the eminent women we studied, many of whom clearly devalued traditional female roles, were aware that their mothers' lives had been limited because they were female, and felt that society did not allow them to achieve renown while fully acknowledging their femininity. It was not their achievements that caused the problems, but the perceived lack of achievement of their mothers accompanied by society's attitude that high achievers could not be fully female.

Thus, gender ambivalence is rooted in relationships—between increased occupational opportunities for women and decreased prestige of homemaking, between the higher level of opportunities available to one generation and the lower level of the previous generation, and between the heightened importance placed on nondomestic achievement for women and the very real barriers that continue to limit the availability of such achievement. To conclude that increased academic and professional opportunities are bad for women is to ignore the real relationships beneath the superficial and facile conclusions. And, of course, if we avoid finding the underlying relationships, we can also avoid change.

Predicting the Future

One relationship evident in our findings is that between developmental and historical change. The symptoms of anxious somatic depression become common among women who undergo the developmental changes of childhood and adolescence during historical periods of changing gender roles. This pattern, in which changes in development take on a particular significance at particular periods in history, has theoretical implications for our understanding of human behavior and personality. Some psychologists have argued that researchers should place greater emphasis on the connections between people's experiences of particular periods of social history and their stages of personality development.[6] In the United States, childhood during the Great Depression was very different from the childhood experienced during the post-World War II economic boom—each period probably produced major differences in attitudes toward spending and saving. Being a teenager during the 1950s was similar in many ways to being a teenager during the Vietnam era, but also quite different in many other respects, with apparent ramifications on attitudes toward politics and authority. The graphs throughout this book appear to indicate that, in terms of physical and psychological symptoms as well as standards of beauty, education, and marriage, the lives of women born during the 1910s and 1920s were similar to those born after World War II, but quite different from those born during the 1930s. This pattern implies that certain social aspects of psychological development may be, to some extent, historically specific, and that even the results of some psychological research may apply only during certain periods.

Knowledge of the importance of the overlap between development and history also has practical implications in that it may allow us to predict the future occurrence of anxious somatic depression. For example, we have found that major depression becomes particularly prevalent at middle age among women, relative to men, in generations that reached adolescence during periods of great increase in rates of college graduation. Our index of changes in these rates (see Figure 4, p. 56) shows that the largest increase took place during the adolescence of women who were born during and after the 1950s. This generation of women is just beginning to reach age 40. Based on our previous findings, we would expect the next two decades to be a period of high prevalence of depression, which is accompanied by somatic symptoms among middle-aged women. Because many women suffering from anxious somatic depression receive a great deal of medical treatment, one possible consequence of this outbreak is that expensive medical resources will be used inefficiently to treat what is essentially a psychological and social disorder. This is a particularly likely, and particularly costly, possibility in developing nations in which major changes in gender roles are likely to occur in the near future.

Predictions for younger women are more difficult. It is unlikely that rates of college graduation among women will continue to increase much in the near future. To the extent that high prevalence of the symptoms of anxious somatic depression is predicted by increases in these rates, we might expect prevalence to decline in coming years among young women. The problem with this prediction is that conditions confronted by women in the 1990s, at least those living in the United States, may be so different from those of earlier periods as to render predictions based on earlier demographic patterns inaccurate.

One important difference is that at no time in history has the proportion of women graduating from college or working for wages outside the home been so great as now. Paradoxically, this unique situation may lessen the importance of college graduation as an index of the limitations placed on women. Although in previous decades one of the strongest barriers faced by women seeking to achieve in areas traditionally reserved for males was limited access to higher education, recent educational changes may have altered both the form and timing of these barriers. Nowadays, many women may confront their greatest barriers when they graduate from college and seek occupational promotion or encounter the work versus motherhood dilemmas discussed in Chapter 5. As a result, nontraditional girls reaching adolescence today may have mothers who are unhappy or appear limited not because they could not attend college, but because after they graduated they were unable to fulfill their aspirations. Measures of gender ambivalence or concerns regarding gender-related limitations placed on their mothers may continue to predict symptoms of anxious somatic depression, though measures of generational changes in rates of female college graduation may not.

It is possible, however, that the recent educational and professional advances of women may lead to lower prevalence of gender ambivalence and anxious somatic depression in the early twenty-first century. Yet such advances may have produced increases in women's aspirations toward success outside the home that are even greater than the availability of such success. In that case, application of William James's equation—"Self-esteem = Success/ Pretensions"—would predict high levels of gender ambivalence and anxious somatic depression among young women in the near future. Increased competition from Europe, Japan, and some developing nations may also place pressure on the economy of the United States that leads, reminiscent of some effects of the Great Depression, to a disproportionate loss of professional and managerial positions among women.

Whatever happens over the course of generations, we can expect anxious somatic depression to afflict millions of women in the next two decades. To ameliorate some of this suffering, we believe that programs of recognition, prevention, and treatment should be developed and implemented. In the last chapter, we turn to a discussion of these types of programs.

Part IV

PRACTICAL IMPLICATIONS OF OUR FINDINGS

11

Recognition, Prevention, and Treatment

Throughout, we have gathered information from a variety of sources, including historical, anthropological, demographic, biographical, clinical, epidemiologic, survey, and laboratory studies—all of which point to the same conclusion: a syndrome involving several psychological and somatic symptoms that afflicts many women beginning at adolescence, particularly during periods of changing gender roles. The syndrome frequently occurs among women who come to feel that their gender places them at an unfair disadvantage in pursuing their aspirations and who develop a conflicted or confused sense of self. We have called such confusion and conflict over gender and self *gender ambivalence,* and the syndrome *anxious somatic depression.* Our observations and data supporting the existence of a distinct syndrome of anxious somatic depression, and its connection to gender ambivalence and changing gender roles, have direct implications for designing programs for the prevention and treatment of depression, disordered eating, and other symptoms of the syndrome.

Recognizing the Syndrome

The first step in treating the syndrome is to develop a clear set of criteria for research and diagnosis. We use the term "syndrome" precisely because our research appears to connect gender ambivalence with a constellation of symptoms. But it would be unnecesarily restrictive to limit the diagnosis of anxious somatic depression to those women who exhibit every symptom. On the other hand, we would certainly not suggest that every woman who suffers from any one of the symptoms is exhibiting the syndrome.

This problem of specifying a cutoff point somewhere between one symptom and all the symptoms is common in psychology and psychiatry. A variety of methods, samples, and statistical techniques, ranging from epidemiologic research on community samples to clinical research on patient samples, have been used to develop diagnostic criteria for most currently recognized disorders. We aim in future research to apply many of these same techniques to develop criteria for anxious somatic depression. This research would also shed light, we hope, on the biological, developmental, and familial factors that lead different women to exhibit somewhat different sets of symptoms.

Another important step in recognizing and treating the syndrome is to ensure that psychological aspects are not overlooked. Because several symptoms of anxious somatic depression involve such physical problems as headache, breathing difficulties, or heart palpitations and murmurs, many women suffering from the syndrome probably seek medical treatment. Studies have shown that depressed people, particularly those exhibiting depression accompanied by physical complaints, frequently visit their primary-care physicians, but that these physicians often overlook underlying depression when they treat patients with physical ailments.[1] One intriguing study found that by paying particular attention to the existence of multiple somatic complaints, it was possible to identify women with somatization disorder (the DSM diagnosis based on hysteria) from those seeking treatment for somatic ailments. A treatment program based on psychological principles that attempted to avoid unnecessary surgery and hospitalization was devised for these women. This program was found to be as effective as traditional medical practices in dealing with the women's somatic complaints, and at a much lower cost.[2]

By extension, a significant reduction in the pain and inconvenience resulting from surgery and hospitalization, and large savings in medical expenses and utilization of medical resources, might be realized if we could develop a similar program for recognizing and treating anxious somatic depression. If simple measures for identifying women suffering from this syndrome could be developed, physicians, school nurses, school psychologists, chiropractors, and others might administer these measures to patients with symptoms of the syndrome. Patients exhibiting severe forms of the psychological problems associated with anxious somatic depression could be referred to psychotherapists. Others might be treated by counselors or health professionals who have received training in integrating the psychological aspects of these problems into their traditional medical treatments. To the extent that physical symptoms of anxious somatic depression are rooted in psychological and social problems, it may at best be very inefficient to treat them using only physical procedures, and at worst ineffective or may even serve to exacerbate the problems. To avoid these difficulties, health professionals as well as the general public must be educated to recognize the signs of depression in general, and of anxious somatic depression in particular.

Treating Anxious Somatic Depression

Because the syndrome has not been recognized in recent years, nothing has been written about therapies specifically designed to treat it. Several different types of psychotherapy have been found to be effective in treating depression, and several therapists who have treated women suffering from symptoms of the syndrome, notably disordered eating, have discussed how they have integrated into their treatment approaches recognition of the importance of gender roles and psychological responses to gender bias.[3] It is beyond the scope of this book to detail these therapeutic techniques, but we would suggest that combining the more traditional therapies that have been helpful in combating depression with the approaches that specifically focus on issues related to gender may be possible and useful.

We believe that therapies designed to treat this syndrome may be most effective if they take into consideration the syndrome's course of development. For example, we have discussed how women who exhibit this syndrome in adolescence or early adulthood may later develop major depression, particularly as they confront issues that pose particular problems for adult women trying to pursue careers, such as childrearing, caring for infirm relatives, and gender-related barriers that inhibit professional advancement. Many women confront these problems in relative isolation, so that it is difficult for them to fully recognize that the problems are not due to their own inadequacy; such isolation also makes it hard for them to receive the social support they need for optimally coping with these challenges. In our clinical work, in doing the interviews for this book, and even in studying the biographies of eminent women, we have been struck by how often women who are extremely bright and perceptive about psychological issues appear to have internalized these problems, blaming themselves for their difficulties. We would suggest that, whether or not women seek individual psychotherapy, many would benefit from the support of groups of women facing similar circumstances. In some cases, this might take the form of formal therapy groups run by professionals under the auspices of private practices or outpatient clinics. In other cases, such groups might be organized by labor unions, PTAs, and other community organizations. Perhaps these groups would not forestall the development of anxious somatic depression, but they might help reduce or limit the severity of its symptoms.

Early Recognition and Prevention of the Syndrome

Recent experience with problems ranging from cigarette smoking to sexually transmitted diseases suggests that prevention and early treatment are often more efficient than therapy occurring after the behavioral patterns are well established. The studies cited here indicate that, for most females, symptoms associated with anxious somatic depression begin during a relatively brief period around adolescence and early adulthood. In Chapter 8, we discussed the psychological reasons for this age-specific development. Putting this material together, we suggest that it may be possible to recognize the syndrome just as it begins, and perhaps even predict it.

Those young women who report a few symptoms of the syndrome could be interviewed at greater length, allowing assessment of not only their physical symptoms, but also the depression, anxiety, low self-esteem, and gender ambivalence that underlie the physical symptoms. Such recognition may allow some girls to deal with the issues of low self-esteem and gender ambivalence early enough to forestall the development of extreme anxiety and depression characteristic of the syndrome. Even in the absence of a great reduction in anxiety and depression, however, effective techniques (such as relaxation, biofeedback, and cognitive therapy) already exist to help those young women cope with their anxiety and depression to avoid the development of severe headaches, extreme insomnia, or other physical complaints.

The ingredients for predicting onset of the syndrome before it occurs can be derived from studies of the psychological and familial dynamics contributing to development of the syndrome, some of which have already been done and some of which still need to be done. We have identified many indices that come together to predispose a girl to develop symptoms of anxious somatic depression, including the following: reporting that her mother was very limited by being female, that she often feels guilty for living a better life than her mother, that she often minimizes her own accomplishments so that her mother will not feel bad about herself, that her mother was dissatisfied with her own career choices or seems "fed up" with playing the mommy role, that her father considers his wife unintelligent, that her parents believe a woman's place is in the home, that her father wishes she was a boy, and that her father treats a brother as the most intelligent sibling of the family. Most of these indices can be measured before women reach adolescence and begin to develop symptoms, allowing prediction of which preadolescent girls are likely to develop the syndrome.

In health classes given in junior high school, these and other girls might be given the opportunity to attend small group sessions in which they discuss issues that appear relevant to the development of anxious somatic depression: What puberty means for girls who aspire to achieve in areas historically reserved for men; what these girls feel about their mothers not achieving in these areas; whether they see their brothers receiving advantages in these pursuits. The attempt would be made to prepare the girls for the social and psychological changes that will come with puberty and adolescence and help them realize that, to the extent these changes are experienced as negative, they are not due to some inadequacy in the girls—but rather to social and historical processes beyond their own families.

Of course, there is no guarantee that simple talk, even talk that prepares the girls for the changes they are about to experience and heightens their awareness that these changes are not due to their own deficiencies, can overcome the very real, concrete treatment they will receive from their families and the larger society. But this problem applies equally to all forms of psychotherapy that seek to reduce distress through psychological change—change that is variously termed insight, consciousness raising, or cognitive restructuring. As already discussed, despite such limitations, some evidence exists that such psychotherapies are helpful in treating depression. Psychotherapeutic prevention—that is, working toward affecting the mental change before the psychopathology fully develops—may be more likely to help than psychotherapy that occurs after the problem develops.

Other preventive approaches might be directed toward the families of preadolescent girls. Gender intensification might be the focus of one such program. We have discussed how talented, nontraditional girls often dramatically confront increased limitations at adolescence in the form of increasingly rigid sex-role expectations. It might be possible to educate the parents of such girls about the workings of gender intensification and its potential cost to their daughters.

It would be naive to expect that every parent will pay enough attention to such warnings coming from psychologists, social workers, or guidance counselors, to overcome decades of socialization, and suddenly change their beliefs and behaviors regarding the proper roles for women. But major benefits might result if even a minority of fathers and mothers who have been so encouraging about and proud of their young daughters' accomplishments would come to realize how important it is to maintain the pride they feel and the encouragement they give as those daughters mature into women.

Changing Society

Up to this point, our recommendations have been limited to programs with a relatively narrow focus in that they have single, specific objectives or are targeted to women exhibiting specific characteristics at a specific stage of life. We have alluded to the relative costs and benefits of these programs in an attempt to argue that, in the short term, they are quite feasible because in most cases they might actually save money. Our goals have been threefold: to demonstrate the practical implications of the research cited throughout this book; to suggest that these problems are not impervious to intervention; and to offer programs that have a chance of being implemented because they are cost effective.

But there is no denying that the problem has been, and remains, a very large one. The processes that funnel women into sex-stereotyped pursuits and that lead those pursuits to be evaluated as less important and less worthy of reward and respect than pursuits typically associated with male roles are multiple. Solutions must go beyond single-objective programs or programs tailored to specific types of people at particular stages of life, and beyond specific cost-benefit analyses.

One of the aims in doing our research was to attempt to demonstrate, using scientific methods, that gender bias does play a major role in causing psychological and physical problems. Throughout its history, medicine, including psychiatry, has for the most part overlooked or downplayed the possibility that a truly scientific psychiatry could include such "soft" (i.e., nonbiological, political) concepts as gender bias in its theory and research. Even today, in a society greatly influenced by changes in gender roles over the past generation, studies of the effects of gender bias tend to be treated as not truly scientific and are confined primarily to journals devoted to the psychology of women.

Some have argued that this practice occurs because smaller, more physical units like molecules, hormones, and organs are more amenable to scientific study in that they can often be measured more precisely than units at a higher level of organization, such as family structure or gender bias. Others claim that blaming biology for people's problems allows those in power to avoid changing a social structure from which they benefit.

Whatever the case, we would argue that true science cannot specify a priori the variables it uses to explain phenomena under study. Through hard work and replicated research, the variables that might explain particular phenomena are suggested, their measurements are improved, and their ability to predict future research findings is compared with the predictive ability of other variables. In this process, "soft," social, historical, political concepts like gender bias and gender ambivalence can be used, if carefully operationalized and measured with some precision, in just as scientific a manner as "hard," biological concepts, like genetics, are used to study psychiatric problems like depression. So when nineteenth-century physicians who noticed the high prevalence of symptomatology among the first generation of college women in the United States did not attempt to formulate and test a series of hypotheses to explain the connection between symptomatology and the strivings of these women, but instead simply assumed that the fragile biology of females was responsible, they were behaving unscientifically, and obviously were products of the society's gender bias. Thus, it seems to us that another practical implication of our findings for the prevention and treatment of anxious somatic depression is that more attention, more resources, and more respect must be accorded to scientific research on the effects of gender bias.

Finally, medicine is by no means the only major institution that requires changes in order to prevent anxious somatic depression. In the long run, we need deep-rooted, widespread social change in almost every facet of society. Parents must change the attitudes they bring to parenting and the subtle and not so subtle responses they have to female versus male children. Teachers must become aware of the many different ways in which schools reward and encourage the intellectual, academic, and professional aspirations of males and sometimes actually inhibit those of females.[4] Businesses must allow parents to take time off from careers to raise young children without being penalized, restructure workdays and workweeks to allow more flexibility, and improve daycare options. Fathers must be given encouragement and respect for spending more time in childrearing. Boys and girls should be taught at every stage in their education to recognize and resist gender biases.

Our research has not focused on every aspect of gender bias, and many recent books and articles have been able to devote more space and attention to argue for the elimination of such bias. But the only complete "cure" for anxious somatic depression (as opposed to "pure" depression, which appears to be equally distributed between genders) lies in eliminating gender ambivalence. And, in the long run, gender ambivalence will only disappear when women who strive to achieve academically, professionally, or politically are given equal opportunity and when women who strive to achieve domestically are given equal respect. Only then will women cease to pay the cost of competence.

Appendix A

Depression, Disordered Eating, and Somatic Symptoms Among Eminent Women

Writers/Artists

Louisa May Alcott
Depression, possible disordered eating, somatic symptoms—Chapter 4

Jane Austen
Depression—had "often a melancholy disposition," wrote to "dispel melancholy"
Disordered eating—nervous vomiting, indigestion possibly from Addison's disease
Source—Halpern, Johns Hopkins U. Press, 1984

Emily Brontë
Disordered eating, possible depression—Chapter 5

Charlotte Brontë
Depression, possible disordered eating, somatic symptoms—Chapter 5

Elizabeth Barrett Browning
Disordered eating—Chapter 6

Emily Dickinson
Depression, disordered eating—Chapter 7

George Eliot
Depression, somatic symptoms—Chapter 8

Georgia O'Keefe
Depression, somatic symptoms—Chapter 9

George Sand
Depression—Chapter 9

Harriet Beecher Stowe
Depression—Chapter 3

Virginia Woolf
Depression, disordered eating, somatic symptoms—Chapter 5

Scientists/Social Scientists

Hannah Arendt
Depression—Chapter 3

Ruth Benedict
Depression, possible disordered eating, somatic symptoms—Chapter 9

Marie Curie
Depression, disordered eating—Chapter 6

Helene Deutsch
Depression—Chapter 5

Anna Freud
Disordered eating, somatic symptoms—Chapter 7

Karen Horney
Depression—Chapter 5

Melanie Klein
Depression—Described as suffering from "deep," "acute," depression, "depressive exhaustion," and as being "suffocated in depression"
Disordered eating—correspondence refers to "stomach complaints," poor appetite
Source—Gross-Kurth, Harvard U. Press, 1987

Margaret Mead
We were unable to find any signs of the disorders we were studying—Chapter 8

World Leaders

Catherine the Great
Depression, somatic symptoms—Chapter 4

Queen Elizabeth I
Depression, disordered eating, somatic symptoms—Chapter 4

Indira Gandhi
Disordered eating—Chapter 4

Joan of Arc
Disordered eating—Chapter 2

Golda Meir
Depression, somatic symptoms—Chapter 4

Eleanor Rossevelt
Depression, disordered eating, somatic symptoms—Introduction

Queen Victoria
Depression, disordered eating, somatic symptoms—Chapter 4

Helping Professions

Jane Addams
Depression—she wrote of "nervous exhaustion with which I struggled for years," early adulthood she reached "nadir of my nervous depression"
Source—Addams, Macmillan, 1940

Clara Barton
Depression, possible disordered eating, somatic symptoms—Chapter 6

Dorothea Dix
Depression—her symptoms were never specified but she was a lifelong invalid described as suffering from "nervous exhaustion"
Source—Tiffany, Houghton Mifflin, 1918

Florence Nightingale
Depression, possible disordered eating, somatic symptoms—Chapter 4

Beatrice Webb
Depression—Chapter 9

Feminist Activists and Ideologists

Susan B. Anthony
Depression—Chapter 7

Simone de Beauvoir
Depression, possible disordered eating, somatic symptoms—Chapter 8

Elizabeth Cady Stanton
Depression—Chapter 6

Mary Wollstonecraft
Beginning at adolescence, she suffered from "chronic depression," digestive difficulties, and acute headaches
Source—Flexner, Coward, McCann & Georghesan, 1977

Daughters/Sisters of Eminent Men

Henrietta Darwin
Disordered eating, somatic symptoms—Chapter 7

Margot Einstein
Possible disordered eating—Chapter 7

Queen Elizabeth I.
Depression, disordered eating, somatic symptoms—Chapter 4

Anna Freud
Disordered eating, somatic symptoms—Chapter 7

Indira Gandhi
Disordered eating—Chapter 4

Alice James
Depression, disordered eating, somatic symptoms—Chapter 6

Eleanore Marx
Depression, disordered eating, somatic symptoms—Chapter 7

Appendix B

Model of the Development of the Symptoms of Anxious Somatic Depression

The poor body image and preference for slim, noncurvaceous bodies associated with anxious somatic depression appear to derive from ambivalent feelings experienced by some women toward their femininity. The feeling that being female places great limitations on them appears to lead to discontent and resentment toward the breasts, curves, and menstruation that define them as adult women. Studies of symptomatology associated with low body weight indicate that some other symptoms, such as amenorrhea and mitral valve prolapse, probably result, at least in part, when women lose too much weight in an attempt to rid themselves of their curves. Menstrual dysfunction and mitral valve prolapse have also been found to be associated with anxiety and depression.[1] The extreme reduction in food intake involved in anorexia and the expulsion of food once it has been ingested through purgative measures such as vomiting or abuse of laxatives probably also result from the quest of gender ambivalent women for curveless bodies.

More research is needed to determine why women who experience gender ambivalence sometimes tend to overeat or binge. It may be that in order to avoid looking traditionally female some women try to be as thin as possible whereas others try to look large and cover up their curves rather than reducing them. On the other hand, some psychologists have found that people attempting to be very thin sometimes experience the need to binge when they find it impossible to keep their weight as low as they want.[2] We do not know how many women proceed directly to bingeing to cover up curves and how many begin to binge on the rebound after trying to be thin.

In Chapter 5, we argued that sexual indifference and avoidance of marriage might result because both sexuality and matrimony place emphasis on the femininity of women and the limitations of traditional female roles. Thus, we hypothesize that poor body image, preference for slim, noncurvaceous bodies, sexual indifference, and avoidance of matrimony result from the desire to deemphasize one's femininity. Restricted food intake, purgeing, mitral valve prolapse, and perhaps bingeing are secondary effects of the desire to avoid curvaceous, traditionally feminine physiques.

Additional research will be necessary before we fully understand the development of the combination of depression and anxiety among women experiencing gender ambivalence. Low self-esteem probably plays an important role in the process. Like other symptoms of the forgotten syndrome, low self-esteem has been found to be related to depression, anxiety, and poor body image, to be more prevalent among females than among males, and to increase much more markedly during adolescence among females than among males.[3] This pattern suggests that the transition into adult women that occurs at adolescence leads some females to experience a great drop in self-esteem that is accompanied by depression, poor body image, and anxiety. As we discussed above, the basic sense of identity confusion, of feeling somehow inadequate and not accepted, often called "low self-esteem," lies at the very heart of the gender ambivalence experienced by many women. We speculate that feelings of personal inadequacy lead these women to feel both anxious and depressed.

Perceived lack of control over important events is another psychological construct that has been found to relate to depression, anxiety or stress, and disordered eating.[4] It is possible that the gender inequality experienced by females as they reach adolescence leads them to feel that they are losing control over their lives. After all, without any intent on their parts, they find their bodies and the reactions of other people toward them changing and the limitations placed on them increasing. The goals they worked hard to achieve earlier in life appear more difficult to attain simply through their own talent or hard work. In effect, they lose control over their bodies, the reactions of important people to them, and the possibility of attaining their goals. These feelings of loss of control may lead to anxiety and depression. Thus, the development of gender ambivalence may predispose women to develop depression and anxiety through its effect on the women's self-esteem, or on the amount of control they feel they have over their life, or some combination of both with other still unknown processes.

Somatic symptoms, such as headache, breathing difficulties, and insomnia, may result from the combination of depression and anxiety associated with gender ambivalence. In Chapter 4, we cited studies that found the existence of somatic symptomatology to be better predicted by a combination of anxiety and depression than by either anxiety or depression alone.[5] Further research is needed to test this hypothesis and understand how depression may combine with anxiety to produce somatic symptoms.

The difficulties in concentration associated with the syndrome probably result from the anxiety and depression exacerbated by the somatic symptoms. The anxiety, depression, and low self-esteem associated with gender ambivalence may be particularly likely to strike women who feel that their intellectual accomplishments have been limited by their gender at times when they strive to concentrate on intellectual tasks.

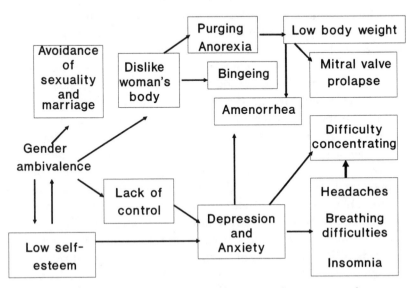

Figure 10 Schematic model of the development of symptoms of anxious somatic depression.

Appendix C

Methods and Results of Unpublished Studies Cited in This Book

Measuring Generational Changes in Headache Prevalence

In order to evaluate the presence of historical fluctuations in gender differences in headache, we reanalyzed data from surveys of headache prevalence with the following characteristics: (1) Data for females and males were reported separately; (2) the prevalence of frequent headache was reported; (3) published data were divided into age cohorts of one decade or less. Data on frequent headache were sought because gender differences in headache prevalence have been found to increase with the severity or frequency of the headache complaint. The criterion limiting the size of cohorts was established to ensure that the relatively brief periods during the century when rates of female college graduation decreased were represented separately from the other periods. In addition, we made particular efforts to find surveys done many years apart so as to minimize the potential confounding of age effects with cohort effects, defined as the effects of particular historical conditions confronting different cohorts of women as they reached adolescence.[1]

Three published surveys met our criteria. One of the three surveys included data from people born at the turn of the twentieth century, allowing us to evaluate the presence of historical fluctuations in gender differences in headache over the entire twentieth century. The other two studies were done more recently and did not include people born at the turn of the century, so we were able to assess gender differences in the prevalence of headache only among people born between about 1905–1910 and the present.[2]

For each survey, we subtracted the ages used to define the cohorts from the year the data were collected in order to calculate the birth years of the members of each cohort—and hence the years respondents reached age 13. Next, we compiled the percentage of females and males reporting frequent headache in each cohort, and subtracted the percentage of males from the percentage of females. The resulting numbers represented a measure of gender differences in prevalence of frequent headache in which positive values indicate a higher prevalence among females and negative values indicate higher prevalence of frequent headache among males than among females.

Figure 5 in Chapter 4 depicts the fluctuations in gender differences in rates of frequent headache over the course of the century reported in the three surveys we reanalyzed. To facilitate comparison of the gender differences, we included data from all the studies on the same graph: The left-hand y-axis depicts the prevalence of frequent headache among females minus the prevalence among males in the 1966 and 1985 studies, and the right-hand y-axis shows female minus male prevalence in the 1980 study. We used two y-axes because the percentages of female and male respondents reporting frequent headache as well as the absolute size of the gender differences in these percentages were smaller in the 1966 and 1985 studies than in the 1980 study. The 1966 study, done in 1962, surveyed the prevalence of "frequent unexplained" headache and the 1985 study, done in 1981, reported the number of respondents who exhibited two or more headaches per week: Gender differences in prevalence of frequent headache in these studies ranged from about −1.5 to about +4.5 percent. In contrast, the 1980 study, done in 1969–1971, reported the number of people exhibiting only one or more headaches per month: Gender differences in this study ranged from about +4.5 to about +20 percent.

For all studies, cohorts were located on the x-axis at the beginning of the decade (1920, 1930 etc.) nearest to the midpoint of the birth years of the cohort. For example, the cohort located at the 1920 x-axis point was born between 1913 and 1922 in the 1966 study, between 1916 and 1925 in the 1980 study, and between 1912 and 1921 in the 1985 study. Because of the limited data available for individuals born prior to 1910, all available data are plotted, including data from two five-year cohorts in the Brewis study and one cohort of indeterminate length, composed of people aged 65 and over, in the 1985 study. From 1910 on, data from the 1966 study are reported in ten-year cohorts to facilitate comparison with the other two studies that are organized into ten-year cohorts.

Calculating Historical Fluctuations in Gender Differences in the Prevalence of Mitral Valve Prolapse

The largest study of the epidemiology of mitral valve prolapse, part of the Framingham study, combined two series of interviews done at different times. As a result, each of the reported age cohorts included people born during different periods, so the reported data cannot be compared to the index of generational change in rates of female college graduation.[3]

Deveraux et al., however, reported a study of the prevalence of mitral valve prolapse (MVP) among 350 relatives of probands referred for MVP, in which the data of the females was reported separately from those of the males, divided into 10-year age cohorts. The data were collected between late 1979 and 1985. Figure 11 presents the ratio of the proportion of females to the proportion of males of each cohort diagnosed as exhibiting mitral valve prolapse,

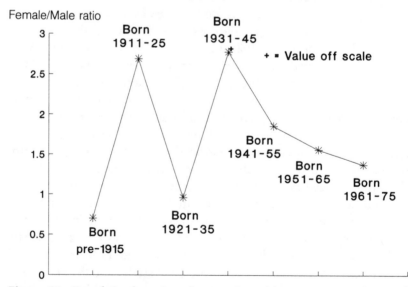

Figure 11 Female/male ratios of proportion of interviewees with mitral valve prolapse organized according to 15-year birth cohorts.

along with the range of years in which the people in each cohort were born.[4]

In the age 70+ cohort, made up of people born at the very latest in 1915 and many born prior to 1910, the rate of MVP was higher among males than among females. In contrast, in the cohort born between 1911 and 1925 the rate was much higher among females. In the cohort born 1921–1935, whose members reached adolescence in the late 1930s and 1940s, females once again exhibited a slightly lower rate than males. But in all the cohorts born after the 1921–1935 cohort, females exhibited higher rates of mitral valve prolapse than males. It should be noted that MVP has been found to be associated with thinness, and, in Chapter 1, we discussed the significant relationship between rates of female college graduation and the emphasis placed by women on thinness, suggesting the possibility that the relationship between rates of female college graduation and mitral valve prolapse may be mediated by thinness. Further research will be necessary before the effects on the gender differences in the prevalence of mitral valve prolapse of age versus year of birth can be unconfounded, as was done in the studies of headache.

Depression Subtypes

SUBJECTS

Subjects were 175 seniors attending two New York City high schools who filled out self-report questionnaires in social studies classes.

INSTRUMENTS

As in Silverstein et al. (1993), depressive symptomatology was measured with the Center for Epidemiologic Studies Depression Scale (CES-D). A high level of depression was defined using the cutoff of 24 or greater on the CES-D found to optimally detect clinically diagnosable cases of DSM-III-R depressive disorders among high school students. In this study, anxiety was measured using the anxiety subscale of the SCL-90-R. A high level of anxiety was defined as scoring at least one standard deviation above the norm for adolescents on this subscale. Additional symptoms were measured by asking respondents to use a 5-point Likert scale ranging from "Never" to "Almost always" to indicate how often they exhibited each symptom. With the exception of "intentional purging of food using laxatives, diuretics, or self-induced vomiting," all symptoms were defined as applying to respondents who reported exhibiting the symptom "Often" or "Almost always." Respondents who reported exhibiting any intentional purging of food were considered to have exhibited this symptom of disordered eating.[5]

Respondents were considered to exhibit anxious somatic depression if they scored above cutoff on depression and anxiety and reported exhibiting at least three of the following symptoms: (1) Frequent severe headaches; (2) frequent trouble breathing for no reason; (3) frequent trouble falling asleep at night or staying asleep without waking up (these two symptoms of insomnia were included in one question); (4) disordered eating (respondents were considered to exhibit disordered eating if they reported frequently avoiding eating for a day or frequently eating uncontrollably to the point of stuffing themselves or ever intentionally purging food by means of laxatives, diuretics, or self-induced vomiting); (5) poor body image/preference for thinness (respondents were considered to exhibit poor body image/preference for thinness if they reported frequently being preoccupied with the desire to be thinner or frequently feeling unhappy or dissatisfied with their overall body shape).

Concerns regarding the limitations placed on oneself or one's mother by being female were measured using scales developed for this purpose. The scale measuring concern regarding the limitations experienced by one's mother was developed using factor analytic methods on an independent sample of college students. This scale consisted of the following questions answered using 5-point Likert scales ranging from "Not at all" to "Extremely": When you were growing up, how much did your mother feel limited by being female? When you were growing up, how much did your mother hope for something better or more out of life? How worried about your mother do you feel? How much do you minimize your own accomplishments so your mother won't feel bad about herself? When you were growing up, how sorry for your mother did you feel? How much do you feel guilty for having a better life than your mother did? When you were growing up, how much did your mother act resentful about her life?[6]

On the female sample in this study, these questions had a Cronbach's alpha of .72. Responses on these questions were summed to obtain a total score. Respondents scoring high on this scale were defined as those who scored in the top 25 percent of this sample.

The scale used to measure feelings of being limited by being female is currently being developed and validated in a number of samples. In this study, items designed to measure this construct were presented with responses indicated on a 5-point scale ranging from disagree very much to agree very much. The following items exhibited a Cronbach's alpha in the female sample of this study of .74: I am dissatisfied being a female. I wish I were born male. My adult life would probably be better if I were male. In general, men lead better lives than women. More people would pay attention to my ideas if I were male. Being female has never held me back (reverse coded in calculating total scale score).

As on the first scale, responses on these questions were summed to derive a total score and respondents whose total scores were in the top twenty five percent of the sample were considered to be high in feeling limited by being female.

Results

Table 1 presents the data of the males and females in this high school sample divided into those who exhibited low depression by scoring below cutoff on the CES-D, those who exhibited pure depression by scoring above cutoff on the depression inventory but not meeting criteria for anxious somatic depression, and those who exhibited anxious somatic depression.

The prevalence of pure depression among males (23%) and females (29) was quite similar, but females were several times as likely (11% versus 1%) to report the combined symptoms of anxious somatic depression ($\chi^2 = 8.82$; $f < .02$).

In order to allow for legitimate statistical analysis of the relationship among females between symptomatology and gender-related concerns regarding achievement, it was necessary to com-

Table 1 Male and Female High School Seniors Reporting Low Depression, Pure Depression, or Anxious Somatic Depression

	Low Depression	*Pure Depression*	*Anxious Somatic Depression*
Males	68 (76%)*	21 (23%)	1 (1%)
Females	51 (60%)	24 (29%)	9 (11%)

*Numbers in parentheses indicate the percentage of respondents in each row exhibiting each type of symptomatology.

Table 2 Females Reporting and Those Not Reporting Gender-Related
Achievement Concerns Who Report Low Depression,
Pure Depression, or Anxious Somatic Depression

		Low Depression	*Pure Depression*	*Anxious Somatic Depression*
Gender-related achievement concerns	Low	25 (74%) *	8 (24%)	1 (3%)
	High	10 (46%)	6 (27%)	6 (27%)

* Numbers in parentheses indicate the percentage of respondents in each row exhibiting each type of symptomatology.

bine into one group the female respondents who scored high on either scale. The resulting analysis, presented in Table 2, indicated that female high school seniors who expressed concerns regarding the limitations placed on themselves or their mothers were nine times as likely as female high school seniors who did not score high on either scale to report the symptoms of anxious somatic depression (27% versus 3%; Fisher's exact test two-tailed $p = .02$).

Of particular interest is the finding that the proportion of respondents who scored above cutoff on the depression inventory but did not meet criteria for anxious somatic depression differed very little between the females who scored in the top quartile of either scale (27%) and those who did not (24%). These findings are almost identical to those reported by Silverstein et al. (1993) for another high school sample.

References and Notes

Introduction

1. Cook, B. W. (1992). *Eleanor Roosevelt: Vol. 1: 1884–1933.* New York: Penguin, pp. 37–39, 137, 156, 168, 199, 232, 235, 300, 332.

Chapter 1: Curves and Competence

1. Morell, P. (1940). *Lillian Russell: The era of plush.* New York: Random House.
2. Venus quote—Ibid., p. 144.
   Flowers of Spring quote—Ibid., p. 97.
   Raging beauty quote—*New York Times Magazine*, "A century of pinups," 12/22/46, p. 28.
3. Morell, op. cit., p. 100.
4. Banner, L. (1983). *American beauty.* New York: Knopf, p. 106.
5. White elephant quote—Morell, op. cit., p. 185.
   American Venus quote—*New York Times*, "Flapper lines oust Venus de Milo plan," 4/10/23, p. 12.
6. Exercise regime—Banner op. cit., p. 203.
   Motion pictures—Morell op. cit., p. 281.
7. Hutchinson, W. "Fat and fashion." *Saturday Evening Post*, 8/21/26, p. 58.
8. Blyth, S. G. "Get rid of the fat." *Saturday Evening Post*, 4/23/27, p. 11.
9. Silverstein, B., Peterson, B., & Perdue, L. (1986). Some correlates of

the thin standard of bodily attractiveness in women. *International Journal of Eating Disorders, 5*(5), 895–905.

10. *New York Times*, 2/8/21, p. 17.
11. *New York Times*, 1/4/25, p. 10.
12. *New York Times*, 9/19/25, p. 7.
13. Cited in Johnston, J. A. (1953). *Nutritional studies in adolescent girls and their relation to tuberculosis.* Springfield, Ill.: Charles C Thomas, p. 7.
14. Starving themselves quote—*New York Times*, 10/12/26, p. 13.
    Dieting fad quote—Diet causes fatigue. *Scientific American*, March 1930, p. 223.
15. *New York Times*, 10/6/33, p. 33.
16. *New York Times*, 2/22/26, p. 3; 2/23/26, p. 7; 2/24/26, p. 6.
17. Bromley, D. D. (1927). "Feminist—New Style." *Harper's*, October, pp. 552–560.
18. Durant, W. (1927). "The Modern Woman." *Century*, February, pp. 418–429.
19. Blyth, op. cit., pp. 10–11.
20. Tolman, R. (1973). *Guide to fashion merchandise knowledge.* White Plains, N.Y.: Milady, p. 49.
21. Emasculated male quote—Durant, op. cit., p. 37.
    Masculine physique quote—Bromley, op. cit.
22. Women in the professions. *Monthly Labor Review*, May 1974, pp. 34–39.
23. Bureau of the census. (1975). *Historical statistics of the United States: Colonial times to the present.* Washington, D.C.: U.S. Government Printing Office.
24. *New York Times*, 9/26/31, p. 1.
25. *New York Times*, 9/27/37, p. 23.
26. Women in business I. *Fortune* July 1935, pp. 50–57, 90, 92, 95–96; quote p. 90.
27. Cited in Laver, James (1938). *Taste and fashion from the French Revolution until to-day.* New York: Dodd Mead, p. 214.
28. *New York Times*, 11/9/42, p. 20.
29. Garner, D. M., Garfinkel, P. E., Schwartz, D., & Thompson, M. (1980). Cultural expectations of thinness in women. *Psychological Reports, 47*, 483–491.
    Silverstein, B., Perdue, L., Peterson, B., & Kelly, E. (1986). The role of the mass media in promoting a thin standard of bodily attractiveness for women. *Sex Roles, 14*, 519–532.
30. Silverstein, B., Perdue, L., Peterson, B., Vogel, L., & Fantini, D. A. (1986). Possible causes of the thin standard of bodily attractiveness for women. *International Journal of Eating Disorders, 5*(5), 907–916.
31. Broverman, I. K., Vogel, S. R., Broverman, D. M., Clarkson, F. E., & Rosenkrantz, P. R. (1972). Sex-role stereotypes: A current appraisal. *Journal of Social Issues, 28*(2), 59–78.

Survey of women in upper management positions by Frantzve, J. L., Carter, J. L., & Lips, H. M. cited in Mednick, A. (1993). World's women familiar with a day's double shift. *A.P.A. Monitor, 24*(5), 32–33; quote p. 33.

32. Cash, T. F. & Janda, L. H. (1984). The eye of the beholder. *Psychology Today*, December, pp. 46–52.

33. Data from study reported in Silverstein, B. & Perdue, L. (1988). The relationship between role concerns, preferences for slimness and symptoms of eating problems among college women. *Sex Roles, 18*(1/2), 101–106. See method note A.

34. Kleinke, C. L. & Staneski, R. A. (1980). First impressions of female bust size. *Journal of Social Psychology, 110,* 123–134.

35. Redundant breasts quote—Women in business II. *Fortune,* August 1935, pp. 50–55, 85–86; quote p. 55.

    Bixler, S. *The professional image.* (1984). New York: Putnam, p. 92.

36. Beck, S. B., Ward-Hull, C. I., & McLear, P. M. (1976). Variables related to women's somatic preferences of the male and female body. *Journal of Personality and Social Psychology, 34,* 1200–1210.

37. Hawkins, R. C., Turell, S., & Jackson, L. J. (1983). Desirable and undesirable masculine and feminine traits in relation to students' dieting tendencies and body image dissatisfaction. *Sex Roles, 9*(6), 705–717.

    Silverstein, Perdue, Peterson, Vogel & Fantini, op. cit.

38. Rodin, J., Silberstein, L. R. & Striegel-Moore, R. H. (1985). Women and weight: A normative discontent. In T. B. Sonderegger (ed.), *Nebraska Symposium on Motivation: Vol. 32. Psychology and Gender.* Lincoln: University of Nebraska Press, pp. 267–307.

    Hawkins et al., 1983, op. cit.

    Stern, S. L., Dixon, K. N., Jones, D., Lake, M., Nemzer, E., & Sansone, R. (1989). Family environment in anorexia nervosa and bulimia. *International Journal of Eating Disorders, 8*(1), 25–33.

39. Silverstein & Perdue, op. cit.

40. Silverstein, B., Carpman, S., Perlick, D., & Perdue, L. (1990). Nontraditional sex role aspirations, gender identity conflict, and disordered eating among college women. *Sex Roles, 23*(11/12), 687–695.

41. Data from study reported in Silverstein & Perdue, op. cit. See method note B.

42. Rost, W., Neuhaus, M., & Florin, I. (1982). Bulimarexia nervosa: Sex role attitude, sex role behavior, and sex role related locus of control in bulimarexic women. *Journal of Psychosomatic Research, 26,* 403–408.

43. Bruch, H. (1978). *The golden cage.* Cambridge, Mass.: Harvard University Press.

    Gordon, R. A. (1990). *Anorexia and bulimia: Anatomy of a social epidemic.* Cambridge, Mass.: Basil Blackwell.

Schwartz, H. J. (1988). Bulimia and the mouth-vagina equation: The phallic compromise. In H. J. Schwartz (ed.), *Bulimia: Psychoanalytic treatment and theory.* Madison, Ct.: International Universities Press, pp. 255–298.

44. Hopkins, M. A. Women's rebellion against fashion. *New Republic,* 8/16/22, p. 332.

Bartos, R. (1982). *The moving target: What every marketer should know about women.* New York: Free Press, p. 166.

45. Women in business I. *Fortune,* op. cit.; quote p. 95.

46. Gross, J. & Rosen, J. C. (1988). Bulimia in adolescents: Prevalence and psychosocial correlates. *International Journal of Eating Disorders,* 7(1), 51–61.

Jampala, V. C. (1985). Anorexia nervosa: A variant form of affective disorder? *Psychiatric Annals, 15,* 698–704.

Ledoux, S., Choquet, M., & Flament, M. (1991). Eating disorders among adolescents in an unselected French population. *International Journal of Eating Disorders, 10*(1), 81–89.

Levy, D.. & Savage, D. (1987). Prevalence and clinical features of mitral valve prolapse. *American Heart Journal,* May, 1281–1290.

Rosen, J. C. (1990). Body-image disturbance in eating disorders. In T. F. Cash & T. Pruzinsky (eds.), *Body images: Development, deviance and change.* New York: Guilford.

Vollrath, M., Koch, R., & Angst, J. (1992). Binge eating and weight concerns among young adults: Results from the Zurich Cohort Study. *British Journal of Psychiatry, 160,* 498–503.

Method Notes

A. Female college students were presented with the pictures portrayed in Figure 2 and asked to select the one most likely to be a homemaker. The scale used for the answers was as follows:

The slimmer woman is			Both are	*The plumper woman is*		
Much more	Somewhat more	Slightly more	About equal	Slightly more	Somewhat more	Much more
0	1	2	3	4	5	6

For this analysis, we combined choices 0–2 and choices 4–6. Of the respondents 6.5% selected the slimmer woman, 46% indicated they felt that both women were equally likely to be homemakers, and 44% selected the plumper woman.

B. Women exhibiting symptoms of disordered eating were those who reported purgeing themselves of food using laxatives, diuretics, or self-induced vomiting or those who reported "usually" or "always" going on food binges during the previous year on a 5-point scale: "Never-Rarely-Sometimes-Usually-Always." Ratings of slimmer and plumper women were as described in note A above using successful and intelligent as the rating words. Thirty-one percent of the nondisordered females rated the woman with the slimmer figure as more successful compared to 46% of the females who reported symptoms of disordered eating ($X^2 = 3.61$, $p = .058$.) Eleven percent of the nondisordered females rated the woman with the slimmer figure as more intelligent compared to 27% of those who reported symptoms of disordered eating ($X^2 = 7.40$, $p = .007$.)

Chapter 2: The Disease of Young Women

1. Hill, O. W. (1977). Epidemiologic aspects of anorexia nervosa. *Advances in Psychosomatic Medicine, 9*, 48–62.
2. Lefkowitz, M. R. & Fant, M. B. (1982). *Women's life in Greece and Rome.* Baltimore: Johns Hopkins, Ch. VII.
    Littre, P. (1853). *Oeuvres completes d'Hippocrate.* Paris: J. B. Bailliere, p. 503.
3. Lefkowitz et al., ibid., p. 96.
4. Benivieni, A. (1954). *De abditis nonnullis ac mirandis morborum et sanationum causis.* (C. Singer, trans.) Springfield, Ill.: Charles C Thomas, p. 95.
5. Morton, R. (1694). *Phthisiologia or a treatise of consumption.* London: Smith & Walford, pp. 8, 9.
6. Ibid., p. 258.
7. Van Deth, R. & Vandereycken, W. (1991). Was nervous consumption a precursor of anorexia nervosa? *Journal of the History of Medicine and Allied Sciences, 46*, 3–19.
8. Cited in Porter, R. (1986). Love, sex, and madness in eighteenth-century England. *Social Research, 53*, 238.
9. Allbutt, T. C. (1901). Chlorosis. In Allbutt, T. C. (ed.), *A system of medicine by many authors, Vol. V.* New York: Macmillan, pp. 481–518.
    Loudon, I. (1984). The diseases called chlorosia. *Psychological Medicine, 4*, 27–36.
10. Fear of obesity quote—Allbutt, ibid., p. 485. Depression and despair quote—Ashwell, cited in Loudon, op. cit., p. 29.
11. Marmor, J. (1953). Orality in the hysterical personality. *Journal of the American Psychoanalytic Association, 1*, 656–671; quote p. 658.
    Purtell, J. J., Robins, E., & Cohen, M. E. (1951). Observations on clinical aspects of hysteria. *Journal of the American Medical Association, 146*, 902–910.
12. Laycock, T. (1840). *An essay on hysteria.* Philadelphia: Haswell, Barrington & Haswell.

Corning, L. (1888). *A treatise on hysteria and epilepsy.* Detroit: George S. Davis.

13. Emmy von N quote—Breuer, J. & Freud, S. (1893–95). *Studies on hysteria.* New York: Basic, reprinted, pp. 80–81.

14. Anna O.—ibid., pp. 21–47. Rejection of all nourishment quote—ibid., p. 4.

15. Lutz, T. (1991). *American nervousness, 1903.* Ithaca, N.Y.: Cornell University Press.
    Savage, G. (1884). *Insanity and allied neuroses.* Philadelphia: Henry C. Lea, p. 90.

16. Deale, H. B. & Adams, S. S. (1894). Neurasthenia in young women. *American Journal of Obstetrics, 29,* 190–195; quote p. 190.

17. Bell, R. M. (1985). *Holy anorexia.* Chicago: University of Chicago; quote p. 56.

18. Brumberg, J. J. (1988). *Fasting girls.* Cambridge, Mass.: Harvard University, p. 79.

19. Magli cited in Bell, op. cit., p. 55.
    Bynum, C. W. (1987). *Holy feast and holy fast.* Berkeley: University of California, pp. 27, 290.

20. Bell, op. cit., p. 25.

21. Bell, op. cit.
    Warner, M. (1981). *Joan of Arc.* New York: Knopf.

22. Morton, op. cit. p. 8.
    Brumberg, op. cit., p. 79.

23. Woody, T. (1929). *A history of women's education in the United States. Vol 2.* New York: Science Press.

24. Clarke, E. H. (1972). *Sex in education; or, a fair chance for the girls.* New York: Arno Press, p. 93.

25. Woody, op. cit., p. 205.

26. Ibid., p. 154.

27. Clarke, op. cit.
    Meigs, C. D. (1859). *Woman: Diseases and remedies.* Philadelphia: Blanchard & Lea.
    Watson, C. (1901). *Encyclopaedia medica. Vol. VII.* Edinburgh: William Green, p. 10.

28. Meigs, ibid., p. 385.

29. Allbutt, op. cit.
    Simon, J. (1897). A study of chlorosis. *American Journal of Medical Science, 113,* 349–423.
    Gosling, F. G. (1987). *Before Freud: Neurasthenia and the American medical community, 1870–1910.* Urbana: University of Illinois.
    Preston, G. J. (1897). *Hysteria and certain allied conditions.* Philadelphia: P. Blakiston.

30. Deale & Adams, op. cit., p. 191.
    Hammond cited in Gosling, op. cit., p. 100.

31. Cleaves, M. (1910). *Autobiography of a neurasthene.* Boston: Gorhan Press, pp. 43–47.
32. Laycock, T. (1840). *A treatise on the nervous diseases of women.* London: Longman, pp. 140, 141.
33. Breuer and Freud, op. cit., pp. 21, 22.
34. Hunter, D. (1983). Hysteria, psychoanalysis, and feminism: The case of Anna O., *Feminist Studies, 9*(3), pp. 470, 478.

    Freud, S. (1957). The sexual aetiology of the neuroses. In S. Freud, *Collected Papers Vol. I.* New York: Basic Books, pp. 220–248.

    Breuer et al., op. cit., p. 240.
35. Brumberg, op. cit.

    Bell, op. cit.

    Loudon, op. cit.

    Bynum, op. cit.
36. King, M. B. & Bhugra, D. (1989). Eating disorders: lessons from a cross-cultural study. *Psychological Medicine, 19,* 955–958.

    Several other studies have recently found a surprisingly high level of symptoms of disordered eating, measured on traditional inventories of disordered eating or with clinical interviews, among women from non-Western cultures. In all cases, the women came from traditional cultures but were attempting to achieve academically. The people studied include 14 to 16-year-old Asian girls attending school in Britain.

    Mumford, D. B. & Whitehouse, A. M. (1988). Increased prevalence of bulimia nervosa among Asian schoolgirls. *British Medical Journal, 297,* 718.

    Also studied were Egyptian women attending college in London:

    Nasser, M. (1986). Comparative study of the prevalence of abnormal eating attitudes among Arab female students of both London and Cairo Universities. *Psychological Medicine, 16,* 621–625.

    These studies did not measure depression and other somatic symptoms.
37. El Islam, F. (1975). Culture bound neurosis in Qatari women. *Social Psychiatry, 10,* 25–29.
38. Boddy, J. (1989). *Wombs and alien spirits: Women, men and the Zar cult in Northern Sudan.* Madison: University of Wisconsin Press, pp. 127, 130.

    Lewis, J. (1986). *Religion in context: Cults and charisma.* Cambridge, Mass.: Cambridge University Press.
39. Finkler, K. (1989). The universality of nerves. In D. L. Davis & S. M. Low (eds.), *Gender, health, and illness: The case of nerves.* New York: Hemisphere, pp. 79–87.

    Cayleff, S. E. (1988). "Prisoners of their own feebleness": Women, nerves and Western medicine—A historical overview. *Social Science and Medicine, 26*(12), 1199–1208.

Nations, M. K., Camino, L. A., & Walker, F. B. (1988). "Nerves": Folk idiom for anxiety and depression? *Social Science and Medicine,* 26(12), 1245–1259.

Low, S. M. (1989). Gender, emotion, and nervios in urban Guatemala. In D. L. Davis & S. M. Low (eds.), op. cit., 23–48.

40. Barnett, E. A. (1989). Notes on nervios: A disorder of menopause. In D. L. Davis & S. M. Low (eds.), op. cit., 67–78.

Finerman, R. (1989). The burden of responsibility: Duty, depression, and nervios in Andean Ecuador. In D. L. Davis & S. M. Low (eds.), op. cit., 49–66.

41. Clark, M. H. (1989). Nevra in a Greek village: Idiom, metaphor, symptoms, or disorder? In D. L. Davis & S. M. Low (eds.), op. cit., 103–126.

As is evident in the citations above to several chapters in a single book, the disorder nerves has been studied throughout the world. The articles and chapters cited also discuss connections between nerves and other disorders such as neurasthenia and hysteria. This is the one case in which various forms taken by what we are calling "anxious somatic depression" have been related to one another.

42. Lambo, T. A. (1960). Further neuropsychiatric observations in Nigeria. *British Medical Journal,* December 10, p. 1699.

Murphy, H. E. (1964). Cross-cultural inquiry into the symptomatology of depression. *Transcultural Psychiatric Research Review, 1,* 5–21.

43. Ullrich, H. E. (1987). A study of change and depression among Havik Brahmin women in a South Indian village. *Culture, Medicine and Psychiatry, 11,* 276.

44. Showalter, E. (1985). *The female malady: Women, madness, and English culture, 1830–1980.* New York: Pantheon.

Smith-Rosenberg, C. (1985). *Disorderly conduct: Visions of gender in Victorian America.* New York: Knopf.

Chapter 3: Depression

1. Young-Bruehl, E. (1982). *Hannah Arendt: For love of the world.* New Haven: Yale University Press, pp. 51, 52.

Stowe, C. E. & Stowe, L. B. (1889). *The life of Harriet Beecher Stowe.* Boston: Houghton Mifflin, p. 37.

Stowe, C. E. (1911). *Harriet Beecher Stowe: The story of her life.* Boston: Houghton Mifflin, pp. 77–78.

2. McGrath, E., Keita, G. P., Strickland, B. R., & Russo, N. P. (1990). *Women and depression: Risk factors and treatment issues.* Washington, D.C.: American Psychological Association.

Nolen Hoeksema, S. (1990). *Sex differences in depression.* Stanford: Stanford University Press.

Weissman, M. M. & Klerman, G. L. (1977). Sex differences and the epidemiology of depression. *Archives of General Psychiatry, 34,* 98–111.

    Carlson, G. A. & Miller, D. C. (1981). Suicide, affective disorder, and women physicians. *American Journal of Psychiatry, 138*(10), 1330–1335.

    Pitts, F. N., Schuller, A. B., Rich, C. L. et al. (1979). Suicide among U.S. women physicians. *American Journal of Psychiatry, 136,* 694–698.

    Weiner, Marten, S., Wochnick, E., Davis, M. A., Fishman, R., & Clayton, P. J. (1979). Psychiatric disorders among professional women. *Archives of General Psychiatry, 36,* 169–173.

3. Verrulst, F. C., Prince, J. Vervururt-Pool, C., & Dejong, J. (1989). Mental health in Dutch adolescents: Self-reported competencies and problems for ages 11–18. *Acta Psychiatrica Scandinavica, 256*(Suppl.)

    This study did not follow the adolescents over time. Age comparisons are based on cross-sectional data.

    Petersen, A. C., Sarigiani, P. A., & Kennedy, R. F. (1991). Adolescent depression: Why more girls? *Journal of Youth and Adolescence, 20*(2), 247–271 did follow people from sixth to twelfth grade. They reported that depressive mood over this period was stable among males but increased among females at eighth grade.

4. Nolen Hoeksema, op. cit.

    Weissman, M. M. & Klerman, G. L. (1977). Sex differences and the epidemiology of depression. *Archives of General Psychiatry, 34,* 98–111.

5. Burke, K. C., Burke, J. D., Regier, D. A., & Rae, D. S. (1990). Age at onset of selected mental disorders in five community populations. *Archives of General Psychiatry, 47,* 511–518.

    Lewinsohn, P. M., Duncan, E. M., Stanton, A. K., & Hautzinger, M. (1986). Age at first onset for nonbipolar depression. *Journal of Abnormal Psychology, 4,* 378–383.

    These two studies on age of onset exhibited other methodological differences that may have also accounted for the differing ages of onset reported but the definition of major depression versus depressives symptoms appears to us to be the most likely explanation of the differences.

6. Barnett, op. cit.

7. Pruzinsky, T. (1990). Psychopathology of body experience: Expanded perspectives. In Cash & Pruzinsky (eds.), op. cit.

    Baron, P. & Joly, E. (1988). Sex differences in the expression of depression in adolescents. *Sex Roles, 18,* 1–7.

    Hammen, C. L. & Padesky, C. A. (1977). Sex differences in the expression of depressive responses on the Beck Depression Inventory. *Journal of Abnormal Psychology, 86,* 609–614.

Vredenburg, K., Krames, L., & Flett, G. L. (1986). Sex differences in the expression of depression. *Sex Roles, 14,* 37–49.

Allgood-Merton, B., Lewinsohn, P. M., & Hops, H. (1990). Sex differences and adolescent depression. *Journal of Abnormal Psychology, 99,* 55–63.

8. Kandel, D. B. & Davies, M. (1986). Adult sequelae of adolescent depressive symptoms. *Archives of General Psychiatry, 43,* 255–262.

9. Jampala, op. cit.

Levy, A. B., Dixon, K. N., & Stern, S. L. (1989). How are depression and bulimia related? *American Journal of Psychiatry, 146,* 162–169.

Strober, M. & Katz, J. L. (1987). Do eating disorders and affective disorders share a common etiology? A dissenting opinion. *International Journal of Eating Disorders, 6,* 171–180.

Swift, W. J., Andrews, D., & Barklage, W. E. (1986). The relationship between affective disorder and eating disorders: A review of the literature. *American Journal of Psychiatry, 143,* 290–299.

Dryman, A. & Eaton, W. W. (1991). Affective symptoms associated with the onset of major depression in the community: findings from the U.S. National Institute of Mental Health Epidemiologic Catchment Area Program. *Acta Psychiatrica Scandinavica, 84,* 1–5.

Frank, E., Carpenter, L. L., & Kupfer, D. J. (1988). Sex differences in recurrent depression: Are there any that are significant? *American Journal of Psychiatry, 145,* 41–45.

Furukawa, T. & Sumita, Y. (1992). A cluster-analytically derived subtyping of chronic affective disorders. *Acta Psychiatrica Scandinavica, 85,* 177–182.

Hawkins, W. E., McDermott, R. J., Seeley, J., & Hawkins, M. J. (1992). Depression and maladaptive eating practices in college students. *Women and Health, 18*(2), 55–65.

Rosen, J. C., Gross, J., & Vara, L. (1987). Psychological adjustment of adolescents attempting to lose or gain weight. *Journal of Consulting and Clinical Psychology, 55*(5), 742–747.

Young, M. A., Fogg, L. F., Scheftner, W. A., Keller, M. B., & Fawcett, J. A. (1990). Sex differences in the lifetime prevalence of depression: Does varying the diagnostic criteria reduce the female/male ratio? *Journal of Affective Disorders, 18,* 187–192.

Young, M. A., Scheftner, W. A., Fawcett, J., & Klerman, G. L. (1990). Gender differences in the clinical features of unipolar major depressive disorder. *Journal of Nervous and Mental Disease, 178*(3), 200–203.

10. Holbrook, M. L. (1878). *Hygiene of the brain and nerves and the cure of nervousness.* New York: M. L. Holbrook & Co., pp. 83–85.

Masson, J. M. (ed.) (1985). *The complete letters of Sigmund Freud to Wilhelm Fliess.* Cambridge, Mass.: Belknap, pp. 98, 111.

11. Brenner, C. (1991). A psychoanalytic perspective on depression. *Journal of the American Psychoanalytic Association, 39,* 25–43; quotes p. 41.

12. Biernat, M. & Wortman, C. (1991). Sharing of home responsibilities between professionally employed women and their husbands. *Journal of Personality and Social Psychology, 60*(6), 844–860.

    Fengler, A. P. & Goodrich, B. A. (1979). Wives of elderly disabled men: The hidden patients. *Gerontologist, 19*(2), 175–183.

13. Stehouwer, R. S., Bultsma, C. A., & Blackford, I. T. (1985). Developmental differences in depression: Cognitive-perceptual distortion in adolescent versus adult female depressives. *Adolescence, 20*(78), 291–299.

14. Fenichel, O. (1945). *The psychoanalytic theory of neurosis.* New York: Norton, p. 241. The citation is from the English translation of the book by Fenichel in which he cites work written in German by Wulff.

    Feigenbaum, D. (1925). Hysterical depression: A clinical and psychoanalytical approach. *Journal of Nervous and Mental Disease, 62,* 634–637.

15. Silverstein, B. & Perlick, D. (1991). Gender differences in depression: historical changes. *Acta Psychiatrica Scandinavica, 84,* 327–331.

    Klerman, G. L., Lavori, P. W., Rice, J., Reich, T., Endicott, J., Andreasen, N. C., Keller, M. B., & Hirschfield, R. M. A. (1985). Birth-cohort trends in rates of major depressive disorder among relatives of patients with affective disorder. *Archives of General Psychiatry, 35,* 773–782.

16. Lucas, A. R., Beard, M., O'Fallon, W. M., & Kurland, L. T. (1991). 50-year trends in the incidence of anorexia nervosa in Rochester, Minn.: A population-based study. *American Journal of Psychiatry, 148*(7), 917–922.

17. Silverstein & Perlick, op. cit. Only among the youngest group, born in the 1940s was there a significant gender difference before age 40. This does suggest the possibility, however, that gender differences in depression may be starting earlier in recent decades.

18. Ibid.

19. McCarthy, M. (1990). The thin ideal, depression and eating disorders in women. *Behaviour Research and Therapy, 28*(3), 205–215.

20. Block, J. H., Gjerde, P. F., & Block, J. H. (1991). Personality antecedents of depressive tendencies in 18-year-olds: A prospective study. *Journal of Abnormal Psychology, 60*(5), 726–738

    Coryell, W., Endicott, J., & Keller, M. (1992). Major depression in a nonclinical sample: Demographic and clinical risk factors for first onset. *Archives of General Psychiatry, 49,* 873–876.

    Hammen et al., op. cit.

    Richards, M. H., Casper, R. C., & Larson, R. (1990). Weight and eating concerns among pre- and young adolescent boys and girls. *Journal of Adolescent Health Care, 11,* 203–209.

Veiel, H. O. F., Kuhner, C., Brill, G., & Ihle, W. (1992). Psychosocial correlates of clinical depression after psychiatric in-patient treatment: methodological issues and baseline differences between recovered and non-recovered patients. *Psychological Medicine, 22,* 415–427.

Vollrath, Koch, et al., op. cit.

Vredenburg et al., op. cit.

Chapter 4: Anxious Somatic Depression

1. Rauste-Von Wright, M. & Von Wright, J. (1981). A longitudinal study of psychosomatic symptoms in healthy 11–18 year old girls and boys. *Journal of Psychosomatic Research, 25,* 525–534.

Headaches have been associated with hysteria, neurasthenia, chlorosis, nerves, Zar possession, and the Hippocratic disease of young women, and were described as symptoms of mental strain among nineteenth-century women who sought higher education. Breathing difficulties are mentioned in descriptions of the disease of young women, chlorosis, neurasthenia, hysteria, and nerves. Insomnia was not mentioned in Hippocratic texts, but it was included in the descriptions of the other disorders. Allbutt's discussion of the symptoms of chlorosis included heart clicks and murmurs. The descriptions of the other disorders do not mention these symptoms of the cardiac disorder now termed by physicians "mitral valve prolapse," but they do refer to heart palpitations, which are sometimes associated with the disorder. These findings are taken from the work cited in Chapter 2 describing the various disorders.

2. Masani, Z. (1976). *Indira Gandhi: A biography.* New York: Thomas Y. Crowell, pp. 8, 20, 36, 46, 54, 65. Correspondence to and from Nehru regarding his daughter Indira's weight is described on pages 36, 49, 54.

3. Lukes, M. M. (1973). *Gloriana: The years of Elizabeth I.* New York: Coward, McCann, p. 64.

Erickson, C. (1983). *The first Elizabeth.* New York: Summit, pp. 77, 187, 252, 281.

Williams, N. (1972). *The life and times of Elizabeth I.* Garden City, N.Y.: Doubleday, p. 25.

4. Weintraub, S. (1988). *Victoria: An intimate biography.* New York: E. P. Dutton, p. 343.

5. Alexander, J. T. (1985). *Catherine the Great.* New York: Oxford, p. 39.

Martin, R. C. (1988). *Golda: Golda Meir—The romantic years.* New York: Charles Scribners, pp. 145, 255.

6.   Higher prevalence among females than males in:
Eating disorders

Halmi, K. A., Falk, J. R., Schwartz, E. (1981). Binge eating and vomiting: A survey of a college population. *Psychological Medicine, 11*, 697–706.

Whitaker, A., Johnson, J., Shaffer, D., Rapoport, J. L., Kalikow, K., Walsh, B. T., Davies, M., Braiman, S., & Dolinsky, A. (1990). Uncommon troubles in young people: Prevalence estimates of selected psychiatric disorders in a nonreferred adolescent population. *Archives of General Psychiatry, 47*, 487–496.

Body image disorders

Freedman, R. (1990). Cognitive-behavioral perspectives on body image change. In Cash & Pruzinsky (eds.), op. cit.

Anxiety

Kashani, J. H., Beck, N. C., Hoeper, E. W., Fallahi, C., Corcoran, C. M., McAllister, J. A., Rosenberg, T. K., & Reid, J. C. (1987). Psychiatric disorders in a community sample of adolescents. *American Journal of Psychiatry, 144*, 584–589.

Weissman, M. M. & Merikangas, K. R. (1986). The epidemiology of anxiety and panic disorders: An update. *Journal of Clinical Psychiatry, 47*(6 Suppl.), 11–17.

Headache

Goldstein, M. & Chen, T. L. (1982). The epidemiology of disabling headache. In M. Critchley, A. P. Friedman, S. Gorini, & F. Sicateri (eds.), *Advances in neurology. Vol. 33 Headache: Physiopathological and clinical concepts.* New York: Raven Press, 377–390.

Linet, M. S. & Stewart, W. F. (1987). The epidemiology of migraine headache. In J. N. Blau (ed.), *Migraine: Clinical and research aspects.* Baltimore: Johns Hopkins, 451–477.

Asthma—see reference 8 below.

Insomnia

Karacan, I., Thornby, J. I., & Williams, R. L. (1983). Sleep disturbance: A community survey. In Guilleminault et al., op. cit., 37–60.

Lugaresi et al., op. cit.

Price, V. A., Coates, T. J., Thoresen, C. E., & Grinstead, O. A. (1978). Prevalence and correlates of poor sleep among adolescents. *American Journal of Diseases of Children, 132*, 583–586.

Sexual indifference

Nathan, S. G. (1986). The epidemiology of the DSM-III psychosexual dysfunctions. *Journal of Sex and Marital Therapy, 12*, 267–281.

Mitral valve prolapse

Devereux, R. B., Brown, T., Kramer-Fox, R., & Sachs, R. (1982). Inheritance of mitral valve prolapse: Effect of age and sex on gene expression. *Annals of Internal Medicine, 97*, 826–832.

Levy & Savage op. cit.

Savage, D. S., Garrison, R. J., Devereux, R. B., Castelli, W. P., Anderson, S. J., Levy, D., McNamara, P. M., Stokes, J., Kannel, W. B., & Feinleib, M. (1983). Mitral valve prolapse in the general population. Epidemiologic features: The Framingham study. *American Heart Journal*, September, 571–576.

7. Verrulst et al., op. cit.

Goldstein et al., op. cit.

Linet et al. op. cit.

The interaction between gender and age is also found in just about all studies of the epidemiology of insomnia but the age at which women begin to exhibit more insomnia than men is inexplicably different in different studies. Nonetheless, many studies report gender differences in insomnia beginning during adolescence or early adulthood:

Dupuy, H. J., Engel, A., Devine, B. K., Scanlon, J., & Querec, L. (1970). *Selected symptoms of psychological distress.* Public Health Service Publication No. 1000-Series 11-No. 37. Washington, D.C.: U.S. Government Printing Office.

Karacan et al., op. cit.

Price et al., op. cit.

Raybin et al., op. cit.

Mitral valve prolapse

Hickey, A. J. & Wilcken, D. (1986). Age and clinical profile of idiopathic mitral valve prolapse. *British Heart Journal, 55*, 582–586.

8. Ago, Y., Sugita, M., Teshima, H., & Nakagawa, T. (1982). Specificity concepts in Japan. *Psychotherapy and Psychosomatics, 38*, 64–73.

Gerstman, B. B., Bosco, L. A., Tomita, D. K., Gross, T. P., & Shaw, M. M. (1989). Prevalence and treatment of asthma in the Michigan Medicaid Population younger than 45 years, 1980–1986. *Journal of Allergy and Clinical Immunology, 83*, 1032–1039.

Ostrov, M. R. & Ostrov, E. (1986). The self-image of asthmatic adolescents. *Journal of Asthma, 23*(4), 187–193.

Resh, J. (1970). Asthma of unknown origin as a psychological group. *Journal of Consulting and Clinical Psychology, 35*, 429.

9. Lewis, G. & Wessely, S. (1992). The epidemiology of fatigue: more questions than answers. *Journal of Epidemiology and Community Health, 46*, 92–97.

Verrulst et al., op. cit.

Ledoux et al., op. cit.

Boudoulas, H., King, B. D., & Wooley, C. F. (1984). Mitral valve prolapse: A marker for anxiety or overlapping phenomenon? *Psychopathology, 17*(Suppl 1), 98–106.

Young, Fogg et al., op. cit.

Young, Scheftner et al., op. cit.

Lutz, op. cit.

Allbutt, op. cit.

El Islam, op. cit.

10. Onset of menstruation was found to be a significant predictor of both dieting and bulimia in sixth-grade girls.

Gralen, S. J., Levine, M. P., Smolak, L., & Murnen, S. K. (1990). Dieting and disordered eating during early and middle adolescence: Do the influences remain the same? *International Journal of Eating Disorders, 19,* 501–512.

Several studies found that early onset of puberty was related to poor body image among females but early pubescence has not been found to be related to poor body image among males:

Clausen, J. A. (1975). The social meaning of differential physical and sexual maturation. In S. Dragastin & G. Elder (eds.), *Adolescence in the life cycle: Psychological change and social context.* London: Halstead, 25–47.

Cohn, L. D., Adler, N. E., Irwin, C. E., Millstein, S. G., Keseleen, S. M., & Stone, G. (1987). Body image preferences in male and female adolescents. *Journal of Abnormal Psychology, 96,* 276–279.

One study found the most common age of onset of migraine headaches to be 10 years for males and 14 for females, and concluded that among females the onset is connected more with the beginning of menstruation than with actual age:

Dalsgaard-Nielsen, T., Engberg-Pedersen, H., & Holm, H. E. (1970). Clinical and statistical investigations of the epidemiology of migraine. *Danish Medical Bulletin, 17*(5), 138–147.

Other studies have not found so close a connection between menarche and onset of migraine:

Goldstein et al., op. cit.

One study reported that among a sample of adolescents, a model based on age and Tanner level of pubescent development explained 64% of the variance in a measure of daytime sleepiness, possibly indicative of insomnia, among females. The comparable figure among males was 38%:

Carskadon, M. A., Orav, E. J., & Dement, W. C. (1983). Evolution of sleep and daytime sleepiness in adolescents. In Guilleminault et al., op. cit., 201–216.

Some cardiologists have speculated that the development of mitral valve prolapse is related to the adolescent growth spurt among young women:

Hickey et al., op. cit.

Aro, H. & Taipale, V. (1987). The impact of timing of puberty on psychosomatic symptoms among fourteen-to-sixteen-year-old Finnish girls. *Child Development, 58,* 261–268.

11. The surveys of headache prevalence that were reanalyzed were: Abramson, J. H. & Hopp, C. (1980). Migraine and non-migrainous headaches. A community survey in Jerusalem. *Journal of Epidemiology and Community Health, 34,* 188–193.

    Brewis, M., Poskanzer, D. C., Rolland, C., & Miller, H. (1966). Neurological disease in an English city. *Acta Neurologica Scandinavica, 42*(Suppl. 24).

    Paulin, J. M., Waal-Manning, H. J., Simpson, F. O., & Knight, R. G. (1985). The prevalence of headache in a small New Zealand town. *Headache, 25,* 147–151.

    For a detailed description of the methods used in this analysis, see Appendix C.
12. MacMahon, S. W., Devereux, R. B., & Schron, E. (1987). Clinical and epidemiological issues in mitral valve prolapse. *American Heart Journal, 113,* 1265–1280.

    For a detailed description of the methods and results of this analysis, see Appendix C.

    We have not performed comparable analyses on insomnia because several studies appear to differ as to the age patterns of gender differences in insomnia. Until the causes of these differences between studies can be ascertained, we have no basis for choosing which studies to reanalyze. The existence of two types of asthma that are never differentiated in surveys of asthma prevalence has rendered analysis of the historical patterns of gender differences in asthma undoable.
13. Elbert, S. (1984). *A hunger for home: Louisa May Alcott and little women.* Philadelphia: Temple University Press, pp. 198, 213.

    Strickland, C. (1985). *Victorian domesticity: families in the life and art of Louisa May Alcott.* University: University of Alabama Press, 47, 49, 54.
14. Allen, D. R. (1975). Florence Nightingale: Toward a psychohistorical interpretation. *Journal of Interdisciplinary History, 6*(1), 23–45; quotes pp. 30, 37.

    Cook, E. (1914). *Life of Florence Nightingale.* London: Macmillan, p. 493.

    Huxley, E. (1975). *Florence Nightingale.* London: Weidenfeld & Nicolson, p. 34.
15. Headache:

    Merikangas, K. R., Angst, J., & Isler, H. (1990). Migraine and psychopathology. *Archives of General Psychiatry, 47,* 849–853.

    Merskey, H. (1987). Psychological factors in migraine. In J. N. Blau (ed.), *Migraine: Clinical and research aspects.* Baltimore: Johns Hopkins, pp. 367–386.

    Asthma

    Creer, T. L. (1978). Asthma: Psychological aspects and management. In E. Middleton (ed.), *Allergy: Principles and practice.* St. Louis: CV Mosby, pp. 799–815.

Lipowski, Z. J. (1990). Somatization and depression. *Psychosomatics, 31*(1), 13–21.
Insomnia

Liljenberg, B., Almwista, M., Hetta, J., & Roo, B. E. (1989). Affective disturbance and insomnia: A population study. *European Journal of Psychiatry, 3*(2), 91–98.

Vollrath, M., Wicki, W. & Angst, J. (1989). Insomnia: Association with depression, anxiety, somatic syndromes and course of insomnia. *European Archives of Psychiatry and Neurological Sciences, 239*(2), 113–124.
Menstrual disorders

Bloom, L., Shelton, J., & Michaels, A. (1978). Dysmenorrhea and personality. *Journal of Personality Assessment, 42,* 272–276.

Fava, G. A., Evangelisti, L. P., Trombini, G., Santarsiero, G., Grandi, S., Orlandi, C., & Bernardi, E. (1984). Depression and anxiety associated with secondary amenorrhea. *Psychosomatics, 25,* 905–908.
Sexual dysfunction

Derogatis, L. R., Meyer, J. K., & King, K. M. (1981). Psychopathology in individuals with sexual dysfunction. *American Journal of Psychiatry, 138,* 757–763.

Insomnia and other measures of disordered sleep have been found to be correlated with headache, breathing difficulties, and decreased appetite and anorexia.

Jampala, op. cit.

Lugaresi, E., Cirignotta, F., Zucconi, M., Mondini, S., Lenzi, P. L., & Coccagna, G. (1983). Good and poor sleepers: An epidemiological survey of the San Marino population. In C. Guilleminault & E. Lugaresi (eds.), *Sleep/wake disorders: Natural history, epidemiology, and long-term evolution.* New York: Raven Press, 1–12

Raybin, J. B. & Detre, T. P. (1969). Sleep disorder and symptomatology among medical and nursing students. *Comprehensive Psychiatry, 10,* 452–462.
Reduced sex drive has been related to asthma:

Thompson, W. L. (1986). Sexual dysfunction in asthmatics. *Medical Aspects of Human Sexuality, 20,* 131–137.

and to anorexia: Jampala, op. cit.

Even when compared to males who are depressed, depressed females have greater sleep difficulties, disordered eating, gastrointestinal symptoms, genital symptoms, and somatic problems:

Dryman et al., op. cit.

Frank et al., op. cit.

Young, Fogg et al., op. cit.

Young, Scheftner et al., op. cit.

Zetin, M., Sklansky, G. J., & Cramer, M. (1984). Sex differences in inpatients with major depression. *Journal of Clinical Psychiatry, 45*(6), 257–259.

Perugi, G., Musetti, L., Simonini, E., Piagentini, F., Cassano, G. B., & Akiskal, H. S. (1990). Gender-mediated clinical features of depressive illness: The importance of temperamental differences. *British Journal of Psychiatry, 157,* 835–841.

16.   North Carolina study:

Swartz, M., Blazer, D., Woodbury, M., George, L., & Landerman, R. (1986). Somatization disorder in a U.S. Southern community: Use of a new procedure for analysis of medical classification. *Psychological Medicine, 16,* 595–609.

Silverstein, B., Perlick, D., Clauson, J., & McKoy, E. (1993). Depression combined with somatic symptomatology among adolescent females who report concerns regarding maternal achievement. *Sex Roles, 28,* 637–653.

17.   Study of relationship between headache and depression that was re-analyzed: Ziegler, D. K., Rhodes, R. J., & Hassanein, R. S. (1978). Association of psychological measurements of anxiety and depression with headache history in a non-clinic population. *Research and Clinical Studies of Headache, 6,* 123–135.

Silverstein, B., Clauson, J., McKoy, E., Perdue, L., & Kelly, E. (in press). The correlation between depression and headache: The role played by generational changes in female achievement. *Journal of Applied Social Psychology.*

18.   Blazer, D., Swartz, M., Woodbury, M., Manton, K. G., Hughes, D., & George, L. (1988). Depressive symptoms and depressive diagnoses in a community population. *Archives of General Psychiatry, 45,* 1078–1084.

Maser, J. D. & Cloninger, C. R. (eds.) (1990). *Comorbidity of mood and anxiety disorders.* Washington, D.C.: American Psychiatric Press.

Katon, W., Lin, E., Von Korff, M., Russo, J., Lipscomb, P., & Bush, T. (1991). Somatization: A spectrum of severity. *American Journal of Psychiatry, 148*(1), 34–40.

Katon, W. & Roy-Byrne, P. P. (1991). Mixed anxiety and depression. *Journal of Abnormal Psychology, 100*(3), 337–345.

Several studies have found somatic symptoms to be better predicted by a combination of anxiety and depression than by either anxiety or depression alone:

McCauley, E., Carlson, G. A., & Calderon, R. (1991). The role of somatic complaints in the diagnosis of depression in children and adolescents. *Journal of the American Academy of Child and Adolescent Psychiatry, 30*(4), 631–635.

Merikangas, K. R., Angst, J., & Isler, H. (1990). Migraine and psychopathology. *Archives of General Psychiatry, 47,* 849–853.

Orenstein, H. (1989). Briquet's syndrome in association with depression and panic: A reconceptualization of Briquet's syndrome. *American Journal of Psychiatry, 146*(3), 334–338.

Eaton, W. W., Dryman, A., Sorenson, A., & McCutcheon, A. (1989). DSM-III Major Depressive Disorder in the community: A latent class analysis of data from the NIMH Epidemiologic Catchment Area Progamme. *British Journal of Psychiatry, 155,* 48–54.

Morrison, J. & Herbstein, J. (1988). Secondary affective disorder in women with somatization disorder. *Comprehensive Psychiatry, 29*(4), 433–440.

Kandel & Davies, op. cit.

Clancy, J., Noyes, R., Hoenk, P. R., & Slymen, D. J. (1978). Secondary depression in anxiety neurosis. *Journal of Nervous and Mental Disease, 166*(12), 846–850.

Percentages were calculated based on reanalysis of the published data.

Morrison et al. compared depressed women treated at a group psychiatric practice with women who exhibited depression combined with symptoms of somatization disorder accompanied by anxiety, anorexia, and insomnia. The women exhibiting this combination of symptoms suffered more frequent and more extended episodes of depression, and had undergone more psychiatric hospitalization than the women exhibiting depression alone. On average, these women had begun to suffer from the somatic symptoms at age 12, whereas they had not developed clinical depression until age 24.

In our last chapter we described the Kandel et al. study that found that females, but not males, who exhibited depressed mood in high school were particularly likely in their twenties to report health problems, to have seen a mental health professional, and to have been hospitalized for a mental illness. A closer look at this study indicates that the measure of depressed mood given to the high school students also included questions about anxiety and insomnia. Similarly, the Clancy et al. study of the records of patients attending general medical clinics at the University of Iowa found that among patients who exhibited anxiety in early adulthood along with somatic symptoms such as headache, breathing difficulty, insomnia, nausea, or vomiting, over half the females compared to only about a quarter of the males subsequently developed clinical depression.

19. Craighead, W. E. (1991). Cognitive factors and classification issues in adolescent depression. *Journal of Youth and Adolescence, 20*(2), 311–326.

20. Katon, W. (1982). Depression: Somatic symptoms and medical disorders in primary care. *Comprehensive Psychiatry, 23,* 274–287.

Marks, G., Goldberg, D. P., & Hillier, V. (1979). Determinants of the ability of General Practitioners to detect psychiatric illness. *Psychological Medicine, 9,* 337–353.
21. Bibb, R. C. & Guze, S. B. (1972). Hysteria (Briquet's Syndrome) in a psychiatric hospital: The significance of secondary depression. *American Journal of Psychiatry, 129,* 138–142.
Cloninger, C. R., Martin, R. L., Guze, S. B., & Clayton, P. J. (1986). A prospective follow-up and family study of somatization in men and women. *American Journal of Psychiatry, 143,* 873–878.
Guze. S. B. (1967). The diagnosis of hysteria: What are we trying to do? *American Journal of Psychiatry, 124,* 491–498.
Guze, S. B. (1975). The validity and significance of the clinical diagnosis of hysteria (Briquet's Syndrome). *American Journal of Psychiatry, 132,* 138–141.
Guze, S. B. & Perley, M. J. (1963). Observations on the natural history of hysteria. *American Journal of Psychiatry, 119,* 960–965.
Briquet, P. (1859). *Traite Clinique et Therapeurtique a l'Hysterie.* Paris: J. B. Baillere & Fils.
22. American Psychiatric Association. (1987). *Diagnostic and statistical manual of mental disorders,* 3rd ed., rev. Washington, D.C.: Author.
American Psychiatric Association. (1994). *Diagnostic and statistical manual of mental disorders,* 4th ed. Washington, D.C.: Author.
23. Hyler, S. E. & Spitzer, R. L. (1978). Hysteria split asunder. *American Journal of Psychiatry, 135,* 1500–1504.
Cloninger et al., op. cit.

Chapter 5: Tying the Knot

1. Lefkowitz et al., op. cit.
Porter, op. cit.
Laycock, *Treatise on the nervous diseases of women,* op. cit.
2. Bell, op. cit.
3. Breuer and Freud, op. cit., p. 140.
Nightingale quote—Cook, op. cit., p. 107.
4. Lasegue, C. (1873). On hysterical anorexia. *Medical Times & Gazette, 2,* 265–266.
5. Bureau of the Census. (1975). *Historical statistics of the United States: Colonial times to the present.* Washington, D.C.: U.S. Government Printing Office.
Bureau of the Census. (1984). *Statistical abstract of the United States.* Washington, D.C.: U.S. Government Printing Office.
See Method note A below.
6. Bair, D. (1990). *Simone De Beauvoir: A biography.* New York: Summit, p. 106.
7. Ibid., p. 170.

8. Lefkowitz & Fant, op. cit., p. 96.
   Savage, op. cit.
9. Boddy, op. cit.
   El Islam, op. cit.
   Low, op. cit.
10. Quinn, S. (1987). *A mind of her own: The life of Karen Horney.* New York: Summit, pp. 129, 154, 158, 170.
    Rubins, J. L. (1978). *Karen Horney: Gentle rebel of psychoanalysis.* New York: Dial.
11. Roazen, P. (1985). *Helene Deutsch, a psychoanalyst's life.* Garden City, N.Y.: Anchor/Doubleday, p. 12.
12. Deutsch, H. (1973). *Confrontations with myself: An epilogue.* New York: Norton, pp. 80, 85, 121, 122, 132.
13. Malhotra, I. (1989). *Indira Gandhi: A personal and political biography.* Boston: Northwestern University Press, 26.
14. Morton, A. (1992). *Diana: Her true story.* New York: Simon & Schuster.
    Hoffman, B. (1993). "Princess and the peeve: Rumor's bullimia." *New York Post, November 5, 1993,* p. 3 cites Buckingham Palace statement that Diana had a migraine headache.
15. Maurat, C. (1969). *The Brontes' secret.* London: Constable.
    Roazen, op. cit.
16. Maurat, op. cit., pp. 128, 131.
    Chitham, E. (1987). *A life of Emily Bronte.* London: Basil Blackwell.
    Frank, K. (1990). *A chainless soul: A life of Emily Bronte.* Boston: Houghton Mifflin.
17. Kalucy, R. S., Gilcrist, P. N., McFarlane, C. M., & McFarlane, A. C. (1985). Evolution of a multi-therapy orientation. In D. M. Garner & P. E. Garfinkel (eds.), *Handbook of psychotherapy for anorexia nervosa and bulimia.* New York: Guilford, 458–490.
    Mogul, S. L. (1989). Sexuality, pregnancy, and parenting in anorexia nervosa. In J. R. Bemporad & D. B. Herzog (eds.), *Psychoanalysis and eating disorders.* New York: Guilford, 65–88.
18. Binswanger, L. (1958). The case of Ellen West: An anthropological-clinical study. In R. May, E. Angel, & H. F. Ellenberger (eds.), *Existence: A new dimension in psychiatry and psychology.* New York, Basic Books, 237–298; quotes pp. 237, 239, 252, 260.
19. Chlorosis—Loudon, op. cit.
    Hysteria—Purtell et al., op. cit.
    Briquet's syndrome—Guze, 1967, op. cit.
    Anna O.—Breuer et al., op. cit., p. 21.
    Freud, S. (1918). From the history of an infantile neurosis. In *Standard Edition,* vol. XVII. London: Hogarth Press, 1955.
20. Nathan, op. cit.

Avery-Clark, C. (1986). Sexual dysfunction and disorder patterns of working and nonworking wives. *Journal of Sex and Marital Therapy, 12*(2), 93–107.

21.   Erikson, E. (1980). *Identity and the life cycle.* New York: Norton, p. 135.

22.   Pribor, E. F. & Dinwiddie, H. (1992). Psychiatric correlates of incest in childhood. *American Journal of Psychiatry, 149*(1), 52–56.

Aiosa-Karpas, C., Karpas, R., & Pelcovitz, D. (1991). Gender identification and sex role attribution in sexually abused adolescent females. *Journal of the American Academy of Child and Adolescent Psychiatry, 30,* 266–271.

23.   DeSalvo, L. (1989). *Virginia Woolf: The impact of childhood sexual abuse on her life and work.* Boston: Beacon; quotes, pp. 45, 125.

Caramagno, T. C. (1992). *The flight of the mind: Virginia Woolf's art and manic depressive illness.* Berkeley: University of California Press.

Method Notes

A.   The rate of never married females and males was calculated by dividing the number of single females (or males) by the total number of females (or males). The female-to-male ratio of never married individuals was calculated by dividing the female rate by the male rate. These census data are reported for several age groups. In selecting the age group on which to focus, we confronted two conflicting constraints. On the one hand, the median age of first marriage for both males and females tends to be in the 20 to 24-year-old age range. As a result, being an unmarried individual in this, or younger, age groups is modal and not particularly indicative of anything unusual. On the other hand, to date we have available census data up to 1980. As a result, data on individuals in their thirties is available only for people born before 1950. An index created from these data would have very few points. As a compromise between these two constraints, we selected the age group 25–29 in creating an index of a female-to-male ratio of never married individuals over the course of the twentieth century.

Chapter 6: Daughters and Sons

1.   These and other discussions of the case are reprinted in Bernheimer, C. & Kahane, C. (eds.) (1985). *In Dora's case.* New York: Columbia University Press.

See also Decker, H. S. (1991). *Freud, Dora, and Vienna 1900.* New York: Free Press.

2.   Freud, S. (1983). *Dora: An analysis of a case of hysteria.* New York: Collier, pp. 33, 34, 35, 38, 39, 45, 74, 101.

3. Breuer et al., op. cit., pp. 140, 155.
4. Ibid., pp. 161.
5. Bruch, H. (1973). *Eating disorders: Obesity, anorexia nervosa and the person within.* New York: Basic.
   Bruch (1978), op. cit.
   Perlick, D. (1978). An exclusive disease—A review of *The Golden Cage* by Hilde Bruch. *Contemporary Psychology, 23*(11), 942–943.
6. Bruch (1978) ibid., pp. 24, 25, 33, 52, 52.
7. Pryor, E. B. (1987). *Clara Barton: Professional angel.* Philadelphia: University of Pennsylvania Press, pp. 45, 154.
   Williams, B. C. (1941). *Clara Barton: Daughter of destiny.* Philadelphia: J. B. Lippincott.
   Barton, W. E. (1969). *The life of Clara Barton, founder of the American Red Cross.* New York: AMS Press.
   Epler, P. H. (1932). *The life of Clara Barton.* New York: Macmillan.
8. Curie, E. (1939). *Madame Curie.* New York: Doubleday, Doran, p. 39.
   Curie, M. (1929). *Pierre Curie.* New York: Macmillan, p. 163.
   Reid, R. (1974). *Marie Curie.* New York: Saturday Review Press, p. 20.
   Pflaum, R. (1989). *Grand obsession: Madame Curie and her world.* New York: Doubleday.
9. Silverstein, B., Perdue, L., Wolf, C., & Pizzolo, C. (1988). Bingeing, purging, and estimates of parental attitudes regarding female achievement. *Sex Roles, 19*(11/12), 723–733.
10. Allen, op. cit., p. 30.
11. This question was included in the questionnaire administered in the study reported in Silverstein et al. (1993), op. cit. This analysis was not reported. See method note A.
12. Lewis, C. R. (1982). Elizabeth Barrett Browning's "family disease": Anorexia nervosa. *Journal of Marital and Family Therapy*, January, 129–134, quotes pp. 131, 132, 133.
13. A detailed description of the methods and results of this study appears in Appendix C.
14. Banner, L. W. (1980). *Elizabeth Cady Stanton: A radical for women's rights.* Boston: Little Brown, pp. 4, 11, 13.
15. Horney cited in Westkott, M. (1986). *The feminist legacy of Karen Horney.* New Haven: Yale University Press, p. 122.
16. Silverstein, Perdue et al. (1988), op. cit.
17. Strouse, J. (1980). *Alice James: A biography.* Boston: Houghton-Mifflin, pp. 99, 113, 121.
    Yeazell, R. B. (ed.) (1981). *The death and letters of Alice James.* Berkeley: University of California Press, p. 130.
18. Strouse, op. cit., p. 89.
    Silverstein, Perdue et al. (1988), op. cit.
19. Ibid.

20. Mussen, P. & Rutherford, E. (1963). Parent-child relations and parental personality in relation to young children's sex-role preferences. *Child Development, 34,* 589–607.

Method Notes

A. We asked all the females attending a suburban high school how frequently their fathers wished they were boys or treated them like boys. Those who answered "often" or "always" on a 5-point Likert scale ranging from "never" to "always" were scored as high on this question. Symptomatology was measured as described in Silverstein et al., 1993, op. cit. Of the 23 respondents (9% of the sample) who reported that their fathers often wished they were boys or treated them like boys, 35% reported high levels of depression combined with at least two of the somatic symptoms, compared to only 9% of those who did not report that their fathers often wished they were boys (Fisher's exact probability = .0018.)

Chapter 7: Idealized Fathers, Devalued Mothers

1. Stern, K., Doyon, D., & Racine, R. (1959). Preoccupation with the shape of the breast as a psychiatric symptom in women. *Canadian Psychiatric Association Journal, 4*(4), 243–254; quotes pp. 244, 248, 249.
2. Chernin, K. (1985). *The hungry self: Women, eating & identity.* New York: Times Books.

    Wooley, S. & Wooley, O. W. (1986). Thinness mania. *American Health, 5*(8), 68–74.
3. Clark, R. W. (1984). *Einstein: The life and times.* New York: Avon, pp. 247, 748.

    Highfield, R. & Carter, P. (1994). *The private lives of Albert Einstein.* New York: St. Martins, p. 193. They also report that Einstein fathered an illegitimate daughter he never met.

    Sayens, J. (1985). *Einstein in America.* New York: Crown, p. 130.

    Vallentin, A. (1954). *The drama of Albert Einstein.* Garden City, N.Y.: Doubleday, pp. 140, 212, 236, 294.

    Silverstein, Perdue et al. (1988), op. cit.
4. Silverstein, Perdue et al. (1988), op. cit.
5. Gay, P. (1988). *Freud: A life for our time.* New York: Anchor, pp. 59, 60.

    Young-Bruehl, E. (1988). *Anna Freud.* New York: Summit, p. 56, 59, 129.
6. Silverstein, Perdue et al. (1988), op. cit.
7. West, G. (1938). *Charles Darwin: A portrait.* New Haven: Yale University Press, pp. 215, 275, 317.

Colp, R. (1977). *To be an invalid: The illness of Charles Darwin.* Chicago: University of Chicago Press, p. 120.

Raverat, G. M. D. (1958). *Period piece: A Cambridge childhood.* London: Faber & Faber, p. 123.

8. Banner (1980), op. cit., p. 10.

    Bair, op. cit., p. 60

    Silverstein, Perdue et al. (1988), op. cit.

9. Silverstein, Perlick, Clauson, & McKoy, op. cit. See method note A.

10. Kapp, Y. (1972). *Eleanore Marx. Vol. I.* New York: Pantheon, pp. 21, 41, 162, 183, 224, 229.

    Thomas, H. K. (1988). Emily Dickinson: "Renunciation" and anorexia nervosa. *American Literature, 60,* 205–225.

11. Silverstein, Perdue et al. (1988), op. cit.

12. Cody, J. (1971). *After great pain: The inner life of Emily Dickinson.* Cambridge, Mass.: Belknap Press, pp. 94, 134, 261, 262, 263.

13. Perdue, L., Pizzolo, C., & Norman, C. (1991). Depressive mood, disordered eating, and women's reports of low achieving, discontented mothers. Paper presented at annual meeting of the American Psychological Association, San Francisco, August 17.

    Silverstein, Perlick, Clauson, & McKoy, op. cit.

14. Klerman et al., op. cit.

    Silverstein et al. (1991), op. cit.

    Coryell et al., op. cit.

15. Addams, J. (1910). *Twenty years at Hull-House.* New York: Macmillan.

    Barton—Pryor, op. cit.

    Stanton—Banner (1980), op. cit.

    Ellen West—Binswanger, op. cit., p. 237.

16. Geist, R. A. (1989). Self psychological reflections on the origins of eating disorders. In J. R. Bemporad & D. B. Herzog (eds.), *Psychoanalysis and eating disorders.* New York: Guilford, 5–28; quote p. 19.

    Schwartz, H. J. (1988). Bulimia and the mouth-vagina equation: The phallic compromise. In H. J. Schwartz (ed.), *Bulimia: Psychoanalytic treatment and theory.* Madison, Ct.: International Universities Press, 255–298.

Method Notes

A. The methods used for this analysis were identical to those described in method note a in Chapter 6 save for the replacement of the question regarding fathers treating respondents like boys with "How often do you think your mother was fed up with playing the 'mommy' role?" Of the 64 respondents (24% of the sample) who reported that their mothers were often or always fed up with the mommy role, 23% reported high levels of depression combined with at least two somatic symptoms. Of those who reported that their mothers were not often fed up, only 8% reported high levels of depression and at least two somatic symptoms $(X=9.09, p<.003.)$

Chapter 8: Adolescence

1. Verrulst et al., op. cit.
2. Cohn, L. D., Adler, N. E., Irwin, C. E., Millstein, S. G., Kegeleem, S. M., & Stone, G. (1987). Body-figure preferences in male and female adolescents. *Journal of Abnormal Psychology, 96*(3), 276–279.

   Simmons, R. G., Blyth, D. A., & McKinney, K. L. (1983). The social and psychological effects of puberty on white females. In J. Brooks-Gunn & A. C. Petersen (eds.), *Girls at puberty: Biological and psychosocial perspectives*. New York: Plenum, 228–272.

   Dornbusch, S. M., Carlsmith, J. M., Duncan, P. D., Gross, R. T., Martin, J. A., Ritter, P. L., & Siegel-Gorelick, B. (1984). Sexual maturation, social class, and the desire to be thin among adolescent females. *Developmental and Behavioral Pediatrics, 5*(6), 308–314.

   Clausen, J. A. (1975). The social meaning of differential physical and sexual maturation. In S. E. Dragastin & G. H. Elder, Jr. (eds.), *Adolescence in the life cycle: Psychological change and social context*. London: Halstead, 25–47.

   Graham, P. & Rutter, M. (1985). Adolescent disorders. In M. Rutter & L. Hersov (eds.), *Child and adolescent psychiatry: Modern approaches*. Oxford: Blackwell Scientific Publications, 351–367.
3. American Association of University Women. (1991). *Shortchanging girls, shortchanging America: Executive summary*. Washington, D.C.: Author.
4. Study reanalyzed—Battle, J., Jarratt, L., Smit, S., & Precht, D. (1988). Relations among self-esteem, depression and anxiety of children. *Psychological Reports, 62*, 999–1005.

   Block et al. (1991), op. cit.

   Rauste-Von Wright (1981), op. cit.

   Richards et al., op. cit.

   Williams, S., McGee, R., Anderson, J., & Silva, P. A. (1989). The structure and correlates of self-reported symptoms in 11-year-old children. *Journal of Abnormal Child Psychology, 17*(1), 55–71.

   See method note A.
5. A. H. Stein cited in Hill, J. P. & Lynch, M. E. (1983). The intensification of gender-related role expectations during early adolescence. In J. Brooks-Gunn et al., op. cit., 202–228; quote p. 202.
6. Hill & Lynch, ibid.

   E. J. Tilt cited in Showalter, E. (1985). *The female malady: Women, madness, and English culture, 1830–1980*. New York: Pantheon, p. 57.

7. Redinger, R. V. (1975). *George Eliot: The emergent self.* New York: Knopf, pp. 33, 54, 137, 257.
8. Bair, op. cit., pp. 44, 60, 61, 469.
9. Blos, P. (1962). *On adolescence.* New York: Free Press of Glencoe, pp. 35, 36, 37, 45.
10. Deutsch, op. cit.
    Banner (1980), op. cit.
    Barry, K. (1988). *Susan B. Anthony: A biography.* New York: New York University Press, pp. 48, 50.
    Roberts, R. E., Lewinsohn, P. M., & Seeley, J. R. (1991). Screening for adolescent depression: A comparison of depression scales. *Journal of the American Academy of Child and Adolescent Psychiatry, 30*(1), 58–66.
    Ledoux et al., op. cit.
    Allbutt, op. cit., p. 484.
    Mercier cited in Showalter, op. cit., p. 131.
11. Garner, D. M., Olmsted, M. P., & Polivy, J. (1983). Development and validation of a multidimensional eating disorder inventory for anorexia nervosa and bulimia. *International Journal of Eating Disorders, 2,* 15–34.
    Charcot's patient cited in Janet, P. (1907). *Major symptoms of hysteria.* New York: Macmillan, p. 234.
12. Plaut, E. A. & Hutchinson, F. L. (1986). The role of puberty in female psychosexual development. *Review of Psychoanalysis, 13,* 417–429. Another developmental task that females have been said to be less successful at completing during childhood is moving from a position of dependency on the mother for gratification to one of seeking libidinal gratification from the opposite sex parent at the beginning of the Oedipal phase. More recently, however, weekly observation of babies and toddlers developing over many years has led other psychoanalysts to conclude that this view is inaccurate and that despite individual differences in timing, girls on the whole successfully completed this task.
    Parens, H., Pollock, L., Stern, J., & Kramer, S. (1976). On the girl's entry into the Oedipus complex. *Journal of the American Psychoanalytic Association, 24*(5), 79–108.
    Parens, H. (1990). On the girl's psychosexual development: Reconsiderations suggested from direct observation. *Journal of the American Psychoanalytic Association, 38*(3), 743–772.
13. Schafer, R. (1974). Problems in Freud's psychology of women. *Journal of the American Psychoanalytic Association, 22,* 459–485; quote p. 464.
14. Horend, I. & Perdue, L. (1990). Bingeing, purgeing, and developmental changes in parental concern for achievement. Paper presented at annual meeting of the American Psychological Association, Boston, August 10.

15. Bateson, C. (1984). *With a daughter's eye: A memoir of Margaret Mead.* New York: Morrow.

Howard, J. (1984). *Margaret Mead: A life.* New York: Simon & Schuster.

Mead, M. (1972). *Blackberry winter: My earlier years.* New York: Morrow.

Method Notes

A. In the Battle et al. study, among elementary school children, the correlation between academic self-esteem and depression for girls was $-.51$ and for boys $-.44$, $Z = 0.95$. Among junior high school students the correlations were $-.61$ for girls and $-.47$ for boys, $Z = 2.2$, $p < .05$. Comparable correlation between academic self-esteem and anxiety in elementary school were $-.44$ for girls and $-.48$ for boys. In junior high school they were $-.57$ for girls and $-.49$ for boys. The changes from elementary to junior high school in the association between academic self-esteem and anxiety among females versus males were similar but not strong enough to be statistically significant.

The data on the increased relationship between self-esteem and weight and eating concerns among girls but not boys at adolescence are from Richards et al. The correlations are: girls in grades 5 and 6— $-.10$; girls in grades 8 and 9— $-.34$, $p < .01$; boys in grades 5 and 6— $-.11$; boys in grades 8 and 9— $-.21$, $p = $ ns.

Chapter 9: Gender Ambivalence

1. Barry op. cit., p. 123.
2. Modell, J. S. (1983). *Ruth Benedict: Patterns of a life.* Philadelphia: University of Pennsylvania Press, p. 89.

Sand, G. (1979). *My life.* New York: Harper & Row, p. 161.

Hippocrates—Lefkowitz and Fant, op. cit.

Alcott—Strickland op. cit., p. 49.

Dickinson—Cody, op. cit., p. 121.

Nightingale—Allen, op. cit., p. 30.
3. Blos, P. (1941). *The adolescent personality.* New York: Appleton-Century, pp. 57, 87, 95.
4. Stoller, R. J. (1976). Primary femininity. *Journal of the American Psychoanalytic Association,* 24(5), 59–78.

Money, J. & Ehrhardt, A. A. (1972). *Man and woman, boy and girl: The differentiation of gender identity from conception to maturity.* Baltimore: Johns Hopkins Press.
5. Block, J. H. (1984). *Sex role identity and ego development.* San Francisco: Jossey-Bass.

6. Money, J. (1985). Gender: History, theory and usage of the term in sexology and its relationship to nature/nurture. *Journal of Sex and Marital Therapy, 11*(2), 71–79.
7. Blos, op. cit., p. 96.
8. Dickinson—Cody, op. cit., p. 121.
   Benedict—Modell, op. cit., pp. 42, 70, 78, 81.
9. Deutsch, op. cit., p. 132.
   Nord, D. E. (1985). *The apprenticeship of Beatrice Webb.* Amherst: University of Massachusetts Press, p. 101.
   Freud—Young-Bruehl, op. cit., p. 129.
   James—Strouse, op. cit., p. 121.
10. Lisle, L. (1986). *Portrait of an artist: A biography of Georgia O'Keefe.* New York: Washington Square Press, pp. 258, 259, 267.
11. Catherine Clement, cited in Warner, op. cit., pp. 157, 158.
12. Silverstein, Carpman, Perlick, & Perdue, op. cit. See method note A.
13. David, D. (1987). *Intellectual women and Victorian patriarchy.* Ithaca, N.Y.: Cornell University Press, p. 147.
14. Bair, op. cit., p. 137.
15. Silverstein, Perlick, Clauson, & McKoy, op. cit.
16. Lewicki, P. & Hill, T. (1987). Unconscious processes as explanations of behavior in cognitive, personality, and social psychology. *Personality and Social Psychology Bulletin, 11*(3), 355–362.
   Also see July 1992 issue of the *American Psychologist* for several articles discussing evidence for unconscious processing of information.
17. Eliot—Redinger, op. cit.
   Freud—Young-Bruehl, op. cit.
   Horney—Quinn, op. cit.
   Nightingale—Allen, op. cit.
18. Bretall, R. (ed.) (1946). *A Kierkegaard anthology.* New York: The Modern Library, pp. 100, 351.
   Erikson, E. H. (1980). *Identity and the life cycle.* New York: Norton, p. 183.
   Waterman, A. S. & Waterman, C. K. (1974). A longitudinal study of changes in ego identity status during the freshman to the senior year in college. *Developmental Psychology, 10,* 387–392.
19. Berger, P. L. & Luckmann, T. (1971). *The social construction of reality.* New York: Penguin.
   Hogg, M. A. & Abrams, D. (1988). *Social identifications.* New York: Routledge.
   Mead, G. H. (1934). *Mind self, and society.* Chicago: University of Chicago Press.
20. Erikson, ibid., p. 109.
21. Clark, K. B. & Clark, M. B. (1958). Racial identification and prefer-

ence in Negro children. In E. E. Maccoby, T. M. Newcomb, & E. L. Hartley (eds.), *Readings in social psychology*. New York: Henry Holt, 602–611.

Fanon, F. (1967). *Black skin, white masks*. New York: Grove.

Kardiner, A. & Ovesey, L. (1951). *The mark of oppression*. New York: World Publishing Company.

22. Kardiner & Ovesey, ibid.

Malcolm X. (1966). *The autobiography of Malcolm X*. New York: Grove Press, p. 54.

23. Erikson, op. cit., p. 31.

24. Ibid., p. 120.

Method Notes

A. To eliminate subjective bias, all drawings were looked at by at least two trained raters who were in great agreement with each other regarding their ratings, and were also unaware of which women exhibited symptoms of eating disorders.

Chapter 10: Anxious Somatic Depression During Periods of Changing Gender Roles

1. James, W. (1950). *The principles of psychology*, Vol. I. New York: Dover, p. 310.

Gove, W. R. & Herb, T. R. (1974). Stress and mental illness among the young: Comparison of the sexes. *Social Forces, 53*(2), 256–285.

2. Gordon, op. cit.

Hagnell, O., Lanke, J., Rorsman, B., & Ojesjo, L. (1982). Are we entering an age of melancholy? Depressive illnesses in a prospective epidemiological study over 25 years: The Lundby Study, Sweden. *Psychological Medicine, 12*, 279–289.

3. Cott, N. (1977). *The bonds of womanhood: Woman's sphere in New England, 1780–1835*. New Haven: Yale University Press.

Bledstein, B. (1976). *The culture of professionalism*. New York: W. W. Norton.

Kessler-Harris, A. (1982). *Out to work: A history of wage-earning women in the United States*. New York: Oxford University Press.

4. Curtis, B. (1980). Capital, the state and the origins of the working-class household. In B. Fox (ed.), *Hidden in the household*. Toronto: Women's Press.

Kessler-Harris, ibid.

5. Silverstein, Perdue, et al. (1988), op. cit. See method note A.

6. Stewart, A. J. & Healy, J. M. (1989). Linking individual development and social changes. *American Psychologist, 44*(1), 30–42.

Gergen, K. J. & Gergen, M. M. (1984). *Historical social psychology*. Hillsdale, N. J.: Erlbaum.

Method Notes

A. Among college students who reported that their fathers did not agree that "a woman's place is in the home," 6% of the nontraditional women reported using laxatives, diuretics, or intentional vomiting to control their weight compared to 9% of the other women. Among those who reported that their fathers did believe a woman's place is in the home, 22% of the nontraditional women purged compared to 11% of the others.

Chapter 11: Recognition, Prevention, Treatment

1. Katon, op. cit.

  Marks et al., op. cit.

  Bibb, R. C. & Guze, S. B. (1972). Hysteria (Briquet's syndrome) in a psychiatric hospital: The significance of secondary depression. *American Journal of Psychiatry, 129*(2), 138–142.

  Morrison, J. & Herbstein, J. (1988). Secondary affective disorder in women with somatization disorder. *Comprehensive Psychiatry, 29*(4), 433–440.

  Smith, G. R., Monson, R. A., & Ray, D. C. (1986). Patients with multiple unexplained symptoms: their characteristics, functional health, and health care utilization. *Archives of Internal Medicine, 146*, 69–72.

2. Smith, G. R., Monson, R. A., & Ray, D. C. (1986). Psychiatric consultation in somatization disorder: A randomized controlled study. *New England Journal of Medicine, 314*, 1407–1413.

3. Elkin, I., Shea, T., Watkins, J. T., Imber, S. D., Stosky, S. M., Collins, J. F., Glass, D. R., Pilkonis, P. A., Leber, W. R., Doherty, J. P., Fiester, S. J., & Perloff, M. B. (1989). National Institute of Mental Health Treatment of Depression Collaborative Research Program: General effectiveness of treatments. *Archives of General Psychiatry, 46*, 971–982.

  Several approaches are discussed in Fallon, P., Katzman, M., & Wooley, S. (eds.) (1993). *Feminist perspectives on eating disorders.* New York: Guilford.

4. Orenstein, P. (1994). *School girls: Young women, self-esteem, and the confidence gap.* New York: Doubleday.

  Sadker, M., & Sadker, D. (1994). *Failing at fairness: How America's schools cheat girls.* New York: Charles Scribner's Sons.

Appendix A

In addition to the works cited in the body of the text, the following references were used to compile Appendix A.

Addams, op. cit.

Flexner, E. (1972). *Mary Wollstonecraft.* New York: Coward, McCann.

Gross-Kurth, P. (1987). *Melanie Klein: Her world and her work.* Cambridge, Mass: Harvard University Press.

Tiffany, F. (1918). *Life of Dorothea Lynde Dix.* Boston: Houghton Mifflin.

Halpern, J. (1984). *The life of Jane Austen.* Baltimore: Johns Hopkins University Press.

Appendix B

1. Amenorrhea is a criterion for the diagnosis of anorexia nervosa— American Psychiatric Association, op. cit.
   Menstrual dysfunction associated with anxiety and depression—
       Fava et al., op. cit.
       Bloom et al., op. cit.
   Mitral valve prolapse is prevalent among thin males and females—
       Levy & Savage, op. cit.
   MVP has been found to be associated with panic disorder—
       Margraf, J., Ehlers, A., & Roth, W. T. (1988). Mitral valve prolapse and panic disorder: A review of their relationship. *Psychosomatic Medicine, 50,* 93–113.
2. Polivy, J. & Herman, C. P. (1985). Dieting and binging: A causal analysis. *American Psychologist, 40,* 193–201.
3. American Association of University Women, op. cit.
       Battle et al., op. cit.
       Freedman, R. (1990). Cognitive-behavioral perspectives on body-image change. In Cash & Pruzinsky, op. cit., pp. 272–295.
4. Abramson, L. Y., Seligman, M. E. P., & Teasdale, J. (1978). Learned helplessness in humans: Critique and reformulation. *Journal of Abnormal Psychology, 87,* 49–74.
       Glass, D. & Singer, J. E. (1972). *Urban stress: Experiments on noise and social stressors.* New York: Academic Press.
       Bruch (1978), op. cit.
       Rost et al., op. cit.
5. See note 23 for Chapter 4.

Appendix C

1. Goldstein et al., op. cit.
       Klerman et al., op. cit.

2. Abramson et al., op. cit.

   Brewis et al., op. cit.

   Pauling et al., op. cit.

3. Savage, D. S., Garrison, R. J., Devereux, R. B., Castelli, W. P., Anderson, S. J., Levy, D., McNamara, P. M., Stokes, J., Kannel, W. B., & Feinleib, M. D. (1983). Mitral valve prolapse in the general population. Epidemiologic features: The Framingham Study. *American Heart Journal*, September, 571–576.

4. Devereux et al., op. cit.

   Devereux, R. B. Personal communication, April 16, 1991.

5. Silverstein et al. (1993), op. cit.

   Radloff, L. S. (1991). The use of the center for epidemiologic studies depression scale in adolescents and young adults. *Journal of Youth and Adolescence, 20*(2), 149–166.

   Derogatis, L. R. (1983). *SCL-90-R administration, scoring & procedures manual-II.* Towson, MD.: Clinical psychometric research.

   Roberts et al., op. cit.

6. Perdue, L, DeCarlo, L., & Pizzolo, C. (1993). Scales measuring college women's feelings about their mothers: Their construction and relation to women's eating and depression. Paper presented at the annual meeting of the Eastern Psychological Association, Arlington, Va., April 16.

Index

Riley